Myth and Ritual
in Women's
Detective Fiction

Myth and Ritual in Women's Detective Fiction

Christine A. Jackson

McFarland & Company, Inc., Publishers
Jefferson, North Carolina, and London

Library of Congress Cataloguing-in-Publication Data

Jackson, Christine A., 1951–
  Myth and ritual in women's detective fiction / Christine A. Jackson.
    p.   cm.
  Includes bibliographical references and index.

  ISBN-13: 978-0-7864-1311-9
  (softcover : 50# alkaline paper) ∞

  1. Detective and mystery stories, American — History and criticism.
  2. Detective and mystery stories, English — History and criticism.
  3. American fiction — Women authors — History and criticism. 4.
  English fiction — Women authors — History and criticism. 5. Rites
  and ceremonies in literature. 6. Women detectives in literature. 7.
  Fairy tales in literature. 8. Mythology in literature. 9. Folklore in
  literature. 10. Ritual in literature. 11. Myth in literature. I. Title.
  PS374.D4 J33   2002
  813'.0872099287 — dc21   2002000113

British Library cataloguing data are available

©2002 Christine A. Jackson All rights reserved

No part of this book may be reproduced or transmitted in any form or by any means, electronic or mechanical, including photocopying or recording, or by any information storage and retrieval system, without permission in writing from the publisher.

Cover image ©2002 PhotoSpin

Manufactured in the United States of America

McFarland & Company, Inc., Publishers
  Box 611, Jefferson, North Carolina 28640
  www.mcfarlandpub.com

To the Mystery Lovers,
with Gratitude

CONTENTS

Introduction	1
1. Anatomy of a Mystery	13
2. Magic and Transformation in Domestic Mysteries	27
3. A Bodiless Dream: Forensic Mysteries and Myths of Identity	49
4. Religion in Mysteries: Of the Essence	67
5. Blood Dues: Rites of Initiation in Career Thrillers	90
6. Tracing the Razor's Edge	114
7. V.I. and Kinsey: Death and Renewal	130
8. Life Restored	159
Works Cited	163
Index	169

Introduction

Mystery novels featuring women sleuths and detectives crowd the shelves at libraries and bookstores. Over the past decade, this literary genre has shown a "bullet" market development with no end in sight. Observers cite two reasons for the growth. One is effective marketing through mega-bookstore chains. Readers like a little crime with their cappuccinos. Offering more books geared to women in many different roles builds readership, especially for the mystery series. People are turning the pages much faster than writers' word processors can churn them out.

The women's movement is another cause. Today's fiction reflects the expanded range of women's opportunities in today's job market. The trend toward more women in law enforcement, for example, results in more authors depicting women characters on the police force, the crime scene, or a judge's bench. In addition, the traditional detective character represents the ultimate in independence and freedom. So it is no surprise that women with widened horizons would be attracted to books featuring women detectives. On a demographic level, increased interest in women's mysteries is not hard to fathom.

The problem with these explanations, however, is that they focus on factors outside the texts, like merchandising, the job market, and career goals. How do these factors clarify what the recent mysteries are about? How do they explain and evaluate women-featured detective fiction as meaningful literature?

Many works of women's mystery fiction conform to a pattern, and these configurations afford a perspective beyond the single crime of passion uncovered or the serial killer finally nailed for long-ago crimes. In many instances, we can read these novels as an analyst would dreams. "The individual may feel that his dreams are spontaneous and disconnected. But over a long period of time the analyst can observe a series of dream images and note that they have a meaningful pattern" (Henderson 107). Similarly, a mystery reader on the lookout for significance can draw conclusions about the fictional cases.

This comparative approach uncovers repetitions in women's detective fiction that echo many motifs from the world of myth. In scores, perhaps hundreds of books, the themes emerge in varied guises. Myths of identity lost and found, quests for connection, tests of worthiness, attempts to alter time, rituals of risk and betrayal, guilt and self-recrimination, all play a part in energizing the so-called "whodunit."

Myths themselves might not literally serve as a source for the writer, or at least a conscious source. Instead, repeated images, metaphors, or bundles of ideas constitute the author's "principle of selection" (Frye, *Myth and Metaphor* 3). To achieve a particular effect, a writer will call upon these patterns for structure and meaning. Their use does not diminish the originality of the author's work. On the contrary, myths serve as powerful underlying structures capturing human experience. They are evidence that the writer has penetrated to the marrow of a human truth and will create living images to portray it. Clearly, relegating these novels to a single category or labeling them escapist fare renders a disservice to the works, mystery writers, and to serious readers. Detective fiction represents a broad pattern of literary and cultural significance. Because the genre reflects and in turn shapes our culture, it deserves to be better understood.

The myriad types of mysteries on the market today represent a substantial investment of writer creativity and reader interest. As literature, the works warrant sustained critical consideration. The best-written mystery novels, some of which are also best sellers, include in-depth character development, complex narrative lines, and polished, distinctive styles. They present complexities of experience by exploring the moral ambiguities implicit in violence and justice. Some works weave mythic themes into conflicts sparked by expanded or changing roles of women. Others recast the ancient quest narrative into the realms of art and writing. Mystery fiction can achieve the quality and intensity of "serious" literature in its portrayal of women sleuths, amateurs and professional detectives. We might call them the night sirens. Imagine something like the following scene:

> *He drew her toward him, warm, insistent. She met his embrace, but then an annoying squawk in the background, a parrot or monkey, broke the spell. The noise finally pulled her from her dream.*

"Yup," she said into the phone.

"Customer for you. A cold one." She recognized Ted Stewart's brusque voice from "C" shift. Last year, she and Officer Stewart had a fling. Now it was over. That was the best either of them could say about it. They had celebrated with a beer at Flynn's.

"Where are you, Ted?"

"Behind an abandoned building on the corner of Northeast Second and Central. Neighbors say they heard shots."

"I'm on my way."

As part of her job, a woman investigator is called to a murder scene in the middle of the night. She is one of them, a night siren. She may once have been a *femme fatale* for Ted Stewart, but literal night sirens, black-and-whites screaming to a crime scene with "party lights" flashing, also play a central role in her life. She responds to the call of sirens beating through the dark streets. The alarms introduce challenging conflicts and draw her toward death. Today's mystery protagonist not only issues tempting night songs; she heeds their call.

In Homer's rendition, sirens sing to lure Odysseus and his crew to doom on the rocks. They fail, however. Odysseus plugs up the ears of his men with wax, then has his crew bind him to the mast. It's not that Odysseus is so smart or clever. He merely responds to another woman's singing before giving in to the sirens. He and the crew survive because he listens to Circe's lurid prophecy: "First you will come to the Sirens, who bewitch every one who comes near them … There in a meadow they sit, and all round is a great heap of bones, mouldering bodies and withering skins" (*The Odyssey*, Trans. Rowse 138-39).

This mythic narrative is hardly a favorite with feminist critics. Coming from the perspective of the male gaze, it conveys a confining image of women as luring and deadly. However, let us imagine that women work side by side with men on a contemporary crew of the *Calypso*. We can rethink the narrative in non-sexualized terms. It is an emblem for the mystery novel. Life stands in the center of a ring of death. The temptation to cheat death is no respecter of gender. The will toward immortality is equally strong for men and women.

The sirens serve as a powerful symbol on several levels. In the fictional worlds, women sleuths pick through those piles of corpses toward the goal, restored vitality. From the reader's perspective, today's women sleuths are themselves like the sirens. Death is their trade. Every adventure finds the lethal ladies surrounded by fallen bodies.

Whether amateur or professional, these updated sirens post themselves in the sunlight and entice us with their songs. Their stories promise suspense, romance, and intellectual challenge. Still, death is at the core. This is true even in the so-called "cozy" mystery, a mystery subgenre that could also be called "death go lightly." It often includes a murder reported off the page or a murder scene where the narrative glosses over details. Death is hardly ignored, however. References to the murdered person are numerous. As the sleuth advances in solving the murder, we see the recently departed as a person among others with a home, family, profession. A tea cozy keeps the pot warm. A mystery cozy keeps the body warm.

The cozy marks the "innocuous" end of a spectrum of murder details. At the opposite "upsetting" end, a forensic mystery sheds a harsh fluorescent light on the processes of decay. Reports from the crime scene spare no sensibility. A cruel chalk line separates from humanity the person who once was. Yellow tags mark bullet holes. Blood spatters and bloating portray a violent, dehumanized end that is ultimately all too natural. In the interests of authenticity, autopsy reports might represent an integral part of the murder solver's follow-up investigation. Some forensic-focused mystery writers even lead readers into the morgue for a close-up of the autopsy itself.

Regardless of where on the spectrum a mystery falls in terms of pathologist's details, the spectre of death haunts every page. The protagonists of these books, like the sirens, are ringed with corpses.

Readers of all levels find these books irresistible. If we read one, we must read more to satisfy our reading appetite, especially if the character we love in one novel reappears as part of a series. Despite the slag heaps of victims' bones, we read on for the closure of seeing the murderer caught, the detective or sleuth shutting the open case. Listening to the call of these sirens is pleasurable, not perilous. The detective novel perpetrates a great lie — that death is knowable.

We consciously know that inevitably, death wrestles us to the ground. Through our intense wishes that death be defeated, myth steps in.

Most people consider myths to be collections of stories from ancient cultures. Look up "mythology" in a bookstore or on the Internet, and note all the references to Greeks and Romans. Bill Moyers tells the story that some of his acquaintances greeted his preparations to interview mythologist Joseph Campbell with skepticism. Why, they wondered, do you need to talk about "all these Greek gods and stuff?" (Moyers xiv).

Because many myths involve magical events impossible in the real world, such as human beings turning into animals or trees, people often consider myths to be "untrue" or "mistaken" concepts. Maureen Murdock's excellent study of *The Heroine's Journey* uses the term *myth* in this way. Her book includes chapter titles such as "The Myth of Female Inferiority," "The Myth of Dependency," and "The Myth of Never Being Enough." In Murdock's work, myths are erroneous thoughts, falsehoods in need of correction.

The anthropologist's view is that myths express true beliefs about a culture's deepest driving forces. The myth narrative may present a magical or impossible condition in the rational universe, but the pattern it expresses is believed to be true by the culture that tells it. Therefore, myths fall into a liminal realm that is not exactly reality, but not magical or false either. "Myth" is a contranym. It holds two opposing meanings at the same time.

We engage this paradoxical quality regularly in daily life. For example, let us examine the phrase "to have your work cut out for you." A police shift commander may tell a rookie, "At first, you'll really have to hustle. You will patrol all this sector of the city, and you'll have your work cut out for you." The rookie greets the news with glee. New, nervous, and a bit naïve, she might be excused for hearing only that last phrase "for you." She thinks, "It won't be so bad working on this shift if somebody else is going to cut the work out for me. I can certainly do the rest."

Obviously, the rookie is wrong. Work that has been "cut out" presents a tough chore, according to the phrase's generally accepted meaning. This idiom means the opposite of its initial linguistic sense. Yet through the rookie's belief in easy work, the phrase presents another, opposite meaning.

This is not to ascribe inkblot-like meanings to the word "myth," so that it means whatever the teller feels at the time. Nor is myth so slippery as to fall into the same category as the limited perspective of the "blind man and the elephant" story. Instead, a myth differs from other linguistic structures by including diametrically opposed meanings. It gains power from reversed logic.

The phrase "to wind up" presents another example of paradoxical, myth-like ambiguity. At the beginning of a stake out, the private investigator winds up her watch to keep it going for another day. As dawn breaks and it's apparent that the suspect is not going to show, the PI says to her lipstick-marked coffee cup, "That does it. Time to wind it up." The phrase means both "to start" and "to end." In each use, the phrase sets out conditions that are true in paradoxical contexts. Similarly, a myth gains power from these contradictory contexts.

From a cultural anthropologist's overall point of view, myths contain a culture's most ingrained expressions of the experience of life. If myth scholars agree on one aspect of this multifaceted subject, it is that pinpointing the value of "myth" is difficult and problematic. In *Myth and Reality*, Mircea Eliade writes,

> It would be hard to find a definition of myth that would be acceptable to all scholars and at the same time intelligible to nonspecialists. Then, too, is it even possible to find one definition that will cover all the types and functions of myths in all traditional and archaic societies? Myth is an extremely complex cultural reality, which can be approached from various and complementary viewpoints [Eliade 5].

The difficulty of nailing myth down does not keep scholars from trying.

When words fall short, metaphors serve to convey what a myth is and does. Like Eliade, Alexander Eliot expresses a conviction about myth's elusive quality. "[Myth is] not something we can isolate for a closer look. The primal myths are built into our brains, our genes, and our blood. However distant they seem, they still surround, embrace, imbue, and color human consciousness" (Eliot 2).

Cultural anthropologists collect stories from primitive peoples to figure out these colors. To most of us, the tales are relics from ancient times. Yet to scholars, myths persist in modern thought. Joseph Campbell's *The Hero with a Thousand Faces* updates these primal stories. He carries them into today's world by noting that myths have the same sources and fit into similar image outlines as other products of the subconscious mind. To Campbell, "the very dreams that blister sleep boil up from the basic, magic ring of myth" (*The Power of Myth* 3). He summarizes this comparison: "A dream is an experience of that deep, dark ground that is the support of our conscious lives, and a myth is the society's dream" (PM 40). Therefore, myth is a complicated construction carrying repeated patterns of images with psychological origins fundamental to human experience.

This concept characterizes seemingly spontaneous stories in an oral culture. What about myths in a consciously shaped artistic work such as a novel? The application of mythic beliefs and actions to literature needs more explanation.

In his study on *Language and Myth* (1925), Ernst Cassirer equates myths to other symbolic entities, like language and art. To the extent that we can use language to discuss art, or render a literary work in artistic form, we can also use myths as a way to trace patterns in literature. Art, myth, and literature might be seen as three windows through which we view transcendent sights. The wondrous experience that each offers is unique, but each also affords a perspective on the others. Peering through the art window helps us to experience myth. Similarly, the view through the myth window sheds light on literature.

Influential cultural and literary commentators such as Constance Rourke, Daniel B. Hoffman, and Henry Nash Smith hold up mythology as an effective lens for viewing literary history. "Characteristic of the Myth Critics were a distrust of technology, a yearning for spiritual significance, an implicit commitment to the idea of community, and an abiding interest in primordial human consciousness" (Leitch 116). These groundbreaking studies trace how various images and motifs have influenced the development of historical, cultural, or literary tradition.

In his assessment of myth as a critical approach, John B. Vickery asserts and illustrates the important principle that myth precedes and grounds literature. He presents several ways in which myth connects with text:

Introduction

> Myth forms the matrix out of which literature emerges both historically and psychologically. Literary plots, characters, themes, and images are basically complications and displacements of similar elements in myths and folktales. Myth stimulates the creative process and provides patterns and concepts which the critic can use to interpret specific works of literature [80–81].

At first glance, primitive myths would seem an unusual choice for studying a fictional world originally inhabited by Sherlock Holmes. The detective story is supposed to be a layer of ratiocination over chaos. Refusing to fall prey to the same terrors that strain Watson's nerves, Holmes avers the light of rationality to overcome darkness. A civilized mind is the tonic to dispel untoward thoughts while poking into the residue of evil deeds.

Yet, the mystery genre invites and is even integral to mythic thinking. Unsolved death jump-starts a mystery. It also prompts myth. Joseph Campbell says that telling the myth gives listeners the experience of life. Consequently, the reality of death is myth's beginning (PM 70). Most of life encourages us to connect, but in confronting life's final passage, we have to succeed at disconnecting. The murder or crime at the center of the plot places the crisis of disengagement directly in the protagonist's path. Regardless of how well trained, intelligent, or observant, the detective or sleuth is marked or even knocked sideways by the victim's being prematurely unhinged from life. This jarring brings ritual into play.

Emily Dickinson says, "After great pain, a formal feeling comes." Rituals are born from those formal feelings. They are proscribed actions designed to restore order. Funerals are highly ritualized ceremonies. They give mourners a perspective, a place to go, words to say. Ritual also contains a strong element of magic. The worn rut of traditional action generates hope that control and order will return, despite upheaval. According to Northrop Frye, "In ritual, then, we may find the origin of narrative, a ritual being a temporal sequence of acts in which the conscious meaning or significance is latent: it can be seen by an observer, but is largely concealed from the participators themselves" (Archetypes 23).

In mystery fiction, after characters discover the body, the narrative coalesces and begins moving into various rigid ways of dealing with social disorder. Forensic and police procedural mysteries call the professional investigator to the case. The official investigation begins, complete with measurements, evidence collections, hair and fiber analysis, and autopsies. In a cozy mystery, the amateur sleuth attends the funeral of the friend or relative. The PI and client agree to terms and sign the contract in the so-called "paid for hire" mystery.

After dealing with death's aftermath, the narrative proceeds using various repeated patterns or motifs basic to human experience. Arranged around the solution to death, these motifs carry an emotional charge similar to Jung's "primordial images." In this study, we will use "primordial images" and "archetypes" interchangeably.

Jung's theory of archetypes is as complex in its way as a definition of myth (Samuels, Shorter, and Plaut, 187). Although Jung's theory begins with the idea of primordial images, his concept of submerged consciousness evolves into only a potential for behavior. In an essay for *Man and His Symbols*, Jung writes, "The archetype is a *tendency* to form such representations of a motif— representations that can vary a great deal in details without losing their basic pattern" (Jung 67; italics added). Eventually, Jung emphasizes the "unconscious and irrepresentable outline" of ideas revealed in images (Samuels *et al.* 187). He also describes them in a way that keeps them more flexible than types. Archetypes are "dynamic forms that manifest themselves in impulses, just as spontaneously as instincts. Certain dreams, visions, or thoughts can suddenly appear; and however carefully one investigates, one cannot find what causes them" (Jung 76). It's little wonder that critics have skimmed over this later development of the theory, as it places archetypes below conscious control and beyond rational thought.

Joseph Campbell defines archetypes as "certain powers of the psyche that are common to all mankind" (PM 217). Campbell notes additional useful aspects of the concept:

> The psyche is the inward experience of the human body, which is essentially the same in all human beings, with the same organs, the same instincts, the same impulses, the same conflicts, the same fears. Out of this common ground have come what Jung has called the archetypes, which are the common ideas of myth [PM 51].

The best writers are aware of these primary "ground" ideas and use them to mold narrative, color characters, and channel expression. Archetypal components of the myth narrative give impetus to the ordinary. In a genre where suspense and narrative tension heat up the main dish, writers are very likely to throw primal images and gestures into the pot.

We live in puzzling times. Statistics tell us that actual crimes are on the wane, but ironically, we are awash in mystery-centered media. Why? Is this our culture's delayed reaction to high murder rates from the eighties?

Suspense films and television crime dramas exert an unprecedented influence on our culture. Not only do these modes of entertainment earn big profits in film and television, but they also shape how we view the world. Even the reporting of actual events takes on the narrative formula of a mystery.

Nightly broadcasts assail us with current events mysteries in the guise of factual news. Reports on developments in the deaths of Nicole Brown Simpson, JonBenet Ramsey, and Princess Diana arrive in our living rooms as mysteries waiting to be solved. Criminal allegations against politicians warrant obsessive media coverage. Prime time "reality" shows like *20/20, 48 Hours,* and *Dateline NBC* lure viewers with promises of features billed as "real life murder mysteries."

Even daytime television plays off the mystery metaphor. Videos of actual daytime legal proceedings appear on *Court TV,* but more contrived court situations bleed into other channels. Television schedules are dotted with shows featuring strong authority figures like Judge Judy or Judge Wapner. For viewers, "real life" courtroom dramas serve as a calming counterpart to the apparent chaos unleashed on other shows, such as *Jerry Springer, Montel, Leeza,* or *Ricki Lake.* Judge Judy exercises parent-like rulings, while Jerry refuses to cast judgment on his guests, the badly behaved children.

Numerous television shows feature criminals, detectives, or lawyers doing detective work. HBO's series *The Sopranos* about a family involved in organized crime continues to garner high ratings. A new show on HBO entitled *Six Feet Under* features the family of a funeral director. While this offering does not feature a detective *per se,* it still deals with the problem of how to counter death with life.

NYPD Blue, Law & Order, and *Judging Amy* are highly touted shows with crime solving or legal solutions at the core. Although most of these shows feature men in leading roles, with women as foils, more regular women characters are coming into their own.

Judging Amy includes enough investigative work for two women. Amy Gray, the lead character, is a judge in family court. Although she may rely on her court clerk, an African-American man, Amy is sole arbiter of her decisions. Maxine Gray, Amy's mother, is a semi-retired social worker in a child welfare agency. The sleuth role is essentially split. Mother Maxine plays the gumshoe, visiting homes and interviewing juvenile "suspects." Amy is the authority figure in court even as her mother takes charge at home. Between the two of them, they effectively cover mysteries of families.

Our media show us images of real murders made fake on the news and staged murders made real on the shows. Mystery reading gains ascendancy partly by riding this exploitation. The fact that these virtual attempts to overcome mortality are hidden in the guise of entertainment or light reading says something of our culture's reluctance to look at death too closely. We are death-repressed. Casting a serious eye on mystery and its meaning at this time provides insight on the violence that laces contemporary life.

Marcia Muller, widely acknowledged as "mother of the modern mystery," gave birth to this squalling creature, the woman private investigator, in 1977. She published her first mystery featuring PI Sharon McCone (*Edwin of the Iron Shoes*). Since 1977, women's voices have sounded loudly on the mystery scene. In an introduction to a short story mystery anthology, *A Woman's*

Eye (1991), Sara Paretsky writes, "What began as a trickle of strong women [protagonists] a century ago ... has grown into a great outpouring of women's stories" (xii-xiii). Paretsky further sees the developed terrain of these mysteries as a paradigm for the growth of the women's movement. She emphasizes that the varied writing voices "mirror the struggles many American women have gone through in the last twenty years" (xiii).

While Paretsky notes the burgeoning crowd of strong women heroes, she does not provide any insights about the works in which they appear. In fact, she cautions *against* drawing any generalizations: "The one thing these stories have in common is the message that there is no one way to view women" (xiv).

If the number of mysteries has paralleled the women's movement, the categories of mystery have grown in a way to parallel other types of communication. Like cable networks with specialty channels dedicated to history or gardening or food or women, the types of women's mysteries now address various demographics. (Looking for a mystery featuring an equine veterinarian? See character Gail McCarthy in Laura Crum's *Cutter*.) However, these types stand apart from readers' tastes by falling into different mythic patterns. For instance, a culinary mystery emphasizes motifs of transformation, a legal thriller runs through a narrative pattern showing rites of initiation, and a mystery featuring a PI protagonist conforms to a quest narrative.

Willetta Heising's valuable reference *Detecting Women 3* illustrates the exponential increase in publication of mysteries by and about women. Titles are arranged in columns, totaling about three hundred works per page. Heising's list of mysteries published between 1940 to 1970 fits on one and a half pages. An index of mysteries published through the eighties takes up four pages. Entries for 1990 to 1995 fill nine pages. A list of mysteries published during a four-year span, between 1996 to 1999, sprawls across over eleven pages (Heising 357-85). The category has expanded from one and a half pages, to four, to nine, to eleven pages. The increase is astonishing by any standard. Critical literary commentary has not kept up.

Although the manor house mysteries of Agatha Christie remain prominently on two or three bookstore shelves, colorful paperbacks and hardcovers more recently written represent diverse settings and characters. The contemporary mystery is set in locales from Alaska to Miami, from New York City to small town America. Of course, there are mysteries set in bookstores.

Mystery-solving protagonists are similarly all over the map in temperament and occupation. Police detectives, lawyers, and private investigators are paid to poke their noses into the crime. They develop a thick skin about death and obstructionist suspects. When amateur sleuths or everyday folks find a corpse, they are more likely to scream, or at least be surprised over the dead body. They also kick up a powerful motivation for finding the murderer.

Modern amateur sleuths represent many rungs on the socioeconomic ladder, from the idle rich to professionals to cleaning women. Still, patterns emerge in the backgrounds of amateurs solving crimes. Characters working with food or in other domestic spheres constitute one disproportionately large group. Bookish types, authors, journalists, professors and lawyers form another. Nuns, former nuns, and women priests seem to run across more murders, percentage-wise, than their real world counterparts. The protagonists' singular occupations equip them for gaining access to evidence and reading clues surrounding that particular murder.

Animals play a surprisingly prominent role in suspense fiction from *The Hound of the Baskervilles* to the present. Many sleuths have pets. V. I. Warshawski's neighbor Mr. Contreras has dogs who keep V. I. company. In *"O" Is for Outlaw*, Kinsey Millhone faces a particularly growly dog as she tries to search a suspect's house by breaking in through the pet's door. In a few cases, animals take the lead away from their human owners and solve the crime, as in Lillian Jackson Braun's *The Cat Who ...* series or Rita Mae Brown's mysteries about Sneaky Pie, the clever feline. What is the significance of these animal motifs? Are the pets alter-egos for the human characters? Are they a touch of nature to counter a death-saturated landscape? Guardians of the gates of hell? A blend of human and vegetative worlds? A totem to represent magic and transformation of the self? Far from just trotting beside the sleuth, animals represent numerous concepts in myth.

Mystery fiction places front and center the solution to an untimely death or ways to smooth over an aberration in the human community. Where mystery thrives, romance is never far behind.

"Romance" mostly denotes a broad spectrum of genre fiction specializing in love and passion. However, "romance" also means "nonrepresentional images." Hawthorne sets out the parameters of this term in the preface to *The House of the Seven Gables* (1851):

> When a writer calls his work a Romance, it need hardly be observed that he wishes to claim a certain latitude, both as to its fashion and material ... If he think fit, also, he may so manage his atmospherical medium as to bring out or mellow the lights and deepen and enrich the shadows of the picture [Hawthorne 243].

What is the source of the long-standing prejudice about mysteries being light reading, not as respectable as mainstream novels?

In a *New Yorker* essay, influential literary commentator Edmund Wilson generally dismisses detective novels as "entertainments" unworthy of critical attention (1945). Puzzled by rabid mystery readers around him, he gives mysteries another college try. Ultimately, he sniffs, "I did not care for Agatha Christie and I hope never to read another of her books" (1950). For over thirty years, Carolyn G. Heilbrun, a distinguished professor at Columbia, wrote mysteries using the pen name "Amanda Cross." "Despite having tenure, Heilbrun was careful to preserve the pseudonym, to avoid being 'ridiculed or professionally demolished' for the extracurricular work she knew her colleagues would label frivolous" (Pervushina 33). For half a century, too many people have shared in Edmund Wilson's mistaken indictment of mysteries.

Detective fiction as a genre has generally not been subjected to the forensic light of literary critics. That unwarranted prejudice about the lower quality of "genre" or "formula" fiction has posed an obstacle. The myth approach has certainly been neglected, perhaps because of the perception that myth goes against the logical. People have taken too literally Poe's idea that "ratiocination" drives the tale of detection. In addition, myth to non-mythologists is only vaguely or incorrectly understood.

Whodunits signify serious business in our death-repressed culture, and they deserve close scrutiny. Mysteries are not less than novels; they are full-fledged novels that happen to be mysteries.

Myth is hardly the only path to meaning in these works. John Cawelti notes that examining aspects of the mystery formula is fruitful, but the results are not to be used as a "universal tool for unlocking the secrets of a culture" (297). Still, between claiming to know all and being satisfied with parts of a formula there lies considerable room for more insight.

CHAPTER 1

ANATOMY OF A MYSTERY

The Body Drops

In life, we measure our mortality every day in small ways, a wrinkle here, an ache there. On the page, an actual corpse sends a big, sudden mortality message. "Somebody has to die in order for life to emerge" (Campbell, *Power of Myth* 106).

The murder may even happen before page one. More frequently, for maximum effect, death enters when a character stumbles over a body, pursues an action leading to death, or discovers a planned death that will turn out to be impossible to thwart. Regardless of when the body drops, the corpse places a heavy burden onto the sleuth. Police investigators may refer jokingly to a body as "a cold one" or "a floater." In Kathy Reichs's *Death DuJour*, forensic anthropologist Tempe Brennan attends an arson scene. A volunteer fireman announces that he has found a body in the basement. "And better bring a spoon. There's not much left of this one" (Reichs 34). However casual or offhand the body collectors seem, the enormity of death poses a major conflict for the feeling character, the siren, at the center of the work. The reality of death hits home, suspending or altering the protagonist's routine.

The Summons

The night sirens call the sleuth to the murder scene. The summons and events to follow are striated with rituals. A trained crime-fighter goes through carefully regulated, scientific procedures. A protagonist may change identity and go undercover, in effect donning a mask. A first-person narrator, the "I" and "eye" of the tale relates events from the scene, simulating a type of confession. While trailing the chief suspect, a detective or criminal hunter participates in hunt rituals. She may even enact a ritual sacrifice, or recreate the crime by committing another, more acceptable murder.

How does the detective/sleuth mingle with the murder scene? For the professional, an official inquiry or call for consultation can set events into action. Murder is part of the job. For the amateur sleuth, the problem is different. People drop dead every day, but it is an unlikely coincidence that the same character will casually encounter a body more than once. Twice, maybe. Three times is really straining credulity. As a result of being at the wrong place at the wrong moment, the amateur sleuth may herself be accused or suspected of the crime. The amateur may witness a crime or have a relative die under suspicious circumstances. A deceased's relative may then employ a private investigator and share information about the case.

Entrance into people's homes is a practical matter. One has to be invited or break in. The other option for the sleuth is to go undercover. An altered identity makes it possible for the detective to come into the world sullied by the crime. Detailed databases in Heising's *Detecting Women* list mystery protagonists' occupations. This lengthy list evidences the many inventive ways mystery authors have found to bring the investigator into a home, office, or morgue. To paraphrase Campbell's "the masks of god," the masks of the sleuth play a ritualistic role as admission tickets. The altered or specialized identity makes possible a privileged entrée into the world of the deceased.

A variant to the masked sleuth motif is that of the masked corpse. Novels by Linda Fairstein, Kathy Reichs, and Patricia Cornwell exemplify this "Jane Doe" forensic type of narrative. The protagonist, usually a coroner or medical examiner, follows ritualized procedures to identify the deceased. DNA, X-rays, forensic etymology, dentistry, and other technological measurers of the death process aid in unmasking the corpse.

In a *New York Review of Books* article on Raymond Chandler's novels, Joyce Carol Oates sees the forensic mystery as a modern "resuscitation" of Poe's "The Gold Bug," with its "codes, ciphers, [and] secret messages" buried as clues (Oates 2–3). This ingenious explanation is only partly right. It fails to take into account that in contemporary forensic narratives, the purpose of the investigation is to name or identify the deceased. Often, the ritual develops into the sleuth identifying *with* the deceased. These high-tech methods of detection are metaphors for knowing the self.

DNA sequences and X-rays bring the protagonist up close to the bone, both literally and figuratively. Literally, the death-efficient professional moves

1. Anatomy of a Mystery

nearer to a name. To learn the name is to know. Figuratively, she seeks to understand Death.

The sleuth identifies so completely with the murdered victim that she undergoes, symbolically, the same method of death as the victim, but she survives. Since it is, of course, impossible to "know" Death completely, except as Other, the search shifts so that the character understands more about experiencing life. She is left with knowing herself. The medical examiner's title, professional name, is often abbreviated, interestingly, as M.E. or "ME."

Confession forms another ritual act common to mysteries, not just at the denouement but throughout the narrative. The "spoken" aspect of confession comes across through first-person narration, a mystery staple since Poe. Watson provides an "I" for Conan Doyle's works. Chandler's Philip Marlowe continues the convention with the private "eye." What is there about the genre that prompts a first-person angle of perspective?

Certainly first-person narration affords the reader a seat inside the yellow crime scene tape. Having a character relate what's going on, seemingly as it happens, makes more obvious that the story is somehow being told. The first-person perspective links the written narrative more closely to the ritual of telling stories, an essential part of harmonizing our lives with reality (Campbell, PM 5).

A person confesses to relieve guilt. Death begins myth, and self-recrimination is its aftermath. "Man lives by killing, and there is a sense of guilt connected with that" (PM 72). Here is where ratiocination enters the mythic narrative.

A rational process like a medical procedure or the legal system ritualizes and codifies guilt for the reader and the protagonist. Mystery readers generally remain twinge-free about wallowing in crime. They do not feel grief or guilt about the murder. Why should they? They buy the book for the fun of following the case. They often perceive that they can "solve the murder" along with the sleuth if they pay close enough attention. However, in most mysteries, regardless of the narrative's overall logic, the plot is so byzantine or strewn with inconsistencies that from the reader's limited vantage point, seeing the correct solution is impossible. The reader-solved mystery is an elaborate ruse, less a way to undo the social upheaval of the crime and more an immediate, ritualized response to overcome guilt that is *not felt* after the reader experiences death on the page.

Although explicit guilt rests squarely on the perpetrator, which is where it ostensibly belongs, the narrative works out another ritual of guilt, the sleuth's re-enactment of the crime. Despite a buzzard-like participation in death, the sleuth generally has no guilt, at least initially. She has to stay two steps ahead of the mourner's grief to keep a clear head. However, later, the protagonist may be forced toward violent acts, perhaps as despicable as the original killing. We see the crime through the culprit's eyes. We may even come to condone the sleuth's actions, to rationalize the murder as an acceptable means to an end.

In Lisa Scottoline's *Rough Justice,* lawyer Marta Richter has been on the run for over ten chapters. Bogosian, her stalker, is a hired killer, a sociopath whose only redeeming feature is that he likes dogs. Eventually, Marta takes matters into her own hands.

> *Please, God, help me.* Marta raised the forge hammer and brought it down on Bogosian's head with brute force, driving the iron ball through his crown. His skull cracked like a pavement. Blood gushed from the wound, hot and wet, splattering Marta's face. She screamed in horror.
> Bogosian's eyes went round as the moon and they stared at her.
> He was dead as he stood [281].

Scottoline tries to humanize Bogosian the killer by making him an animal lover, but essentially he himself is an animal, the prey of Marta's hunt. In a few spots through the rest of the novel, Marta reminds herself of the act. "Marta was a killer now. The thought nauseated her" (286). She still suffers, eleven chapters later: "Marta's stomach felt queasy" (372). However, by the end of the book, the character's guilt is nearly dissipated.

Telling about the murder, that is, the story itself, expiates culpability. "Guilt is what is wiped out by the myth. Killing the animal is not a personal act. You are performing the work of nature" (Campbell, PM 74). We make excuses for Marta's crime, viewing it as self-defense or fair retaliation against Bogosian's bestial nature. The villain is a scapegoat.

This confrontation between the sleuth and villain is often regarded merely as a requisite "woman in peril" convention. In many cases, the encounter takes on the scapegoat ritual significance, along with other mythic meanings of altering time, as we will explain. The investigation, a search for the aberrant personality, can be seen as a ritual hunt to override the original murder. The detective goes after the criminal, the one who committed the murder and lied to cover it up. In doing so, the sleuth may commit a similar crime of murder, but we condone this taboo, because the killing is an act of nature, a cleansing of the culture. Ironically, in many mysteries an animal is anthropomorphic. Here on the hunt, the human villain becomes less than human.

Quests and Tests

The detective/sleuth is a hero in the mythic sense. She may begin as an ordinary person, but after an encounter with murder, life changes. She attempts to solve the mystery, essentially trying to control mortality, an arduous quest by any measurement. Still, people are not born heroes, and to achieve hero-status, the protagonist must face a series of tests. The difficulty of solving the crime measures the sleuth's worthiness.

Campbell says that among heroes there are "some that choose to undertake the journey and some that don't" (PM 129). This serves as a most accurate description on the difference between a professional investigator and an amateur sleuth. Often the amateur needs more coaxing to move into the mystery. However, once thrust onto the stage of action, the character learns the value of working for a cause larger than the self, restoring the broken human circle. "This person then takes off on a series of adventures beyond the ordinary, either to recover what has been lost or to discover some life-giving elixir" (PM 123).

In a mystery, what's lost, of course, is life. As part of the process for regaining life, the seeker must name and face the murderer. Sometimes, as we have seen, she even has to fight the murderer.

She also has to do this alone.

The sleuth is the only one with the special knowledge to pass the test. "One authoritative voice and one infallible solution are required; the detective alone holds the alpha position as the binaries of crime solving are unfolded" (Klein 183). Campbell approaches this same phenomenon of the solitary solver from a mythic angle. "Privation and suffering alone open the mind to all that is hidden to others" (PM xiii). The ending to Campbell's *The Hero with a Thousand Faces* emphasizes that the loneliness of the quest increases its ultimate worth:

> It is not society that is to guide and save the creative hero, but precisely the reverse. And so every one of us shares the supreme ordeal — carries the cross of the redeemer — not in the bright moments of his tribe's great victories, but in the silences of his personal despair [391].

Solving the murder helps everyone. Despite the solution's value to the human community, the sleuth alone bears the full burden of answering the question of who committed the murder.

The Line-Up

After a homicide, a witness tells police she saw a bearded man running outside the zoo, which is the crime scene. In a police procedural, the detective stages a sort of *tableau* of bearded men for the witness. Most of the bearded faces are unfamiliar or strange to the witness, innocent "ringers" brought in to play a role in the drama. The witness finds one bearded face familiar; he could therefore be the guilty party or a conduit to additional information.

Whether the line-up takes place at the station or in seventeen different apartments in the same neighborhood as the zoo, this drama of the search for words characterizes this phase of the narrative. The sleuth gathers verbal clues of varying relevance. The words' relevance to the crime may be obvious or not obvious right then, as with the precinct line-up. The amateur sleuth does not explicitly have the power to arrange a formal line-up, but the drama proceeds nonetheless via telephone calls, visits, or chance meetings. Informal, casual conversations can later take on significance.

The object of the sleuth's quest differs in various plots. In some cases, the narrative conforms to myths of searches representing mother and child bonds or myths of artistic creativity. Along with the solution to the crime, many fictional women private investigators manage to restore a family or in some way satisfy their own lack of families. The detective may have a sidekick character with whom he or she shares a surrogate family bond. The prize, therefore, is a restoration of "the harmonious rhythm of relationships" (Campbell, PM 220).

Family ties figure prominently in myths, and so do artists: "Creative artists ... are mankind's wakeners to recollection; summoners of our outward mind to conscious contact with ourselves" (Campbell, *Creative Mythology* 92). The detective's impulse toward creativity finds realization through a renewal of vision or completion of an artistic task. Private eye narratives, therefore, generally involve archetypes such as the White Goddess, the Dark Mother, the Earth Diver, the Cosmic Egg.

The sleuth poses questions and compares witness stories, alibis, and motives. She picks her way through falsehoods to see who has something to hide. When she finds that person, has she found the murderer?

Red Herrings

In some mysteries, the detective learns that everyone has something to hide. Red herrings or false clues are more than a bit of razzle-dazzle to trick the reader. John Cawelti calls the interviewing phase of a detective narrative "a complex process of changing implications" (146).

As the detective proceeds with the search, she sees words in a new light. The process is complex because the very concepts of guilt and innocence are often what change. Delivering a keynote address at the first Private Eye Writers Convention (Eye Con Milwaukee 1995), Sue Grafton notes that in some books, the writer may frame every character, making them all seem guilty. "I try to keep everybody innocent," Grafton says. Mistaken impressions in themselves have meaning. The detective can go on the proverbial "wild goose chase" and still maintain respect as a savvy crime fighter. The difficulty of solving the crime tests the hero's resolve (Campbell, PM 126). From the wrong turns and errors in conclusions, the sleuth gains strength and experience to face the next hurdle.

This kaleidoscope of slippery meanings, half-truths and misperceptions could proceed forever except the search must eventually answer the question, Who killed X? Through a series of three or four increasingly difficult dilemmas, lies and deceptions are pinpointed, and the detective's learning curve reaches its height. Events then move quickly, as she rearranges the kaleidoscope wheel to match words with meanings.

Academic and bookstore mysteries, suspense dealing with works of art or rare manuscripts, psychological and legal thrillers all emphasize nuances of verbal meaning as part of the narrative. Clues may appear as types of riddles the hero must solve to be worthy. Sleuths with word expertise and an ability to gauge ambiguity figure prominently in these mystery types. These would include writers, professors, book collectors, journalists, psychologists, and lawyers. "The adventure is symbolically a manifestation of [the hero's] character" (Campbell, PM 129). These are the searchers best qualified to pass the verbal tests.

This quest for truth proceeds through *Logos*, or what Joseph Campbell calls in *Creative Mythology*, "the word behind words." In mythology, possessing this knowledge opens the door to revelation. To arrive at this word is to connect "one's own truth and depth to the depth and truth of another in such a way as to establish an authentic community of existence" (CM 84). With the true killer dead or behind bars, the human community resumes its experience with life.

Skulking in the Labyrinth

G. K. Chesterton cites the role of landscape in detective fiction as crucial in conveying "the poetry of modern life" (Chesterton 4). The mystery writer is no different from other writers in relying more or less upon actual locations for fictional settings. However, in the hands of a skilled novelist, the world of the sleuth clings like a silk blouse. Atmosphere and territory contribute mightily to the mission of the detective. Rarely does the setting serve as mere backdrop. In many works, the landscape comes alive to lend symbolic significance to the action.

The world surrounding the mystery protagonist may come into sharp or soft focus through the accuracy of its details. The city becomes a character in its own right. Linda Barnes presents a comprehensive tour of Boston through the journeys of cab driver–turned–PI Carlotta Carlyle. Elaine Viets's journalist sleuth Francesca Vierling travels both the mean streets and ritzy neighborhoods of St. Louis. Carolina Garcia-Aguilera is the creator of Miami-based private eye Lupe Solano. She tells how a geography professor from Dartmouth contacted her regarding her references to Miami streets and landmarks. His purpose was to obtain permission to use Garcia-Aguilera's books as texts in his geography course (Garcia-Aguilera, February 25, 2000, Fort Lauderdale). These authors integrate actual landscape so completely into the work, the mystery's setting emerges as a New Local Color. We travel the territory as we read.

Despite pinpoint accuracy of setting, a novelist has no obligation to paint an exact representational landscape. Sue Grafton's PI Kinsey Millhone lives and works in Santa Teresa, "ninety-five miles north of Los Angeles." There is no actual place called Santa Teresa, but Grafton spends part of the year in Santa Barbara, and Kinsey's territory could be regarded as that town's fictional counterpart.

Comparing reality to fiction with landscape is instructive on one level, but it does not take us very far into the pattern of the work. The pulse of landscape on the page comes from its mythic meaning in relation to the protagonist, and that's a different order of geography. As Northrop Frye reminds us, literature exists in a nonrepresentational realm: "An image is not merely a verbal replica of an external object" (Archetypes 22). The murder thrusts events into a liminal sphere halfway between life and death, or what Alexander Eliot calls a "mythosphere" (1–13), a mythological space. In this sphere, the sleuth struggles to realize the vision quest or reach the *axis mundi*, the center of the world (Eliade 39–45). The reward for reaching this destination is precious — renewal of the human community.

After the murder, mythic space pressures the sleuth to undertake the mythic journey. The hero may be ambivalent about his direction, but he suddenly finds himself in a transformed realm, a landscape that most addresses his weaknesses. Campbell reiterates that the hero gets the landscape he deserves. "You leave the world you're in and go into a depth or into a distance or up to a height. There you come to what was missing in your consciousness in the world you formerly inhabited" (PM 129). On the foggy heights of San Francisco, Marcia Muller's PI Sharon McCone seeks clarity of vision. In Nevada Barr's novel *Blind Descent*, park ranger Anna Pigeon is forced onto a rescue team inching along a gopher city of caves. Anna, of course, is claustrophobic.

A mystery's setting, then, can express the opposite of the sleuth's psyche. However, we can take additional steps toward examining the dynamism of landscape by incorporating narrative, or the book's forward motion into the model. In interviewing suspects and double-checking clues, the woman sleuth walks or drives the terrain. She traces a line on the earth, and each successive episode in the narrative advances this line. While many contemporary mysteries present the transformed realm as antagonist or arena of conquest, the landscape can also meld narrative and protagonist through the image of the labyrinth.

In Athenian mythology, on commission from King Minos, Daedalus fashions an unsolvable maze. "A multiplex of courts and cloisters blind/where misdirections led, in mazes long,/The cheated eye circuitously wrong" (Ovid VIII, 152).

This Escherian palace serves to hold the beastly minotaur in as much as to keep mortals out. Theseus volunteers as minotaur food and boldly enters the crooked paths. He has a safety line, the thread from Ariadne, the king's daughter. Theseus kills the minotaur, rolls up the thread, and makes good his escape (Grant 338–39).

This myth's version of the labyrinth presents significant ramifications for contemporary mysteries. Like Theseus, the detective must overcome initial qualms about facing the killer, a human equivalent of the murderous minotaur. Keeping in mind that she, too, could be sacrificed, she must enter the maze of the case. Ambiguous evidence, complicated emotions, and mixed motivations from suspects all act to keep her from the killer's ugly reality. She attempts to leave a trailing thread, an envelope mailed to herself or a message to a friend that she has gone to the murderer's apartment. In the end, when the sleuth unmasks the murderer, the monster is slain and all of Athens rejoices.

The myth of the labyrinth is but one pattern that can explain the role of setting in a mystery. Others involve the body of the goddess embedded in the land and the myth of the Razor's Edge.

In this narrative pattern, the hero must walk the line exactly or all is lost. The Razor's Edge also explains how an apparently new twist in mysteries, cybercrime, or clues hidden in programs or hard drives, falls into a mythic pattern. Computer use or word processing duplicates the heroic journey. One step to either side, such as tapping a key out of sequence or failing to hit "save" at the crucial time, can lead the searcher off the edge, and all is lost.

Mythic Time

In a murder investigation, time is obviously important. The entire correct solution can hinge on time of death and alibi times, intervals in a suspect's existence that others can account for. For the mystery series especially, time plays a key role. The sleuth has a life beyond the last page, and succeeding episodes in the series have to make some effort to be consistent in chronology as well as character.

Many mysteries invoke a more overriding meaning for time by defining the sleuth's quest toward the solution according to days, months, or seasons.

Several series link time, mystery, and religious sleuths. Harry Kemelman's Rabbi Small day-of-the-week series was among the first with titles related to time.

Rabbi Small solves crimes using his special knowledge of *pilpul*, a type of logic akin to Poirot's "little grey cells." Although the Rabbi series relies partly on the ratiocination convention, the actions of a holy man intensify, almost consecrate, the ritual aspect of the solution.

Several other ecclesiastical series create links with time. Books by Lee Harris feature former nun Christine Bennett and center mysteries around holidays. The Decker-Lazarus series by Faye Kellerman includes religious settings noted in the titles. Sister Carol Anne O'Marie, herself a nun, writes mysteries featuring Sister Mary Helen. The titles of these works relate to the liturgical calendar of the Catholic Church. A clerical sleuth makes sense in terms of location and character. Places of worship, churches, temples, convents, or monasteries, can be notoriously spooky places. The holy site clashes with the unholy crime. Spiritual leaders have access to a closed community. Cynthia Manson's introduction to *Thou Shalt Not Kill*, a short story anthology focusing on "ecclesiastical sleuths," notes the contrast between sacred and profane: "The darker side of humankind seems all the more sinister when probed by the devout followers of the church" (Manson xi). This explains the conjunction of murder with men or women of the cloth, but why include time? Again, myth provides an insight on this pattern.

Some mystery writers give their books titles with holiday-themes as a marketing hook. However, the progression of time in any mystery is much more complicated. Time, or change, is really mortality in another guise. Like death, it is another of life's great mysteries.

Many levels of time unravel in the mystery. Concepts from Northrop Frye serve as a guide to these timescapes. "We may call the rhythm of literature the narrative, and the pattern, the [reader's] simultaneous mental grasp of the verbal structure, the meaning or significance" (Archetypes 22). Like poetry, mystery is a literary type in which narrative and significance are unified. A mystery's manipulations of time result in a broken narrative rhythm. This ruffled surface reflects a deeper disruption of life due to unexpected death. Form and meaning become one.

As the narrative unfolds, events proceed in a linear, causal fashion until a death occurs. At that moment, mundane life hangs unfinished, and liminal, mythic time takes its place. In this dimension, reasons are not apparent, and the sleuth must question causes. This world of suspended time is the temporal dimension to the spatial "mythosphere." Man-made time markers fall to either side of the lost life. We have only "before" and "after." Depending on when in the book the murder occurs, nearly the entire narrative could exist in suspended, mythic time.

The inexorable movement of clock hands gives way to a clock with no hands. Seasonal holy times lend themselves to a mystery because sacred time or a holiday is an equivalent to mythic time. It has its own rhythm apart from daily life. Intense and emotion-charged, mythic time also lacks individuation of minutes or hours. It bends, like Dali's clocks. Either all things happen at once or nothing happens at all. For a simple understanding of the transition from linear to mythic time, compare the pre-holiday rush with the actual holiday.

As events in the mystery move toward a resolution, the narrative rhythm varies. The plot may race backward, forward, or even pause, as if the person running the show has an itchy finger on the video remote.

The video rewinds. We might think that the narrative function of flashbacks is practical, to refresh the reader's memory about the investigation and re-examine various clues as they accumulate. However, does it make logical sense to "pause" events at this juncture? Shouldn't the narrative line step smartly toward a conclusion? Time shifts, flashbacks, pauses, and fast-forwards logically complicate matters. The book's energy should wind down for a denouement, not pulsate like a dying star.

Time shifts in the nearly completed narrative arc represent the sleuth's struggle to regulate time. She has to re-establish natural rhythms for life to proceed as it had been. The goal, according to Frye, is "to synchronize human and natural energies" (Archetypes 23). One reversal of time's arrow occurs through the sleuth's lecture. At this point in the narrative, usually within fifty pages of the ending, she runs through her understanding of the crime. She may speak the lecture to herself, a group of suspects, or the killer. In telling how the death occurred, the sleuth illustrates mastery over linguistic falsehood. Finally, the word version of the crime matches its actuality, showing the way to *Logos*, the word behind words.

Sometimes the villain initiates the flashback through a confession. While holding the detective at gunpoint, knifepoint, or some other precarious situation, the killer confesses how the whole crime happened and why. The veracity of this "confession" is rarely an issue, although why would the killer bother to tell the truth at this point? Still, we as readers generally believe the confession. The fact that the murderer claims to "reveal all" means that the sleuth will be killed. Dead men tell no tales. The flashback heightens suspense. This pause in the forward progression gives the protagonist time to make a run for it or plan an escape. In any event, she gathers strength for the final battle.

The flashback takes on mythic meaning in conjunction with guilt rituals. We discussed earlier how the protagonist may re-enact the original crime by hunting the killer and mimicking the murder. In this case, the sleuth essentially "takes back time." By understanding death and punishing the killer, she pulls the world of the unsolved murder out of its suspended state and moves the narrative onto a forward time track.

In this world of shifted timescapes, there can also be time lags, as when an overused videotape balks at moving forward. The key piece of evidence leading to the suspect is some special knowledge the protagonist used to know but has forgotten. A clue or phrase may jog a vague memory, but the insight is beyond the detective's cognition. It takes a trauma to bring the memory to the surface.

In mythic terms, this time lag is extremely significant. It suggests lost time or amnesia, and the annals of myth are filled with myths of forgetting and remembering. In myths, forgetting is a kind of sleep, even a symbolic death. Ironically, the sleuth has to undergo the exact fate of the murdered victim in order to understand how the death happened. Then, when the murderer's name flashes onto the sleuth's consciousness like a lightning bolt, the quest vision is fulfilled. "Waking implies anamnesis, recognition of the soul's true identity, that is, re-cognition of its celestial origins" (Eliade 129).

To further complicate temporal matters, the writer may delay revealing the sleuth's leap of intuition to the reader. This flash of insight leaves the reader behind, but enables the sleuth to make a heroic leap forward to unmask the killer.

The Killer Unmasked

At the moment when the sleuth discovers or reveals the murderer, time stands still. It is forever high noon. Northrop Frye says that "Patterns of imagery ... or fragments of significance, are oracular in origin, and derive from the epiphanic moment, the flash of instantaneous comprehension with no direct reference to time" (Archetypes 23). As literary turning points go, the unmasking is intense and Janus-like, looking both backward and forward. It achieves in time what the razor's edge phenomenon stands for in space. For an instant, time stops, and the face of Insoluble Death is revealed. Then, the clock resumes its ticking, and death falls into the background as the unsolvable reality of our experience.

These tests of the detective or sleuth make the killer the equivalent of a monster in myth. Joseph Campbell's definition of a mythic monster corresponds neatly to the villain in a mystery. The mythic monster is a creature with "powers too vast for the normal forms of life to contain them" (PM 222). The sleuth's discovery of the killer's identity unleashes these powers. The sleuth then tries to contain the destructive energies, by wounding the murderer or presenting him or her to the police to be arrested. "By a monster, I mean some horrendous presence or apparition that explodes all of your standards for harmony, order, and ethical conduct" (PM 222).

Life Restored

Mickey Spillane has said that a book's first page sells that particular book, and the last page sells the next one. Marketing considerations aside, the mystery's ending assures the reader that the series will continue, that these characters will have a life off the page doing whatever they do until we next meet up with them, working cases, starting love affairs, playing with dogs or babies. The bodies are carried completely offstage, and tomorrow is another day.

These usual descriptions of satisfactory endings fall short in characterizing the stark contrast between the hero's suffering to complete the quest and the end of the quest itself. "When the Angel of Death approaches, he is terrible. When he reaches you, it is bliss" (Campbell, PM 222). The narrator's suffering beforehand makes the conclusion of life restored all worthwhile. The self reaffirms its existence. The labyrinth releases its terrors. The rhythm of narrative resumes its harmony with nature.

At the end of Nancy J. Cohen's *Permed to Death* (1999), hair stylist Marla Shore fends off a ghastly attack from the murderer. In the process, she injures her hands. She has put herself to the test and risked what was most important to her.

After Marla endures the encounter with evil, her rescuer and love interest arrives. She transcends the mythic landscape. "Her body became weightless as he lifted her to his chest" (Cohen 287). Later, that same rescuer checks in on the patient, who is now recovering at home. For the first time, Marla sees him as serious relationship material. Since her divorce, she had avoided men.

> Vail cleared his throat. "I was wondering if you'd like to go out to dinner tonight since you can't cook until your hands recover."
> A silly grin split her face. "Sure that sounds great" [293].

With the re-introduction of love and laughter, the barren landscape blooms once more. Marla finds the benefit from her sacrifice. The mystery completes its pattern of death and rebirth, restoring life's broken vessel.

Graham Greene once wrote that detective novels are our modern fairy tales. Mysteries certainly contain the submerged power of fairy tales. At times, a detective story or cozy mystery appeals out of all proportion to the work's stated solution. Despite realistic details of geographical and historical setting, the timelessness of mystery narratives indeed places them in a "once upon a time" landscape. As in a fairy tale, the overall arc of the mystery narrative reaffirms survival. Characters may not necessarily live "happily ever after," but life continues, changed — maybe even transformed — but solidly on the scene.

Graham Greene's comment is true for mystery beginnings and endings, but what about the narrative in between? To a mythologist, fairy tales present stories of children's rites of passage. Very often, a mystery is a fairy tale for adults. It will not lull us to sleep, if we ask the right questions. When we do, we see that the death-centered mystery fizzes with embedded truths about the struggles of living — violence and healing, fantasy and reality, conflict and harmony, beginnings and endings.

CHAPTER 2

Magic and Transformation in Domestic Mysteries

Few would argue that it's so nice to have a homicide around the house. Still, more women joining the ranks of murder writers have updated and adapted the cozy murder mystery developed by Agatha Christie. Today's writers of non-violent mysteries present a fresh look at traditional women's roles by casting wives, mothers, caterers, hairdressers, and housekeepers as suburban sleuths. "Heroism for the woman mystery detective is not in the extraordinary. It is lived in the ordinary" (Dilley xii). This "ordinary" woman engaged in catering, adornment, or housecleaning not only brings light into the realms of death. She is a mediator, bridging the gap between the outer world of appearance and an inner sense of self.

In part, amateur sleuths embody a kind of wish fulfillment. Readers enjoy the vicarious thrill of spying on neighbors or chasing a clue around the block. However, a more fundamental reason for amateur murder solving among the soccer moms is that the books often present a disguised version of deep, painful truths of experience. These mysteries are fairy tales for adults. The amateur sleuth of a domestic mystery is unambiguously caught between past and future. To move away from this liminal state, she either has to make her current situation fit or re-establish herself in a new role.

Bruno Bettelheim's *Uses of Enchantment* (1977) points out the fairy tale's formative role in child development. In a similar way, domestic mysteries address difficult conflicts basic to modern adult experience. Plots involve stalking, poisonings, assaults, and homicide. In the reformulated world of the domestic mystery, these dangers dramatize psychological risks and realities involved in personal growth. Transformation of clues or suspicious figures represents a release of the spirit (Jung, FA 81). Loss of consciousness, fainting, or sleeping all represent a ritual rebirth. They give the protagonist time to gather energy to combat the dark forces thwarting her inner development.

In Agatha Christie's novels, Miss Jane Marple is rarely in trouble. Miss Marple fixes the death and disorder in her village almost to entertain herself, like doing a jigsaw puzzle or working out a cross-stitch. The new sleuth on the suburban scene has a past, and it isolates her from her community. She has not yet fit her inner world with the outer one. For these updated sleuths, tying the loose ends of their own lives is nearly as crucial as bringing the murderer to justice.

Domestic sleuths are amateurs at crime solving and isolation. They differ from private investigators, who have adapted to being alone. V. I. Warshawski and Kinsey Millhone, for instance, do not belong to a highly socialized culture. They are isolated. Though domestic sleuths are adamant about being independent, they are indeed dependent financially on a highly socialized group — the upper middle-class society that can afford to hire a caterer, visit the hair salon weekly, or engage housecleaners.

Faith Fairchild is a fugitive from a big city — New York. There she had run her own catering business. Married to a minister and with a new child, Faith feels imprisoned by the small town environment of Aleford, Massachusetts. In *Body in the Belfry* (1990), Faith worries that her life is becoming "terribly quaint."

> Time was when village meant the Village and "town" was up or down. And when did she start using phrases like "time was"? She let another sigh escape into the pollution-free landscape and longed for a whiff of that heady combination of roasted chestnuts and exhaust fumes that meant autumn to her [2].

Like Faith Fairchild, China Bayles has also fled the big city. The sleuth in Susan Wittig Albert's series, China left a Houston law firm to open a spice and herb shop in a small Texas town. China's shop does not technically dispense food, but the shop's inventory carries the same life-giving properties. Spices are a means of preserving food. Herbs may be dried up, or smoked, but like food, they convey the message that the stuff of life finds significance beyond ripeness or fertility. As China Bayles ages, she finds new life in this occupation. Ultimately, Faith's and China's problems fitting into the small town reflect their fears of facing the future, and their adventures in mystery solving involve their struggles to work out problems of aging and change.

2. Magic and Transformation in Domestic Mysteries

Diane Mott Davidson's culinary series features Goldy Bear Korman, a caterer. Goldy is divorced. Her ex-husband, John Richard Korman, is a physician, charming, and handsome. Unfortunately, he was also abusive and drank too much. She left him after he pounded her hand with a hammer. She took her son Arch with her and never looked back. As a former doctor's wife, she is also exiled from her former social and economic circle in the upscale Colorado suburb of Aspen Meadow. Goldy has begun her own business with the motto "Goldilocks' Catering, Where Everything Is Just Right!"

Nancy J. Cohen's protagonist Marla Shore in the "Bad Hair Day" series is a successful hairstylist. She is also divorced and childless in a hothouse, not to say, steamy subculture where women's major topics of conversation revolve around husbands and children. *Permed to Death* (1999) opens with the poisoning death of an elderly client in Marla's salon. The police suspect Marla, who had a good reason to want Mrs. Kravitz dead. The dead woman knew secrets from Marla's past and had been blackmailing her. Another nagging ache from Marla's past occurred when she was nineteen. She had been babysitting, and the child placed in her care had drowned. Marla feels compelled to solve the murder of Mrs. Kravitz, not only to exonerate herself, but because she is attracted to Dalton Vail, the handsome police lieutenant in charge of the investigation.

Callahan Garrity, created by Kathy Hogan Trocheck, had been on the Atlanta police force. Tired of working inside a law-enforcement bureaucracy, emotionally and spiritually bankrupt, Callahan now lives with her mother and runs a housecleaning service, called The House Mouse. Along with her mother, her mother's elderly friends, and one particularly astute young man named Cheezer, Callahan is mostly content to clean houses. Still, when crimes cross her path, she follows them up.

These life difficulties let loose a Pandora's box of trouble for the sleuth from the beginning. However, the main character's conflicts also link her ritually with the deceased. The tinge of death in life has already darkened the detective.

Although each is employed in a creative endeavor, these crafts used to sustain life are ironically the very ones that can also make it most artificial. Food, cosmetic adornment, and household cleaning depend on a certain suspension of disbelief for their rejuvenating effects. As a practitioner of those magic arts, the sleuth has intimate knowledge of where artifice to cover an ugly truth ends and where beauty begins. Through her magic, she restores life to the same community that has rejected her.

The sleuth must also reconcile personal inner realities with this social circle. As a character, she shows two dimensions, the self she used to have and the self she has now. She achieves hero status by traveling the road toward solving the mystery and healing her own spirit. The sleuth overcomes her past and blends with the present, essentially working what Joseph Campbell calls a "creative mythology":

> Thus it corrects the authority holding to the shells of forms produced and left behind by lives once lived. Renewing the act of experience itself, it restores to existence the quality of adventure, at once shattering and re-integrating the fixed, already known, in the sacrificial creative fire of the becoming thing that is no thing at all but life, not as it will be or as it should be ... as it is, in depth [*Creative Mythology* 7–8].

The sleuth's journey follows a narrative propelled by the same forces of magic and transformation that power fairy tales. Instead of being motivated by causation or logic, the story line moves in the spasmodic actions similar to those of dreams. "Mythology and the psychology of dream are recognized as related, even identical" (CM 358). The reader has no sense of a gradual accumulation of events or subtle changes resulting from character action. Things happen at once, as if through sympathetic magic. Food, hair, or houses have cloud-like auras around them, affecting people for good or ill.

For the most part, characters react to events, instead of precipitating or shaping them. Events happen in the narrative suddenly, or by a type of sympathetic magic. While characters achieve psychological insight at times, the narrative lurches ahead according to whim or immediate upset. The sleuth is attacked out of the blue. A clue appears or disappears. Highly suspicious characters or romantic figures pop out of the dark suddenly, almost as a wish fulfillment. Events are ambiguous, not in themselves, but only because the character is limited by her own ill-fitting perspectives. She cannot "see." Once she does arrive at a clear vantage point, the mystery is cleared up, but even these scenes take on the blurred edges of nightmare.

Most domestic mysteries are written in limited third person. This perspective offers the reader only a narrow view of the main character's mind. Instead, we are invited along as a fellow dreamer. The mind of the dreamer is largely uncomplicated, after all. It is the world out there that is nuanced and perilous.

These motifs of a frightening "world beyond the self" link domestic mysteries even more tightly to fairy tales. "Fairy tales are images of processes in the collective unconscious when consciousness does not understand them. They are like not-understood dreams that are not integrated into the cultural consciousness or that are integrated only partially" (Von Franz 144). Stories where transformation and magic are touchstones for safety are very prevalent in fairy tales with European origins. Goldilocks samples food and bounces on the furniture in the home of the three bears. A kiss transforms a beast into a handsome

2. Magic and Transformation in Domestic Mysteries

prince. A touch from a magic wand changes Cinderella from a housemaid to a princess. Witches in tales from the pages of Grimm turn children into swans or ravens.

Folklorists often consider that American storytelling includes no major streak of transformation. On the contrary, near-magical transformation plays key roles in American thinking that we may not want to acknowledge. Despite enormous odds, people close their eyes and hope for automatic riches. I *will* win the lottery, or the magazine sweepstakes are on their way to my house. Advertising, too, works its magic, as consumers believe that a mere touch from a fashion model's cosmetic or European car will grant them sex appeal and success.

American popular culture also perpetuates the transformation theme via supernatural creatures. The wolf man, vampires, the Blair witch, and the evil twin all have extensive development in films or other commercialized media. Recently the Pinocchio motif has received much attention as a non-human creature such as a robot or alien wishes to become human. These transformation narratives all have considerable viability in contemporary American culture. So it is no surprise that domestic mysteries tap into this suspension of disbelief.

A sizable dollop of the cozy mystery subgenre shows the sleuth solving a death and reviving a famished community through the transformative powers of cooking. Culinary mysteries feature caterers or chefs as protagonists. Virginia Rich was among the first to scatter recipes like bread crumbs among the crime-solving (*The Cooking School Murders*, 1982). Nancy Pickard's recent collaboration with Rich (*The 27-Ingredient Chile Con Carne Murders*, 1993) and Pickard's reincarnation of Rich's charming character Eugenia Potter has generated new interest in Rich's contribution to the culinary mystery. An ever-lengthening shopping list of mystery novelists places food and cooking as central to the book. A partial list of authors with at least three titles in a cooking series includes Mary Daheim, Denise Dietz, Selma Eichler, Nancy Fairbanks, Tamar Myers, Joanne Pence, Phyllis Richman, and Rosemary Stevens.

Diane Mott Davidson's culinary series started in 1990 and continues to sit at the head table. The name of Davidson's sleuth, Goldy Bear, and the motto of her catering firm already suggest a fairy tale setting. As with Goldilocks, the porridge of this Goldy's world is either too hot or too cold. Nothing is "just right." Goldy mediates between the world of authority and power, as represented by John Richard, her hammer-wielding ex-husband, and the world of magic tricks and alchemy, expressed by her son Arch. Arch has a fascination for dungeons and dragons and performs magic shows. Although Goldy considers her act as a single mother a "parenting trick" (*Dying for Chocolate* 14), she finds herself perpetually off balance. She resorts to food preparation to ease her problems.

Goldy's food magic melts her troubled outer reality. Her world calls for a mythic solution. Campbell identifies the world needing myth as:

> [A]ny world in which (to state the problem pedagogically) force and not love, indoctrination, not education, authority, not experience, prevail in the ordering of lives and where the myths and rites enforced and received are consequently unrelated to the actual inward realization, need, and potentiality of those upon whom they are impressed [CM, 388].

Only food's ritualistic power is equal to overcoming these dark forces.

Many patterns from ancient sacred art depict the encounter. Campbell describes images from a classical sacramental bowl. Agathodaemon, god of Good Fortune, offers a poppy stalk in one hand and grain of corn in the other (CM 16–17). This emblem suggests both the ritual value of food and its physical function. The poppy, an opiate, represents an altered state of consciousness and the corn stands for food's regeneration and nutrition. Campbell notes that in sacred art, Agathodaemon and food cornucopias are counters to the Lord of the Abyss: "With his hammer in his right hand and on his left arm a cornucopia, this dark and terrible god is enthroned upon a scaly sea-beast ..." (CM 17). While it is unlikely that Davidson had exactly this artwork in mind, as a writer she selected patterns of images to set the conflict between Goldy and John Richard in a mythic realm.

In *Dying for Chocolate* (1992), Goldy and Arch are staying with a wealthy general and his wife, Bo and Adele. Goldy cooks for the couple. The palatial home is a sanctuary for mother and son, although she still does not feel safe. Despite the series' light touch, Davidson provides harrowing details about John Richard's harassing and violent behavior, about late night phone calls, slashed tires, and mangled mailboxes (18). To overcome her terrors, Goldy's pep talk to herself emphasizes her expertise with fine-touch control over small kitchen appliances: "If I could mince with a Cuisinart, I could master this" (29).

Fortunately, the general stands up for her. Bo's military connection and obsession with security devices would seem to make him also a member of the Straightforward Facts club. But when John Richard has a tantrum and throws clay pots, fracturing them into hundreds of pieces, the general brandishes a stick and bars the door. He reminds Goldy of Arch and his magic wand (83).

As is the way of dreams, Goldy stumbles from one troublesome situation into another. Threats come at her unprovoked from many directions. A newspaper food critic named Pierre is trashing her reputation. He writes about throwing up after attending one of her catered dinners (12) and basically tells her to get out of the kitchen: "Since Ms. Bear has no demonstrable skill in the culinary arts and no successful experience in the love department, this reviewer recommends that she try something she's good at. Like carpool" (166). When Goldy hopes that everything will be "Just Right," like her motto, another problem upsets her dessert cart. Even her very identity is under attack. She learns that the name for her company represents a copyright infringement.

These slams against Goldy's professional credibility are minor compared to the murder of Philip Miller. She had felt a romance beginning to bud with this drop-dead gorgeous psychologist. "He scanned the room from behind Ray Bans. A hum of admiration rose from the women. I took a deep breath, let it out" (24). Philip doubles as both a love interest and a shrink. His illuminating discussions are starting to help Goldy grasp her problems. The murder occurs during a blizzard. Philip cannot see, learning the hard way that being "drop dead gorgeous" is not enough (32). The murderer has blinded Philip.

Interestingly, Goldy fails to catch the warning. She has also been blinded. She is falling for a man cut from the same cloth as John Richard, a charming doctor with classic features. On one level of Goldy's mind, Philip the deceased represents her ex-husband.

Goldy resorts to cooking to bring herself and the murder-rocked community back to life. As in the Goldilocks nursery tale, the first thing she goes for is the porridge bowl. "Goldilocks' search for her self and role in the family begins with eating" (Bettelheim 221).

Goldy is a shrewd marketer. She understands the emotional and psychological power of food. People snap up her baked goods for Arch's school. "Perhaps the idea of eating something called Montessori muffins made people think they were learning something. Food can substitute for so many things" (120). When the general asks her to prepare fish filets on Friday, he apologizes for wanting to adhere to the Catholic ritual, but she understands. "We eat for different reasons, I said with great seriousness." On that Friday, grief over Philip hits her hard. She takes comfort in preparing a fish recipe from Julia Child (141).

As a chef, Goldy understands food, but author Davidson takes food a step farther, using it to structure the narrative and motivate characters. She taps into that aspect only dimly understood by Weight Watchers, food's mythic power.

Claude Levi-Strauss's *The Raw and the Cooked* (1983 ed.) points out numerous comparisons between civilized and "primitive" or mythic attitudes toward food. In Western culture, table manners protect us from food. We tuck bibs around the neck of a baby to protect him from the food. We use utensils to keep our hands clean while eating. Interestingly, if we drop a bit of food, we usually throw it away, because it is tainted by the environment and not fit for us to eat. However, there are exceptions. At times, we also lapse into mythic thinking about the power and glory of food.

An example is when the "five-second rule" comes into play. The premise goes something like this: the food is "still good" if it has been on the floor for less than five seconds. Considering how many pieces of cookie or candy have been dropped by little hands, children are most grateful for this rule. Another technique of making sure the food is still edible is to retrieve it quickly from floor or sidewalk and make some blessing gesture, to "kiss it up to God" as a ritual sterilization process. Food on its way to our mouths requires re-consecration, its power restored.

In primitive cultures, the power of food is so potent that food needs protection from the environment, especially from people. It has a power to nourish or to kill. When used as poison, its power is drained away. The toxicity desecrates natural forces.

Davidson makes Goldy's awareness of food psychology a part of her expertise, but the writer also relies on food's mythic power to exert a sympathetic magic, changing whatever it touches. The Harringtons, neighbors of the general, have hired Goldy for a themed affair. "Affair" is right, because the philandering wife of the couple wants a "decadent" feast. Goldy starts her menu with oysters and ends with a load of chocolate. As she prepares the sumptuous dessert, Brian Harrington, the husband, makes a pass at her. Startled, she drops the dessert. The food's power translates into immediate sexual attraction, and too much is destructive. During the dinner Goldy recites stories about food as an aphrodisiac (110, 113).

After the dinner, Sheriff Tom Schulz, her good guy steady, calls to ask when she last saw Brian.

> "When I left, Brian Harrington was asleep on a couch."
> "Alone, I assume."
> "Alone."
> "Doesn't sound as if your aphrodisiacs did the trick, Miss G."
> "Oh, I never was convinced of the science of the thing. Probably suggestion is all there is to it" [119].

As she well knows, food power does not belong to the "science of the thing." Food is a tie with the natural world. The rituals surrounding food, the cocktail party, the need to impress, the catered affair, and the revelry of the feast all override nutritional value. The poppy dominates the ear of corn. We are in the realm of magic. Food clearly wields power to set loose the forces of evil. Philip Miller the psychologist dies in his car, which is "the color of vanilla pudding" (27). Brian Harrington is drowned due to his chocolate-induced lust. The toxic powers of an aphrodisiac come into play again, near the novel's conclusion (301–04). Food can kill.

Goldy's downplay of food's mythic power rings hollow. She herself gives

2. Magic and Transformation in Domestic Mysteries 35

in to food's tonic powers. When she goes on a tear, instead of getting drunk, she wallows in Mozartkugel and London mints (116–17, 168). Food is a vital support for her emotions, consecrated and powerful.

Food exerts a very real impact for and against human actions. Bread almost sprouts legs to assault Goldy in a cafe.

> Loaves of bread toppled down as I landed on the broken table and the tile floor. My body screamed with pain. I couldn't see; I could only hear my voice howling, even as I knew the sound was muffled by loaves of bread. A husky voice came in close to my ear. It said, "Let Philip Miller rest in peace" [147–48].

If *Dying for Chocolate* intersects with the Goldilocks fairy tale through porridge, it also relates to the bear family. Goldy the caterer performs a balancing act between being a single parent and deciding to commit to a serious relationship with bear-like Sheriff Tom Schulz.

Bettelheim analyzes "Goldilocks and the Three Bears" in terms of the child's search for sexual roles. As Goldilocks tries out different beds, she understands that neither the father's nor the mother's role fits her. Conventional variants bring the tale to a happy ending. Goldilocks finds that the baby's bed is "just right," and the bears return home to find her curled up in the baby's bed, fast asleep.

Bettelheim sees this as a bad sign. Without a mature sense of balance or willingness to move into "big bear" world, Goldilocks regresses to an infantile state. In many variants of the tale, she awakes. "Goldilocks receives no help with her growing-up problems from the bears, so all she can do is to run away, scared by her own daring, defeated in her efforts to find herself" (Bettelheim 222).

Tom plays a big role in Goldy's life. In *Catering to Nobody* (1990), Tom is described as "large in height and bulk" (34–35). He has bushy eyebrows and a "mountain-man's body" (56). Goldy's romantic interest in Philip Miller is partially a way to avoid any commitment to Schulz. She sees her cooling romance with Schulz in terms of food.

> I had deliberately let the relationship with Schulz wane until there was little left. We had been like the hot chocolate they sell at the ski resorts. For your buck fifty, a machine first spews dark, thick syrup into a cup. This liquid gradually turns to a mixture of chocolate and hot water. Soon there is just a stream of hot water, and in a moment, drops. You wish the chocolate part would go on gushing forever, but it doesn't [121].

Unlike the Goldilocks who runs away, this Goldy Bear must move beyond sexual attraction to the next plane of a mature, committed relationship.

After Brian Harrington upsets the chocolate mousse, he appears before her suddenly, as is usual in fairy tales. He prepares to confess to Goldy. She asks, "Do I look like a priest?" (260–61). In a way, she is a shaman figure, a white witch, dispensing life forces with magic powers. Jung describes these qualities in the mother archetype. "The place of magic transformation and rebirth, together with the underworld and its inhabitants, are presided over by the mother" (Jung, *Four Archetypes* 16). Mixing, stirring, and mincing, Goldy performs magic tricks that would make her son Arch proud, transforming raw ingredients into cooked magical ones. Her transformations represent a release of the imprisoned spirit (Jung, FA 81). Her cooking shapes order out of disorder.

Like the witch figure, Goldy is allied with the natural world. After Brian's flirtatious behavior, Goldy whips up another delectable dessert under the watchful eye of Scout, the cat hanging around the General's house (96). Scout is like the witch's familiar, overseeing her activity on the replacement dessert, restoring its magic. The cat is in touch with her on some uncharted level. Later, when Goldy feels the house has been broken into, Scout offers a warning. "*Don't venture into the world*, his impassive face said. *It's dangerous out there*" (140–41). Once Goldy begins to act, the cat as her alter-ego disappears and she moves full steam ahead on her own.

Another aspect of Goldy's witch image is that she casts spells through the word magic of her recipes. Recipes essentially represent food coming into actuality. The words become actions, which become substance. In *Dying for Chocolate*, recipes are framed by designs showing food's tonic/toxic identity. Images of eggs, cakes, berries, and chocolate squares make up the border. These are interspersed with a smoking revolver on one side, a dagger on the other, and a skull and cross bones rooting the whole frame front and center. Framing the recipe protects food from the environment and makes all the ingredients whole.

Despite Goldy's understanding of food magic, she fails to spread that magic completely to the community. When she has to make deliveries in the back entrance of a home, she is aware of her slide down the social scale (18). She makes a suggestion about a gourmet product to a clerk at a health food store. "She looked at me as if I'd suggested sex with an extraterrestrial" (20). Goldy regularly thinks about what she looks like to the rest of the community. Throughout the novel she endures people looking down their noses at her. When Arch asks for a swimsuit at a store in town, Goldy imagines one of the mothers who overhears the request thinking "How can *you* afford a pool?" (249).

Her limited ability to provide for her son Arch is a massive sore spot. Goldy can like it or not, but Arch is the product of her marriage with John Richard. He is an amalgam of a physician's scientific bent and destroyer of

2. Magic and Transformation in Domestic Mysteries 37

feminine symbols, the pots, and the mother's dabbling of magical potions. Goldy scoffs at John Richard's attempts to take her son away. However, right after Arch jumpstarts his mother's car, he asks if he can live with his father. The request strikes terror in Goldy's heart. She worries that Arch is moving toward the values of John Richard. Despite this, she swallows her sorrow and agrees: "I wanted to give him his freedom" (273).

Many obstacles undercut Goldy's confidence as a mother. The threats that assail Goldy, slams at her cooking, her copied name, an inability to provide for Arch, all in some way address her maternal worthiness. The killer ultimately represents Goldy's worst suspicions of herself, that she is an evil mother. Through her encounter with the killer, she defeats the specter of herself as an inadequate nurturer. To prove her value as a mother, Goldy must grapple with this mythic monster and ritually bear her son again.

Goldy reads Poe to help Arch with an assignment for school. She learns a lesson from "The Purloined Letter": Think like the villain (269). Instead, the villain subverts Goldy's thought. When the time comes for Goldy to act, she is paralyzed, vulnerable to the killer's use of food as a toxin. Goldy and Schulz mistakenly drink double espressos laced with cantharidin, or the aphrodisiac Spanish fly (302–4). The Dark Mother's black magic does its work.

For Goldy, food preparation had been her way out of an abusive relationship. It is her livelihood, an expression of her independent spirit. When the killer brandishes food as a murder weapon, it adds insult to Goldy's injury. Ingested poison is essentially cursed food, a reversal of nutrition and life.

Goldy imagines an enemy from the outside. The killer is actually a threat very close to home. "I had imagined we were confidantes. And now I was paying the price of my own self-deception, with the poisonous drug mistakenly taken when you tried to make people love you" (303). If Goldy is a white witch dispensing life-giving tonics, the killer is also a witch, a wicked one.

To save her son from drowning, Goldy must again give birth to him. Possessed by a manic energy, she becomes a kind of mermaid or siren as she dives into the pool. She summons all her telepathic powers to revive her child:

> My hair fell like cold seaweed over my eyes and I was blinded ...
> *Come on honey, come on,* I sent my thoughts to him the way I had prayed in childbirth. If we can just get through the next five minutes, I thought, *if we can just get through* ... [309].

After this rebirth, all difficulties become clear to Goldy through a relatively quick solution. She subdues the murderer, discovers the identity of the evil critic, and faces the people who are suing over her copyright infringement. She considers a marriage proposal from Tom Schulz, regains her son, and clears her name. Unlike Goldilocks of the fairy tale, this Goldy has achieved a balance in the family of bears.

Permed to Death is the first novel in Nancy J. Cohen's "Bad Hair Day" series. Marla Shore is a South Florida hairstylist. She is crisp and efficient at her job. As a successful businesswoman, she supervises other employees, but she has more than a few heartaches in her past. As a teenager, she suffered deeply from the drowning of a child placed in her care. In addition, she has another secret; pictures were taken of her in a somewhat compromising position. She had done nothing wrong, but unscrupulous minds could take them the wrong way. Her divorced, childless status makes her an outcast from the community of women who visit her salon.

Haircuts, perms and make-up improve our outer appearance, but as rational beings, we consider that these improvements are only "skin deep," not affecting who we really are. As with food, adornment gains its power from a mythic meaning that reverses the usual thinking. Mythic thought considers that outer markings, adornment, scarification, or tattoos represent an inner state. People in early Briton tattooed themselves blue to show inner reverence to the Goddess of the night-sky (Graves 241). Dilley discusses the British punk movement. "Zippers, seams, and safety pins were worn outside and all over clothing, and in the case of safety pins on the body, to draw attention to what is usually hidden" (Dilley 145). In the story of Samson and Delilah, Samson's strength extends to every strand of him. When Delilah cuts his hair, she drains away his strength, therefore cutting short his life.

Marla's skills as a hairstylist place her as a mediator between inner and outer reality. To shape hair is to control life. She has it in her power to reverse the effects of death in the community and restore her place in it. But first she has monsters to slay.

The quintessential hair-controller from Greek myth is Perseus, who conquers the Medusa. Perseus is half-god, half-mortal. He is the son of Zeus, leader of the gods, and Danae, an unwed mother. When Perseus lacks a gift to bring to a festival honoring his mother, he proudly says he will snag a Gorgon's head.

To do this he must first visit the Gray Women, who hold the secret of the way to the nymphs' abode:

> These women dwelt in a land where all was dim and shrouded in twilight. No ray of sun looked ever on that country, nor the moon by night. In that gray place the three women lived, all gray themselves and withered as in extreme age. They were strange creatures indeed, most of all because they had but one eye for the three, which it was their custom to take turns with, each removing it from her forehead where she had had it for a time and handing it to another [Hamilton, 144].

2. Magic and Transformation in Domestic Mysteries 39

Perseus sees the Gray Women. In the dim light, the women have the shape of swans (145). Perseus bides his time until one of the old women takes out the shared eye. He then steals the eye and blackmails them for information on how to find the dancing nymphs of the north.

Using the Gray Women's directions, Perseus finds the nymphs. These maidens stop dancing long enough to give him the gifts he needs: winged sandals from Mercury, an adjustable silver wallet, and a cap to make the wearer invisible. More gifts come from the gods: a sword from Hermes and a shield from Athena that will serve as a mirror. Armed with his gifts, Perseus proceeds on his mission (Hamilton 143–146).

The Gorgons have wings and golden scales. Their hair is a mass of twisting snakes. Only Medusa is awake. "She was once a beautiful maiden whose hair was her chief glory, but as she dared to vie in beauty with Minerva, the goddess deprived her of her charms and changed her beautiful ringlets into hissing serpents" (Bulfinch 97). One glimpse at her turns the onlooker into stone.

Perseus uses the shield to deflect Medusa's paralyzing image. He lops off her head and saves it in his magic bag, the "wallet of silver." The other two Gorgons awake, but by then Perseus has donned the magic cap, making him invisible to the two monsters. Afterwards, Perseus uses the squirming head as a weapon over enemies and achieves great fame.

Marla has not actually killed Mrs. Kravitz, but it is hard not to see the hairstylist as Perseus on a mission. First, the description of the Gray Women in the myth closely parallels a salon setting, where gray wrinkled women preen like swans. The "eye" worn on the forehead and passed among the women is reminiscent of a hair dryer. This image emphasizes vanity coupled with limited awareness, indeed blindness. Impressed with their own beauty, Marla's clients are blind to her powers in helping them attain it.

When Marla's client, the soon-to-be deceased Mrs. Kravitz, sits in the chair, Marla cringes. The woman complains and tosses out damaging words. She casts her gaze around the salon "like a vulture searching for prey" (Cohen 2).

> Hoping to escape before the woman issued a new command, Marla rushed into the storage area. Her gaze scanned the shelves of chemicals, alighting on the neutralizer solution she'd selected earlier. She plucked it off its perch and was reaching for a pile of towels when a strangled sound struck her ears. A loud crash followed, like glass shattering.
>
> Sprinting into the salon, Marla stared at Mrs. Kravitz, who slumped in the shampoo chair. Her bagged head lolled against the sink. The plastic cap wrapped around her rods had become dislodged, partially shading her face [2].

This entire scene is couched in bundles of motifs from the Medusa myth. Mrs. Kravitz has a sharp, deadly gaze. She intimidates and paralyzes Marla with her questions and demands. To escape, Marla's own gaze is fixed on the deflecting shield of the shelves. The "neutralizer," with its connotations of reducing effects of a noxious substance, is Marla's equivalent of a sword. Holding the neutralizer helps Marla to escape being paralyzed by the demanding Mrs. Kravitz.

The "shattered glass" suggests fragmentation and release from an imprisoning form. As we later learn, Mrs. Kravitz has been blackmailing Marla over the embarrassing pictures. Before the book even opens, Marla has already been encased in stone. The death of Mrs. Kravitz is her freedom. Marla removes herself from the room, and like magic, Mrs. Kravitz and her lethal gaze are gone. Only the bagged head with its horrible rods remains.

This analysis does not suggest that Cohen consciously relies on the Medusa tale, but rather the insightful writer chooses and controls configured images to convey significant human truths. The opening scene is powerful in addressing metaphoric levels of sight, the blind gaze made more ironic when set in an arena for arranging beauty.

The opening scene is also emblematic of how the Medusa Myth plays out over the entire narrative of *Permed to Death*. Healthy hair expresses a natural outer reality. It represents "the life force, strength; energy, the life-substance from the head; the power of thought; virility" (Cooper, *An Illustrated Encyclopedia of Traditional Symbols*, 77). The Medusa's snaky hair represents an outer reality that is deadly and out of control. The writhing snakes are the gossip in Marla's social world that she fears the most. Hard work has won her a place in this community. "Marla was proud of her reputation, one she'd struggled to earn after the tragic incident in her past" (16). A whiff of scandal could bring it all down. The reality that this new life could be ruined by the past keeps Marla "stiff with fear" and "immobilized" through the novel's opening pages.

She clearly seeks absolution from her past. She is first attracted to police lieutenant Dalton Vail for his absolving qualities. One look from him seems "to suck the guilt from her soul" (9). The Medusa's stone-forming gaze comes from within, in the same way that Marla's secrets paralyze her inner world. With Mrs. Kravitz gone, Marla can begin to chisel away at the stony reality that blocks her happiness.

Hair grooming enters Marla's personal life as well as her professional one. Like Goldy, Marla shares living space with an animal, her French poodle Spooks. A soothing tie with the natural world, Spooks gives much and asks little. Marla finds him a "comforting presence" (22). After a blow-up at her ex-husband, Marla clings to Spooks. The little canine looks good by comparison. "His soft form warmed her heart as he licked her chin. Ironic, wasn't it,

2. Magic and Transformation in Domestic Mysteries 41

that her dog cared more about her than her former husband?" (89) Spooks is Marla's familiar, comforting her in a solitary life.

A clue involving hair color tips Marla off to the murderer. Cohen presents Marla's final confrontation with the killer in animal imagery as well. It is as if Spooks has become a dreaded beast so she can throw off her spooked past once and for all. The natural world has turned menacing. The killer has glinting eyes, jumps "with the speed of a cougar," pounces, drools, and lands "shrieking like a wild animal" (285–86). Shattered broken pieces as during the death of Mrs. Kravitz also return. To restore the landscape to fertility from its stony, barren state, Marla must slay Medusa all over again.

In the Grail legend of Parzival, the knight's great love is Condwiramurs (*conduire amours*, French for "the guide of love"). After Parzival returns from battle, he finds that his lady love has put her hair up to signify that they are married. As Campbell notes, "The point here is that it was not a marriage that began with physical sex; when she put her hair up, they were married" (Campbell, *Transformations of Myth* 252). The series name of "Bad Hair" extends its mythic meaning of "staying single" as a curse over the community. If Marla and Dalton Vail indeed wed, bad hair will form into a shapely cloud of good, and the curse of a loveless landscape will be broken.

Like Marla, Callahan Garrity holds a mediator's position between inner and outer worlds. Callahan is a moonlighting P.I. and professional house cleaner. A detective fits nicely into a maid's outfit. What, after all, is the Criminal Investigation Department of a homicide unit except a specialized housecleaning service? This job provides a no-nonsense solution to the sleuth's practical problem of entering a house without breaking in. Being a maid or housecleaner affords maximum opportunity for snooping. It also blends social worlds, giving a working class woman a neat entrée into upper-income neighborhoods.

Callahan's cleaning service is named The House Mouse. The name suggests exterminators, rather than cleaners, but mice appear often in fairy tales. The mouse is associated with ghosts and souls of the dead scraping around the house as they return at night (Von Franz 176). In *Strange Brew* (1997), Callahan's House Mouse troupe also has to clean up after the Dead, the Grateful Dead.

The neighborhood is changing due to gentrification. First one of the developers is found murdered. Then Wuvvy, an aging hippie who resisted the development, is dead of an apparent suicide. Among Wuvvy's effects is her old collection of rock concert T-shirts and classic LPs. Callahan investigates Wuvvy's suicide, which suggests not only the death of the sixties, but that the spirit of youthful love is gone from the world. As with other domestic mysteries, *Strange Brew* is a fairy tale for adults.

The novel begins with an equivalent of "once upon a time." Callahan casts her mind back over Sunday afternoons viewed through "the same grainy, black-and-white quality as those old photographs in the family scrapbook" (Trocheck 1). Callahan and her mother Edna sit on the porch and watch the world go by. In their neighborhood, Callahan says, "Nothing happens, nothing changes. It's a lie we tell each other, a charm to keep us safe ..." (Trocheck 1).

They need this charm. Callahan has good reason to fear change. In *Every Crooked Nanny* (1992), she learns that she has breast cancer. The disease is the worst kind of development, representing destructive "growth." Callahan is a survivor, but memories of the experience are never far away. When the subject comes up again in *Strange Brew*, Callahan clenches her hand over her chest "like a shield that would protect me from recurrence of my own breast cancer" (247).

The forces of darkness are afoot as Edna wields a broom and hose to chase a bum away from her gardenias. No amount of disinfection can counter the forces of social change that will upset the Garrity routine there in Candler Park. As Callahan says, her neighborhood is a "working class kind of place ... The only really significant thing about Candler Park is the fact that it's still here at all" (5).

The deep woods of fairy tales tell us that the world is a dangerous place. Weather stirs up the "strange brew" of forces affecting the House Mouse crew. A Halloween tornado whips into town and makes a clean sweep of the universe. It knocks the governor's mansion flat and lifts a baby out of its mother's arms (10). The wind howls, the lights go out, and a tree blows down in front of the Garrity house, bringing the changing outside world that much closer.

When Callahan was six, it snowed on Halloween. She refused to go out trick or treating with the other kids because "I didn't want to spoil my Cinderella costume by wearing my ugly brown winter coat over it" (8–9). Underneath her housecleaner's uniform, Callahan is still Cinderella, although an overripe one. Throughout the narrative, Trocheck plays with motifs from this fairy tale. Instead of the story turning into "happily ever after," we see Cinderella coping with realities of middle age.

Like Cindy, Callahan dwells in the dust. She is in many ways a displaced figure, out of step at home and with her generation. She lives among many elderly women, but not one volunteers as a fairy godmother. The House Mouse van, her pumpkin carriage, has been crumpled by a tree. She has Prince Charming on a string, but neither of them is willing to commit. Although the story leaves several murders and a long-buried family secret as stains that Callahan must clean, the major crime for her to solve is getting over Cinderella's dreams.

She attends a Halloween party "ball" half-hoping for a magical transformation. "Tonight I was not Julia Callahan Garrity, former cop, cleaning-business

2. Magic and Transformation in Domestic Mysteries 43

owner, private detective. Tonight I was a raven-haired, bell-bottomed tattooed rock goddess with exceedingly bad taste in men" (19). Despite all the "girls" working for House Mouse, no fairy godmother comes forward to help with her "Cher" costume, which barely fits.

At the party, Callahan flops in her attempt to feel comfortable in her own skin. Other revelers mistake her for the Bride of Frankenstein. Men in drag are more attractive than she is. Callahan's cop friend Bucky dresses up as Jackie Kennedy. One woman is the Grapes of Wrath. The Halloween costumes all represent icons displaced by social change. No glass slippers are in sight. Callahan catches a close-up view of Wuvvy the hippie: "Her eyes were dull and bloodshot, her skin dried and tanned to the consistency of an old boot, hands and nails grimy" (33). A masquerade is a ritual to unify time and identity, to sweep away past selves and acknowledge a change into the present.

Callahan is an aging woman worried about her sexual attractiveness. Life with Mac, her Prince Charming, is not a guaranteed happy ending. In one of their few romantic scenes, they are indulgent and infantile. They fingerpaint each other with chocolate (80-81). Goldy would be proud, but Callahan characterizes herself, "I am never satisfied" (156).

Bruno Bettelheim discusses the significance of Cinderella's tale in helping children understand sibling rivalry and deal with jealousy (Bettelheim 243–45). Even though Trocheck parodies the Cinderella role, the tale has a core of truth for Callahan. The character has supposedly reconciled herself to living at home with Edna. Still, she is a fifth wheel among her married siblings interested in raising families. When they come to visit, she avoids going home because "my sister and sister-in-law would be discussing the fine points of ovulation. And the dinner dishes would all still be stacked in the sink, waiting for me" (70).

Callahan's mother Edna approaches the destruction from the tornado with a spirit of commercialism. The House Mouse features a special on post-tornado clean-up (85). Those twin spirits of domestic harmony Baby and Sister Easterbrooks also pitch in.

Baby and Sister are two senior citizen "girls" employed by Callahan's House Mouse cleaning service. They are grannies in tennis shoes. Their names and identities as "girls" reinforce Trocheck's theme of seasons out of alignment. The Easterbrooks turn age stereotypes upside down. They tell about being evacuated during the storm to a motel with porn movies on the cable (87–88). The ladies' names place them in a family context, a racially integrated family. Baby and Sister fluctuate between being guardians of the hearth and wicked step-sisters who displace Callahan yet again.

In her study of classical mythology, Edith Hamilton emphasizes that the Romans wanted practical gods and goddesses to watch over everyday life. Collectively, these gods were the "Numina," or "those above." They were closely connected with simple acts of daily living, especially those household rituals, which therefore gained dignity.

> Every Roman family had a Lar, who was the spirit of an ancestor, and several Penates, gods of the hearth and guardians of the storehouse. They were the family's own gods, belonging only to it, really the more important part of it, the protectors and defenders of the entire household ... a public Lar and Penates ... did for the city what others did for the family [Hamilton 44].

When Callahan awakes after spending the night on the sofa, she finds Baby and Sister making breakfast and singing, "Over my head, there's trouble in the air" (141). Callahan says she can't count how many times she's been ousted from her bed. "Someday I'd have to solve the mystery of why I spend so much time sleeping on makeshift beds in my own home" (140). As a former police officer, Callahan was a public guardian, but at home, she loses out to Edna and two elderly friends, three step-sisters who ostensibly "guard" the house, displacing Callahan.

Trocheck's series takes place in and around Atlanta, Georgia. Callahan's displacement resonates in a psychological realm, but the theme has significance in its Southern setting as well, where debris from the past sets old and new worlds at odds. The novel's denouement presents an intense, nightmarish vision of triplicate images destroyed. Again, as is the way with dreams and fairy tales, a helpless Callahan can merely witness the drama. A past generation presses a gun to the head of the current one and pulls the trigger. Callahan responds internally: "It wasn't me," I wanted to tell somebody. "It all started a long time ago" (313). She acknowledges the fatalism of universal patterns.

The authors of these mysteries may have consciously used scattered motifs from well known fairytales. A lesser known fairy tale of French origin entitled "Nine Brothers Who Were Changed into Lambs, and Their Sister" illustrates many of the same features as the narrative pattern fundamental to domestic mysteries.

Ten orphaned children live in a castle deep in the woods. The oldest child, a girl, cares for her nine younger brothers. One day, the brothers are hunting in the woods and come upon a ramshackle hut. A gruesome old woman lures them into the hut with the promise of water. She has protruding teeth and a tongue so long that it winds "nine times around her body." Despite their suspicion of the woman, the brothers drink the water, because they are thirsty. The old woman then says that they have to pay for their water, and the oldest boy has to marry her. They run to safety back to their sister.

2. Magic and Transformation in Domestic Mysteries   45

The witch arrives at the children's castle, murmurs a curse, and levels the castle "in one terrible bang" (Von Franz 126). Then her eyes glow, and she casts a spell, changing each of the brothers into a lamb. The witch says the sister's curse is to care for them, but if she tells anyone that the lambs are really her brothers, the witch will return and transform the sister into a lamb as well.

For a time, the sister lives happily with her lamb-brothers, petting them and making them garlands. When she is older, she marries a man who really loves her and accepts the lambs as part of their household. Soon the sister is pregnant. They hire a maid. The maid is really the witch's daughter who has come to seek revenge on the happy couple. When the husband is away, the sister is blind to the maid's evil. After a few days, the maid lures the pregnant sister to the well and shoves her in.

When the husband returns, the maid poses as the wife in a room with drawn curtains. She feels ill, she tells the husband. The only thing that will make her feel better is a piece of the biggest lamb. With sadness, the husband goes out to slaughter the lamb, which escapes from his knife but draws the husband's attention to the well. The husband discovers the injured wife and pulls her up. She has given birth to a baby boy.

The couple makes plans for the baby's baptism. The wife insists that the largest lamb act as the baby's godfather. Once the baby is baptized, the largest lamb melts back into human form, and the witch's spell is undone. The priest places his stole over the other eight lambs, and they too change back into human brothers.

As a family, they all hunt down the witch and her daughter. They capture the evil-doers. Four horses tear them apart. Pieces of their bodies are thrown onto a pyre and burned. Then the sister and all her brothers live in happiness (Von Franz 126–29).

The first item to note is that the children are orphans. They have to make their own way in a world without any pre-set notions or moral guidelines. Their castle is in the woods, isolated from other human contact. Goldy, Marla, and Callahan are also essentially alone. Their stories begin with a similar reversal of fortune. Goldy is exiled from her previous social position as a physician's wife. Marla is an outsider in a setting full of married mothers. Callahan is forty, single, and feeling that she is reaching the end of the line. Each character's personal back story is more than a subplot to go along with the murder puzzle. It is integral to the fabric of the narrative.

The sister of the orphaned children has the weighty burden of caring for the brothers, but she handles it well. Likewise, these sleuthing women are off-balance in many ways, but they take comfort in their magical powers with food, hair, and cleaning. The precipitating crisis is that the brothers are placed in harm's way and trouble follows them home in the person of the witch, who completely destroys their castle.

Although Goldy has removed herself and Arch to the relative safety of the general's house, Arch's father finds them there. He wreaks literal havoc on the general's house and figuratively ruins Goldy's maternal culinary world by breaking pots. He also blurts out news of Philip Miller's romantic indiscretions to shatter Goldy's romantic dreams. Marla's flattened castle comes from her feelings of failure after the drowning of Tammy, who had been placed in her care. Mrs. Kravitz lies among broken pieces. In *Strange Brew*, the tornado gains power through the community's rumors that it has hit both the governor's home and hurt a child. Then the storm topples the tree and flattens the van. The house of House Mouse has been blown down. Everyone is vulnerable.

The brothers' transformation into lambs renders them completely dependent. Their human selves are lost to the sister. Their loss punishes her for any thoughts she may have had about ridding herself of their burden. Her caretaker's guilt over not caring properly for her charges makes her even more determined to make their existence better. Goldy tries to be a better mother to Arch, reading his books, helping him at school, picking up his magician costume. Marla seeks to educate parents about drowning dangers. To make the House Mouse stronger financially, Callahan throws herself into the world of entrepreneurship to find out more about the care and feeding of employees. As with the sister's marriage and pending pregnancy, things are looking up.

The sister cares for the lambs because she sees both inner and outer appearance. Yet she fails to see the maid's treachery and falls into the well. Like the sister, the sleuth mediates between two worlds. She maintains "the look that one directs at things, both outward and inward" (Campbell, CM 329). The domestic sleuth is in the middle by virtue of her magical occupation. The caterer knows her client's expectations, food allergies, health or lack of it, and the food itself. The hairstylist ("Only your hairdresser knows for sure") knows the bad hair days and tries to tease them into good ones. The housekeeper, too, is in the middle, with full awareness of the dirt that was swept under the rug. This heightened ability to observe may explain why a momentary lapse of judgment leads to a physical wound.

With this keen perspective of observation comes vulnerability. Campbell notes that "it is not to be supposed that the refinement and alertness of the faculties of observation can be sharpened to an exceptional degree without having one's susceptibility to pain sharpened as well" (CM 329). These amateur sleuths practice their crafts to control the uncontrollable. Of course, perfection in wielding this skill is impossible. These women have already been emotionally wounded by being alone. The physical wound that each one suffers makes tangible the social isolation they feel. The wound ritually opens the way between outer and inner pain. So the stage is set for them to descend, or leave consciousness, in preparation for the final encounter with evil.

2. Magic and Transformation in Domestic Mysteries

The perfidy of the maid removes the sister's budding creativity from the scene, placing the lambs in peril. The sister's fall represents a loss of consciousness, where she has to reach inward for strength to overcome final forces. Goldy is rendered unconscious by the Spanish fly and must submerge herself when Arch is in danger. Marla nearly faints when she grapples with the killer and later yields to "oblivion" (Cohen 287). Callahan has pills shoved down her throat that cause her to "grasp the ladder rails tightly to keep from falling" (Trocheck 287–88). Later, in confronting the ultimate evil, Callahan removes herself from the murder scene with a wish for "my own bed and some peace and quiet" (Trocheck 312).

The fairy tale ends with a transformation of animals, the lambs, returning to the human realm, and beastly dark forces being banished. The four horses as part of the witch's punishment suggest a limited earthly demise, as in the "four corners of the globe." Von Franz notes in her analysis of the tale that the witch image is stopped only temporarily and may again return (Von Franz 144). The figure is of the spirit.

The witch figure poses an especially provocative tie with the modern mysteries. Domestic mysteries are often thought of as feminine empowerment tales, subverting and challenging forms of the detective story, a genre "aligned with oppressive masculinity" (Walton and Jones 86). Kimberly Dilley emphasizes that "while they do not preach feminism, many women's mystery novels introduce a multiple of feminist issues" (Dilley 143). This quality of a feminist perspective may be partly true, but wouldn't it make sense that the woman sleuth's journey ends when she overthrows masculine powers of authority? Given all the evil women of domestic mysteries, this is clearly not the case.

It is not spoiling an ending or giving too much away about killer identities when we mention that more often than not in these books, the murderer is a witch woman, an archetype that Jung calls the Dark Mother. "On the negative side, the mother archetype may connote anything secret, hidden, dark: the abyss, the world of the dead, anything that devours, seduces, and poisons, that is terrifying and inescapable like fate" (Jung, *Four Archetypes* 16).

One explanation for the frequency of Dark Mother villains is that through the confrontation, the women sleuths work out their own difficulties as daughters. The daughter overthrows the mother. "As an adult, the daughter interprets. She says that her mother could no longer accept the limitations of her life. She acknowledges that her mother resented motherhood bitterly, often sabotaged it" (Chernin 55). Yet the up-close, intense encounters in the novels suggest more directly a grappling with the self and an attempt to throw off destiny-shaping secrets. This is a Dark Mother residing in the self, "whose effects are seen as damaging, even paralyzing, to the developing consciousness ..." (Elias-Button 358).

As a guilty mother, Goldy wrestles down evil objectified in the form of a horrible mother. Marla's experience with the drowned daughter has made her ambivalent about becoming a mother. Her first brush with murder involves the dreaded Mrs. Kravitz and the last one pulls in a Kravitz-like figure. The novel has Medusa bookends around its narrative. Callahan's role as a childless cancer survivor juxtaposed with two fertile sisters leads her to tussle with not one, but three generations of imperious women, leading to more echoes of wicked stepsisters. Because these characters are the focus of a mystery series, ding, dong, the witch is not dead, and the dreaded figure is likely to return in the next installment.

The domestic mystery whips up a light soufflé for the reader's taste. We read these novels for humor, romantic escape, and vicarious adventure. Like fairy tales, "they have much the same healing function as a not-understood dream" (Von Franz 19).

However, to call these works "cozies" is a misnomer, in that the shadow of painful truth is never far away. "These tales and traditions are like the stairs going down: by them the people have preserved a means of reconnecting to the unconscious, though the stairs have become hidden or invisible" (Von Franz 56). Our suburban detectives have to accomplish much more than point a finger at the murderer. The sleuth somehow has to reconcile her personal life with an unforgiving social landscape. She does so by wielding the magic language of myth. "Mythological symbols touch and exhilarate centers of life beyond the reach of vocabularies of reason and coercion" (CM 4). By practicing her craft, the sleuth restores the balance between inner and outer life to rid death from the landscape and restore the flow of life.

CHAPTER 3

A BODILESS DREAM: FORENSIC MYSTERIES AND MYTHS OF IDENTITY

In classic mysteries, we know who has been killed; we don't know the killer. The sleuth identifies the murderer by surveying a group of suspects then naming the guilty party. The sleuth or detective stands apart from the group regarding the entire crime as a type of people puzzle. From a distant perspective, the sleuth singles out the crucial jigsaw puzzle piece, the one that is not sky or trees, but has on it the face and figure of the murderer.

In the past, unnamed remains meant unsolved murders, so a scenario with an unnamed corpse was unlikely to find its way into fiction. Recently, more accurate tools for identifying the dead mean that mystery literature can plausibly revolve around the victim's identity. With women having increased access to the high-tech world of forensics, more mysteries feature women detectives working close to the crime scene. The role is fraught with conflict. In some ways, the many facets of women as life-givers enable them to shoulder well the burden of death. In others, women may find it hard to gain acceptance in a previously male-dominated profession.

The mystery's central solver may have an occupation such as a sex crimes prosecutor, forensic anthropologist, or medical examiner. Skulls sometimes talk, and these characters bend very close to listen.

To some extent, all sleuths, amateurs or professionals, have to descend to the world of the dead. Their journeys most often begin with the living. However, the forensic sleuth has only dead remnants, hair and fiber, DNA, or blood types, to launch her journey into the underworld. With little or no living human corroboration, the forensic detective in fiction has to use her own life to fill in the blank spaces on the deceased's resume. She reconstructs the victim's occupation, habits, and relationships through her own context. The sleuth's merging with the deceased creates many tensions, to say the least.

Without traditional rituals to separate living and dead, the detective's own hold on identity comes into question. The search proceeds through a peculiar mathematics of the self. One alive seeks to know one dead. Since the trail follows a ghostly being, the two selves are reduced to one and a half. At one point in the search, the names of the two may be known, and the possibility of complete self-knowledge arises. However, the hunt ends with the two merging, possibly leaving none.

The myth of Narcissus and Echo outlines an identity-seeking narrative. People generally know how this myth's conclusion chronicles the perils of self-absorption. Scholars believe this interpretation came relatively late in Roman history, during medieval times. It shows how the material world of appearances is a poor substitute for the soul's reality (Grant 335). With Narcissus and Echo paired, as Ovid writes, the myth instead discloses multiplicity and reduction in the search for self.

Ovid's *Metamorphoses* (III) tells us that Narcissus is the son of a wood nymph and a river god. At the child's birth, the prophet Tiresias pronounces that Narcissus will live a long life, provided "he never knows himself" (Grant 333–34). In an Egyptian painting contemporary with Ovid's account, Narcissus appears as a figure labeled "Search." The other half of the painting shows "Ignorance," or "Agnoia" (Grant 335). Narcissus grows into a handsome young man, a deer hunter, breaking the hearts of all the nymphs falling for him. The one nymph who pines for him most is Echo.

Echo has a peculiar burden to bear. Previously, Zeus had sought the company of many woodland nymphs, and Echo was among them. One day, Hera came onto the scene and heard Echo's happy chatter. In a fit of pique, Hera cursed the young nymph. Echo could not speak unless spoken to, and could only repeat what another had said to her. The only benefit was that she would always have the last word.

Despite this restricted ability to speak, Echo follows Narcissus on his deer hunts. In every confrontation with the vital young man, Echo can only say back at him the requests he poses of her. When he says, "Come to me," all she can do is issue the same command. In frustration and misunderstanding, he refuses to do her bidding and leaves. She retreats from the light to suffer in dark grottos (Hamilton 87–88). "Her bones were changed into rocks and there was nothing left of her but her voice" (Bulfinch 88).

After that, Narcissus breaks so many hearts, the goddess Nemesis has to take action. "May he who loves not others love only himself" (Hamilton 88). During a busy day of hunting, Narcissus stops to rest by an enchanted spring. "He strove to quench his thirst, but other thirst/Was born — he was bewitched by his own beauty:/Loving a bodiless dream ..." (Ovid III, 407 in Grant 334). The rest, we know. Riveted to his own reflection, Narcissus stares at his own image until death releases him.

The connections between Narcissus the hunter and the ghostly *Döppelganger* of Echo parallel the separation or merging of detective and victim in forensic mysteries. Linda Fairstein, Kathy Reichs, and Patricia Cornwell have each created a series featuring a forensic detective. Their narratives represent variants of the Narcissus and Echo myth.

All three authors are not afraid to show death close-up. Their protagonists handle cases with latex gloves. Details of the crime, rape victim interviews, corpse close-ups, autopsies, bodily fluids, bones, and microorganisms of decomposition comprise the clues to be sifted, sometimes literally. In addition, all authors claim absolute authenticity of their stark realism. Their claims are credible. They have the professional credentials to back up their work. Despite these vigorous claims of verisimilitude, mystery fiction still falls into the realm of romance. All the details of death serve to assert mysteries of life, or identity, forming the core of the narrative. "The symbols of the self arise in the depths of the body and they express its materiality every bit as much as the structure of the perceiving consciousness" (Jung & Kerenyi 92). Jung further asserts that the more palpably physical the symbols, the more universal, or "deeper" the archetype (Jung & Kerenyi 92).

As is common with cosmology or creation myths, mutilation serves as a means to reassemble or assert wholeness.

> The many myths of the Goddess's dismembered body arise from a sense that everything is alive, and yet in pieces. This is not an intellectual construct but rather a deep intuition. And so we create stories of a Goddess who sacrifices Her body to make the world. In the Big Bang theory of modern science, all of existence began as a unit, bound together in a kind of perfect egg called the *ylem*. The ylem exploded into light and energy, some of which converted into particles of matter [Pollack 228].

The forensic investigator's mission is to dissect the body and learn a name. On another level, she seeks to "know." This knowledge from mutilation is one more way to gather up the self, to act out the ritual in which the hunter identifies with the hunted.

Author Linda Fairstein is the creator of Alexandra Cooper, a high-profile sex crimes prosecutor in Manhattan. Fairstein has over twenty years' experience with the Sex Crimes Unit of the District Attorney's office in Manhattan, so we are assured that her books are authentic in their procedural details. In a closing "Acknowledgments" section of *Likely to Die* (1997), the second novel in the series, Fairstein reaffirms this verisimilitude: "Every crime described in this book is based on an actual event" (LTD 417).

The world of Fairstein's protagonist Alexandra Cooper is littered with the results of fine-tooth comb scrutiny.

> The top of my metal desk is covered with a bright red blotter, rarely more than a sliver of which is visible because of the accumulation of manila folders and white legal pads that pile on top. They are house case files and witness interviews, police reports and memoranda from unit prosecutors, laboratory analyses of body fluids and blood types, mug shots of suspects being sought, medical records and DNA profiles of rape survivors, and every other form of detritus of the world of criminal law [*Fatal Jeopardy* 16–17].

In the first novel of the series, Alex needs these life fluids to resuscitate herself, since she begins the day by reading her own obituary in the newspaper.

Alex has rented a car for an old friend, Isabella Lascar, pronounced "la SCAR" we are told. Alex has given Isabella run of the summer place on Martha's Vineyard. Isabella is a famous actress, with "a few minor speaking roles in some major movies in the late eighties ..." (FJ 8). While driving to the house, Isabella is killed by a shotgun blast to the head. Police mistakenly identify the victim as Alex. The police chief tells her, "Hell, it was your driveway, a rented car, and a girl with a similar build and size — it made sense that it was you" (FJ 5).

Alex spends the rest of the book trying to figure out the identity of the intended victim. Was it really Isabella, who had been stalked some months before? Or was it Alex herself, whose prosecutorial record means that the murderer's identity is in one of those case files strewn across her red desk blotter?

This plot twists the "woman in peril" convention into a pretzel. Despite her dispassionate forensic abilities, Alex is too "blinded" by her own prejudices about herself to discern the actual murderer (FJ 298). What draws our attention here is how the *Döppelganger* motif changes in relation to Alex's investigation.

> The news wires were about to explode with the information that the face of the dazzlingly beautiful actress and film star, Isabella Lascar, had been obliterated, and that what was left of her body lay in the tiny Vineyard morgue, with a toe tag mislabeled in the name of Alexandra Cooper [5].

3. A Bodiless Dream 53

Isabella is the disabled Echo shut up in the morgue. Alex's ingenuity and legal mind contrast with her glamorous friend who can speak only when given lines. As Alex first moves to reconstruct Isabella's life, we see two halves of a feminine persona, one emotional and glamorous, and the other rational and science-oriented. Eventually the character forges a third identity.

Alex's professional identity relies on her mind, but she is not completely comfortable with that resolution. "I'm so sick of being strong, I complained to myself" (FJ 27). Isabella Lascar, or The Beauty Scar, reminds Alex of what she now lacks. The glamorous half has been killed off, so what remains? Is it possible for a woman to be in this profession and still maintain an aura of glamour? Alex eventually overcomes this deficiency, and the narrative asserts the validity of a woman in a profession like a sex crimes prosecutor.

Once Alex arrives at her new identity, a blend of both personal and professional selves, she proceeds to the thick of the mystery, which hinges on single-minded obsession, or "erotomania." Alex shares more than a few traits with the murderer. She nearly succumbs to the crime's dark pull, but lifts her eyes up from a Narcissus-like perspective at the river's image just in time to fathom the actual answer to "final jeopardy." In the book's closing paragraphs, Alex rejoices in being alive. "I wanted to keep my three friends around me and talking to me for hours more, despite my exhaustion, until the daylight poured through the windows over the river ... Keep talking, I said to myself. Keep talking" (FJ 310). As a counter to self-absorption, Alex essentially restores Echo's power of speech.

The victim in Fairstein's second novel *Likely to Die* (1997) is not as obvious a *Döppelganger* for Alex. Still, the plot turns on issues of identity. Alex merges with her alter-ego just long enough to administer justice. To solve the murder, Alex symbolically has to become the victim and re-enact the crime to realize herself.

The victim is a highly successful woman neurosurgeon found brutally murdered in her office at the medical center. At the top of the suspect list is a man who's been impersonating doctors through an elaborately concocted identity. Alex's police contact tells her, "Everyone assumes he'll start using a new credit card or ID any hour now. Steal one, buy one, con one off somebody" (LTD 385). At the request of the police, Alex needs to inventory more files to verify the suspect's identity. She debates going to the actual murder scene, the office of the dead woman, Gemma Dogen, but she has no way of getting in.

Instead, she still has the key to the deceased's apartment. She goes to Dr. Dogen's apartment to assess the files. Alex's trip to the dead woman's home has no logical purpose, but it fulfills the mythic pattern of selves merging. While in the apartment, a flood of feeling overcomes Alex. She experiences the "spookiness of being alone with the keepsakes and belongings of the dead woman" (LTD 388).

Alex is a stand-in for the victim in several ways. Both Alex and Dr. Dogen are successful professionals in well-publicized positions. Alex is on the trail of clues to an identity, her own. In a sense she adopts the home of the dead doctor. She goes behind the professional identity to stand very close, almost in the same shoes, to the dead woman.

Unfortunately, she also places herself next to the killer. He is already there, hidden in a closet. The villain delivers a terrible blow to her head. All the files disperse.

> ...my feet slipped on the shiny tops of the dozens of folders that had dropped to the floor and spread across it like a giant-sized version of fifty-two pickup. My left leg slid out from underneath me as I pivoted and fell onto one knee, staring up to see [the villain] plowing his fist into the place on the wall where my face had just been [395].

At this time, weirdly, she imagines herself mimicking Grace Kelly in "Dial 'M' for Murder." Like an actress, Alex's identity could be anyone's. The ID folders trip her up. Her physical being is diminished, as she is in a "giant-sized" game. The reference to cards shows that where she lands is a matter of chance. Her foothold on reality is in question. Because she now has no identity of her own, she takes on Gemma's, becoming a dead woman. "Images of Gemma's mutilated corpse flashed through my mind" (LTD 397). Then in that guise, prey becomes the hunter.

Alex takes the professional instrument of Gemma in hand. She stabs Gemma's murderer in the groin with one of Gemma's awards, a trophy sporting a golden scalpel. "I whirled back with the gold-handled scalpel in my palm and ripped it across the wrist of the mad doctor ... I stabbed at his upper thigh, digging the scalpel in repeatedly" (LTD 400). In the guise of the murdered neurosurgeon, she exacts revenge, not merely thwarting Gemma's murderer, but symbolically raping him. She doesn't kill him, but the cops later say that he'll be "singing soprano with the Attica boys' choir" (LTD 404).

After this ordeal, Alex Cooper resumes her own identity. She's familiar to herself. "I didn't need a mirror to remind myself what shape I was in" (403). She had to break into pieces before she could reassemble herself.

This book's title, *Likely to Die*, refers to a list the villain had made for ferreting out his victims. Alex is afraid that she is on the list. The only mortals *not* in that category are, statistically speaking, no one. All are likely to die. Being on this list, technically in the company of all human beings, is central to Alex's identity. If she blends with all humanity, she is obliterated, with no individual self. Her mutilation of a previous self begins her process for reassembling life. She has to piece together her identity from the beginning. Her encounters with the murderer enable her to step into a ritual death act, and then into life.

3. A Bodiless Dream

In the work of Kathy Reichs, identity loss occurs less as sudden trauma and more through a disintegration process. The fragmentation of the body, and therefore the self, occurs over time, but the myth of life through mutilation continues.

Protagonist Temperance Brennan is a forensic anthropologist. Just as her first name suggests moderation, she forswears getting intoxicated on death. Despite her role as a dissector, her self effloresces. Tempe develops additional selves to counter the death, or loss of self, she deals with everyday.

In *Déjà Dead* (1997), Tempe maintains a healthy distance from death. In a preliminary case, the director of her laboratory informs her that two workers have found some bones near the river. She visits the site. After several pages of rooting and digging, she reaches her expected goal, a paper bag. She has no illusions about what she will find. "Whatever it [the bag] held was heavy, and I had little doubt what that would be. And I was right" (*Deja* 15). She peers into the bag to verify her discovery:

> A human face stared out at me. Sealed off from the insects that hasten decomposition, the flesh had not fully rotted. But heat and moisture had altered the features, converting them into a death mask bearing scant resemblance to the person it had been. Two eyes, shriveled and constricted, peered out from under half-closed lids.... Shaken, I closed the bag [15–16].

Death moves Tempe Brennan, but she is not afraid to look it in the face, literally.

In the follow-up book, *Death DuJour* (1999), Dr. Brennan is summoned to locate the corpse of a nun who had died over a century ago. The nun has been proposed for sainthood. Tempe's role is to identify the bones as part of the sainthood process. There's plenty of paperwork evidence to verify the sister's life but no bones.

Another very old nun of legendary origins shows Brennan and her team where the bones are. Interspersed with the search are Tempe's feelings about herself. Being with the nuns takes her back to her childhood at St. Barnabas' Catholic school (DD 13). She has problems remembering herself as an adult, but gives herself some tough talking. "Stop it, Brennan. You're over forty, a professional. A forensic anthropologist. These people called you because they need your expertise" (DD 13).

Tempe learns from one of the sisters that the bones have been removed and reburied in separate small coffins. "She held her tiny arms out to indicate a child-size dimension" (DD 19). With that clue, they locate the burial site (DD 19–22).

Here Tempe's search takes on a circular shape consistent with the life cycle. Tempe thinks of the beginning of her own life, and then discovers the end through the bones of a giving, saint-like nun. Both are couched in terms of being a child — life full of potential, yet unlived and unexplored.

Dr. Brennan makes numerous ghastly discoveries, but she refuses to allow them to derail her life. *Death DuJour* includes a passage in which Tempe awakens to find herself entombed in a tunnel. She remembers who she is, one acquainted with death, but she has to remind herself. "As I recoiled my head cracked wood and the start of a scream rose in my throat. Goddam it, Brennan, get hold of yourself. You are a crime scene professional, not a hysterical onlooker" (DD 360). She loses her ice scraper, the only tool she has for prying an opening to let in air. Despite the tense situation, she continues to remember who she is. She calls up a systematic procedure for discovery. "Cursing my clumsiness, I began a miniature grid search across the dank clay" (DD 361–62). She seeks her instrument of life in the middle of the "dank clay," symbolic death.

There are no echoes or screams in Tempe's life, regardless how enclosed it may become. "Any world is a valid world if it's alive. The thing to do is to bring life to it, and the only way to do that is to find in your own case where the life is and become alive yourself" (Campbell, PM 149).

Tempe develops a tough talking second persona to keep herself in line. "When it is deep winter, I often have a talk with myself before deplaning. It will be cold, I remind myself" (DD 25). By preparing for the cold, a reality, she can develop the flexible identity to overcome it.

Tempe is Narcissus who follows the prophecy of Tiresias. The secret to a long life is to recognize that some parts of the self are unknowable. As close as Tempe is to death and its mysteries, she knows there are pockets of the uninvestigated in life. By contrast, Kay Scarpetta's character in Patricia Cornwell's books since 1995 shows us a Narcissus who has sunk beneath the river. In an attempt to overcome death, Scarpetta has herself died. She neglects the part of her that is alive. To prove this point, we shall ritualistically do an autopsy. By cutting the character into pieces, we can perhaps resurrect her.

The body in question lies before us on the slab. We read the toe tag, *Scarpetta, Kay*. What happened to transform this once razor sharp professional into a bloodless character of a single dimension? The purpose of our autopsy is to examine the remains, determine time and cause of death, present evidence pointing to the likely murderer, and to note how future deaths of series characters might be prevented.

Ever since Hammett and Chandler, detective fiction has featured violent death, but it took Cornwell's Medical Examiner Kay Scarpetta to zoom in on the visceral violence of death's real brutality laid out on a silent dissecting table. The way Scarpetta cuts into cadavers makes violence in a hard-boiled detective novel pale by comparison.

3. A Bodiless Dream 57

When Scarpetta first emerges from her fluorescent-lit morgue, all brisk and white-coated, she is an appealing blend of professional and personal conflicts. The first Scarpetta saga, *Postmortem* (1990), remains the only novel to garner Edgar, Creasy, Anthony, and Macavity Awards in the same year.

The next four books follow in quick succession. We learn about Luminol and DNA as exculpatory evidence, about the Y-incision and the mutilated body as metaphor for the human condition. We come to understand FBI profiling of killers. We laugh at Captain Marino. Cornwell shows Scarpetta at the top of her game and gives real weight to the emotional complications of staying there.

Around 1995 with the publication of *From Potter's Field*, an illness takes hold. Here, an acute identity crisis undercuts Kay's previous confidence.

In this book, the killer is obvious, the psychopathic Temple Gault. Instead, as with most forensics, mystery surrounds the victim. Kay uses her expertise to make the corpse say its name. The problem, however, is that she merges with the nameless victim, Jane Doe.

In an article on feminist mysteries, Sandra Tomc notes that the female detective often identifies with the woman victim. The pattern extends the idea that one woman's murder is a crime against the entire gender. "Frequently, the confusion is literalized as the detective herself becomes the target of the killer" (Tomc 46–47).

Cornwell takes this confusion one step further. Temple Gault paralyzes Kay so absolutely, she loses all sense of herself. Cornwell moves the main character through the narrative as a kind of shadow for the other characters. Kay Scarpetta has become Echo.

The villain Temple Gault sets a horrific crime scene. In Central Park, a woman's body lies frozen under a fountain draped with bloody ice. Gault has ripped pieces of skin from inside the victim's thighs (FPF 29–30). The frozen fountain suggests male impotence, and the victim is more than a helpless female, the crime being a ritualized castration. (Interestingly, this crime of the slashed thighs, is nearly identical to Alex Cooper's revenge on the insane doctor in Fairstein's *Likely to Die*.) After witnessing the scene, Kay is herself a frozen victim with no identity.

To stay vital through the rest of the novel, Kay hangs herself, like a leech, onto other characters.

She first bleeds dry her married lover, FBI agent Benton Wesley. After they spend a night together, Kay awakes to something wrong: "... this was the first Christmas when someone other than me had been in my bed. I felt I had stolen something" (FPF 43). As they stroll the Manhattan sidewalks, they are mirror images of each other, wearing identical baseball caps (FPF 68). Kay asks Wesley a few times if he is losing weight (FPF 72, 278). Then she brings up The Wife.

Vampire-like, Kay gains stature as she grills him about his failing marriage. She even steels herself against feeling jealous. Kay grows stronger while Wesley drains away. After she reminisces about a previous lover, now dead (FPF 70), we see that Wesley's future looks bleak.

Kay's next vampire fix occurs when she nearly shoots her own niece Lucy by accident. Lucy, computer genius and closeted homosexual, is Kay's closest family member. She looks like Kay and dresses like her, again mirror images. After the near shooting, our intrepid heroine collapses with a case of the vapors.

> The pain was so sharp and I could not catch my breath. Lucy tried to help me up, but I was too weak. My hands were going numb, fingers cramping, and I leaned forward in the chair and shut my eyes as I broke out in a profuse cold sweat. I was breathing rapid, shallow breaths [215].

We now see this for what it is, an old-fashioned case of soap opera-itis. Later, when Lucy shrieks, "you almost had a heart attack," Kay says primly, "I reviewed the cardiogram. I had nothing that a paper bag and a hot bath wouldn't have fixed" (FPF 217–18). Obviously, Kay could not have a heart attack in the middle of her own mystery.

By almost shooting Lucy, her alter-ego, Kay nearly commits suicide. If you think this is so much dimestore psychology, Kay and Benton apply exactly this same logic to Gault, the psychopathic killer.

> "Benton, who is he really killing when he kills these people?"
> "Himself," he said. "Gault is killing himself" [FPF 65].

They have this conversation so we know that when Gault impersonates Kay and she kills him, who is she really killing?

Temple Gault is the serial killer we love to hate. He has a karate black belt and effeminately wears a long coat and floppy hat. He sends love notes to her at the morgue (FPF 180). Kay describes his evil as "beyond description" (FPF 60). In a washed out picture, he could be either a man or a woman (FPF 116).

Kay finally identifies Gault's victim from the corpse's unusual gold foil dental work (FPF 284, 288). The victim is Gault's twin sister. Temple killed off half of himself.

Gault attaches himself to another half-personality, Kay. He steals her gold Amex card, and essentially becomes her, signing K (with the initial K) *Scarpetta* on a credit slip (FPF 75, 254). Gault uses Kay's card to buy her jewelry, a caduceus pin (FPF 254). The clerk tells Kay, "Actually, it's you. The pin is really you" (FPF 255–56).

3. A Bodiless Dream   59

The climactic scene is a confluence of symbol for the self. The two half-people, Gault and Kay, come together. Gault wears the caduceus pin, the virtual Kay, on his lapel (FPF 350), while Kay becomes Gault, the castrator. In the fetid subway tunnels under New York City, she reenacts his original crime against a twin. "I was on my knees. I raised the knife as he got in position to kick and plunged the surgical blade into his upper thigh. With both hands I cut as much as I could as he shrieked" (FPF 351).

Fear of sexuality is a time-worn mystery convention. John Cawelti notes, "Sexual passion is treated as a semimystical moral and religious experience and is often associated with the redemptive and healing qualities of the simpler life" (236). Not so usual is fear of androgyny.

Gault seduces both men and women. By castrating him, Kay hopes to put her own undefined sexual feelings to rest, but the conflict persists. Gault has an accomplice in his crimes, Carrie Grethen, another psychopath, who moves even closer to Kay. Grethen has been Lucy's lesbian lover. Institutionalized for the next two books, Carrie is mostly under wraps, but she serves to "carry" an androgynous menace into *Point of Origin* (1998).

This work marks the time of death for Kay Scarpetta as a credible character. When Carrie escapes from the asylum, Kay's reactions are so overblown that she loses all authority as a smart woman of science. The fatal illness of poor characterization claims its victim.

Now we start the autopsy. Let us begin with the head. A few times in *Point of Origin*, Scarpetta teaches us something new. We receive mini-lectures on the stages of a fire, from point of origin to flashpoint (PO 28, 36, 101). We learn how to calculate the height of a victim from a femur (PO 96). We also see an electron microscope at work (PO 275–77). However, Kay is not the point of origin for this information. Others provide the expertise. More often, we see Kay as hapless or angry, intellectually out of it. As she removes a victim from the crime scene, she is "tense and irritable" (PO 42). We don't see her working smarts.

The reason? Kay has received a crazed message from Carrie. It paralyzes her out of all proportion to the danger. Kay sits at her breakfast table feeling sick, because Carrie is "curdling the air with her foul, evil presence" (PO 3).

Kay has seemingly lost her ability to reason. She jumps to conclusions and overreacts. When Marino tells her he has bad news, she responds, "I immediately thought of Lucy and felt the strength go out of my knees. I swayed and put my hand on his shoulder as my mind seemed to shatter into a million pieces" (PO 78). There's that swoon again, like an eighteenth-century heroine. Marino's bad news is Carrie has escaped from the asylum. The reader knows from the first page that this would happen. Kay is seventy-seven pages behind.

At the same time, she tries to work a big case, a murder arson. Fire completely levels an estate owned by a media millionaire. A woman's body is discovered in what had been the master bath. The body is unburned, a whole corpse pressed and preserved under melted glass (PO 41). She has a hemorrhage near her eye (PO 43), and a ring in her back pocket (PO 78). Eventually Kay learns that the victim's name was Claire.

The owner of the burned house is named, redundantly, Kenneth Sparkes. The house has burned to the ground, but somehow they discover that a Calico submachine gun has been stolen. Kay asks Sparkes, "What else is missing from the house?" (PO 176). Sparkes had collected fine bourbon, and the fire had broken the bottles, so everything was soused in bourbon, including, I think, the main character.

In previous books, Cornwell had deftly used computers. Villains sent Doctor Scarpetta threatening messages. The genius Lucy had designed a computerized criminal database. In *Point of Origin*, Lucy has to download top-secret files to Kay's computer because she cannot get her printer out of the box (PO 159). Kay tells her, "'Don't worry, I'm used to confidential information. I'll make sure no one else gets hold of them.' I knew it was stupid when I said it" (PO 159). We are set up for Carrie to tap the line. This never happens. The whole computer subplot comes to no resolution. Incidentally, Lucy sends all these super-secret death files to Kay over AOL.

We wait for Carrie's insane message to have some meaning eventually, but that never happens, either. When Cornwell held an online discussion with her fans, a reader from Ireland wrote, "*please* put your mailing list 'friends' out of our misery ... What do the letters *GKSFWFY* mean? 'Gretham [*sic*] kills Scarpetta, fire waits for you' was a popular guess." Cornwell's response? "I have too many books in my head to remember everything" (January 18, 1999).

Kay says and does numerous other things that end up being ineffectual. Kay is in Lucy's house, but when Lucy wants something to drink, Kay tells Lucy to help herself (PO 160). Whose house is it? Kay tries to dispense motherly advice, but it falls flat. The way to survive, she tells Lucy is, "You decide you can't give someone more power than you already have" (PO 161) She also says, "It's very lonely being you" (PO 162).

When Marino gets drunk and swears, Kay tries to analyze the power of the "f" word. "In truth, it was a grand word that expressed what one felt by the very act of saying it" (PO 167). What is wrong with Kay? Does she have creeping senility? She claims to know that Marino is thinking about Carrie. Then, two pages later, she asks, "Are you thinking about Carrie?" (PO 162–65).

Literary Examiner's Findings: Assorted samples show localized live cells, but head of the deceased evidences a general softness.

Next we examine the eyes. Kay used to have perfect vision, both inside and out. For instance, she begins an autopsy.

3. A Bodiless Dream

> I attached the victim's films to light boxes where the shadows and shapes of his organs and bones bared their souls to me. Bullets and their multitude of ragged pieces were lethal snowstorms in liver, lungs, heart and brain ... [FPF 18].

By contrast, she prepares to visit the murder arson crime scene by helicopter. It takes off outside The Eye Institute, where no lights are on (PO 16). The Eye Institute is also where she has her vision checked and glasses adjusted (PO 17). This is the first we have heard that she even needs glasses. The helicopter gives her no special vantage point, but instead lifts her, as she says, "into chaos" (PO 15–16).

Kay tells us that as a trained observer she lets her eyes go first onto a murder scene (PO 35). Yet she is too worried about being seen to see fully. Her lover Benton tells her about a peeping Tom in her neighborhood. On several occasions she stumbles around in the dark, fearing the watcher outside (PO 14). At the arson scene, she says, "I was certain McGovern was watching to see how long I would last" (PO 35). Later, she appears at the courthouse to testify on a routine case. The watching reporters cause her to panic. She hides for half an hour. "I shut myself inside the small windowless witness room and sat in a wooden chair. I felt trapped and foolish ..." An attorney comes in and talks to her to calm her down (PO 128). Indeed, there seem to be no lights on at the "I" Institute.

It is certainly acceptable, even realistic for Kay to be emotional, but she is the reader's eyes. When she cannot see, neither can we.

Literary Examiner's Findings: "Windowless witness room" is a perfect phrase for character's extreme myopia about self and relationships. Needs glasses for an inner blindness.

Continuing with our autopsy, we spread the rib cage to expose the heart. Scarpetta's emotional core has three arteries, one to each of her three intimates in life, her lover Benton; Marino, her close associate; and her niece, Lucy.

Benton Wesley, who threatened to disappear due to weight loss in *From Potter's Field*, actually does disappear in *Point of Origin*. Kay and Benton now live together, but in separate wings of her house. During foreplay, the strongest urge she has is to sleep. Benton is "desperate for skin," yet her pillow talk focuses on wound measurement and ruined bodies (PO 11–13). Kay and Benton no longer share a shower or a bed. Their plans for a vacation together are interrupted. Their love is stale.

For those who haven't read this novel and wish to, take note, because here comes the spoiler. Carrie kills Benton, and it's almost a benevolent euthanasia. Cornwell has already drained Benton's character of energy and personality. Here he is an FBI profiler, yet he calls a criminal psychopath "a squirrel" (PO 227). This is what Marino called them in previous books. Even before Benton's demise, his role as Kay's lover was a walk-on.

There is more emotional realism between Kay and Pete Marino, the police captain. He travels with Kay as her bodyguard, despite responsibilities in his own precinct. In Marino, Columbo meets Archie Bunker. Amazingly, he still says "yo" (PO 53, 161–62). He and Kay spar like an old married couple over his smoking and bad eating habits. He even goes shopping with her, to a sports store and a restaurant supply house to find a cookpot big enough for her special dish (PO 131). We discuss more on that later.

In the early books, Marino was married, but he is now divorced, living a pitiful life in a redneck neighborhood. Kay visits his place for the first time. She sees his camper and his Christmas lights, still up in June (PO 187–88). She sheds a quick tear, but soon snaps out of it.

Marino feels old and useless. He is like Sipowicz from *NYPD Blue*, shaking his head over a disintegrating moral order and his own declining body. He tells her, "I keep seeing my time running short. I think about my life, and I've pretty much done it all. If I didn't do nothing else, I still would have done enough, you know?" (PO 189). Scarpetta shows him every sympathy: "And the reality is, if you die, you'll come to me and end up on one of my tables" (PO 189). I guess even a corpse should fear her autopsy.

The third artery connects Kay to her niece, Lucy. Under our scalpel, this vessel shows the most damage. When it comes to Lucy, this heart is hypersensitive and overloaded.

Kay wants to live through her niece. Lucy quit the FBI, which Kay takes as a personal affront: "Lucy had walked off from her heart and was no longer within my reach" (PO 21). Kay is upset that Lucy sometimes ignores her (PO 26). Cornwell laces Kay's reactions to Lucy with phrases such as "a splinter in the heart" (PO 102) or a "blow to the heart" (PO 153). Her heart "turns hard" or "hurts more" (PO 160–61).

To measure Kay's affection for Lucy, let's look at Kay's reactions to Teune McGovern, Lucy's woman supervisor on the arson squad. The major emotion here is jealousy.

The exchanges begin like schoolyard squabbles. Kay thinks McGovern is picking on her (PO 34). McGovern reacts with anger (PO 36). When McGovern tires on the crime scene, Kay is glad (PO 40). Kay learns that Lucy has seen a psychiatrist. McGovern knows, and Kay doesn't. Her reaction is petty and unreasonable (PO 122).

About Lucy, Kay is more a jealous lover than an aunt or mother figure. She has nothing going on with Benton, but is a kid peeping into a circus tent when it comes to Lucy's love life. Kay and Lucy spend a night in a motel, with separate beds. Kay ogles Lucy's body and sees how Carrie might love her. "I felt shamed and confused, when for an electric instant, I envisioned her as

3. A Bodiless Dream

Carrie's supple, hungry lover" (PO 58). Tensions build, and Kay harangues Lucy like a jealous spouse, accusing her without reason of sleeping with McGovern (PO 59–60).

> Teune's gender makes no difference to me. I do not know a thing about her proclivities. But if you are attracted to each other? Why wouldn't anyone be attracted to either of you? Both of you are striking and compelling and brilliant and heroic [PO 60].

Trace evidence under the deceased's fingernails shows that she has her grip on Lucy and will not let go.

Literary Examiner's Findings: The victim's heart has atrophied. Kay manifests neutrality about Benton, irritation with Marino, and a confused love/hate for her niece.

Now for the nervous system. Despite Kay's stiff neck, we find a weak backbone. Kay no longer musters the discipline to complete paperwork or act on her own initiative. When she finds a nick in a victim's skull, she prepares to visit a bone expert at the Smithsonian. Logic dictates that she would set up the appointment first, then call Marino, her guard dog. Curiously, she calls Marino first. "Listen, can you go with me, assuming Dr. Vessey can see us?" (PO 132). She has lost her work ethic and independent spirit.

We may also trace a deterioration of moral fiber. Kay works the hardest on a task involving that oversized cooking pot. She boils the bones of the arson murder victim, Claire, to remove the skin. "I worked very carefully, loosening and defleshing while the rest of the skeletal remains quietly cooked in their steamy pot" (PO 131).

Literary Examiner's Findings: In this spineless corpse of Doctor Kay Scarpetta, the nervous system is completely absent.

Now that the autopsy is complete, we are prepared to discuss the murderer.

The perp in the book's mystery is, surprise, a fashion photographer named Newton Joyce. We have no way of guessing whodunit, because we know nothing about him, except that he owns a Mercedes. Until the end, he has no role in the narrative. What fun is that? Kay and company locate his house and discover mannequins ghoulishly fitted with skin faces. The scene must be truly horrible because it causes even Marino to swear. There are also thousands of pictures, arranged in a requisite shrine to his victims, who were scattered all over the globe. Carrie is thrown in as Joyce's accomplice for an additional helping of evil.

As a monster, Carrie is ineffective. At least we catch glimpses of Gault. Carrie appears only as a background figure on a video. However, Kay perceives her as omnipotent and evil incarnate. "Carrie was not there and yet she was" (PO 267). We never really feel the mythic energy Kay claims for her (PO 46–47).

Because of Kay's overinflated reactions, the novel flat-lines just when its tension should build. In his insightful comments on the art of the mystery, John Cawelti says that the balance between violence and order creates a tension necessary to sustain suspense (108). When Scarpetta's emotional upsets compete with and overthrow the violence of her profession, which is considerable, the morgue ceiling caves in. Noel Carroll analyzes the role of suspense in effective horror tales, noting that suspense equals anticipation plus a worthwhile stake (137). Here both ingredients are absent. The only event that is even half-surprising is Benton's death. If we were paying attention three books ago, we could see it coming.

Newton Joyce and Carrie Grethen are only pawns in this mystery. The true Evil Queen on this chessboard is — the deceased, Doctor Kay Scarpetta. Symbolically, she is the real killer.

Here is the evidence. Newton Joyce drives a Mercedes and lusts after Claire. Kay drives a Mercedes (PO 193) and lusts after Lucy. The names *Claire* and *Lucy* both connote light. As we know, there is a need for light at the darkened "I" Institute.

Newton Joyce the photographer uses a knife to strip beautiful people of their faces. Kay boils off human skin for a portrait of the victim.

Seeing Kay as the symbolic equivalent of Carrie is easy. Because Kay killed Gault, "to die by my hand was to bond me to him forever" (PO 8). Carrie and Gault were the "evil twins" (PO 8), with Kay as a third party. Carrie finally puts Benton out of his misery. He cramped Kay's style. He had to go.

Why does Carrie spook Kay as much as she does? This makes no sense, unless we consider one fact: that Carrie has had Lucy. We see the depth of Kay's anger at McGovern when she thinks they are having an affair. Weirdly dressed and androgynous, Carrie "sucks up every drop of Lucy's life" (PO 125). So does Aunt Kay. Aunt Kay wants to know where Lucy is every minute. "Carrie knew what Lucy would do ... Carrie had been watching all along" (PO 348).

In the symbolic formula of this book, Newton Joyce and Carrie equal Kay. Why? Kay notes that the ugly Joyce killed because he was jealous of youthful beauty and miserable in his own life (PO 342). This matches Kay to a tee. Like Joyce, she finds love only at death scenes. In discovering Benton's body, Lucy is wounded. She falls against Kay, moaning, the two embrace, and almost collapse (PO 250). Just as Newton Joyce seeks to rob someone else of happiness, Kay robs Lucy of McGovern (PO 342). At Joyce's house, Kay passes out and comes to in McGovern's arms (PO 338). McGovern is tender and caring to protect Kay from the horrors (PO 339).

3. A Bodiless Dream 65

The terrible soup in the cooking pot underscores Kay's dissociation from humanity. Just before she cooks her "dish," she tells her secretary that she does not want to feel human yet. "I'm always in enough trouble with God as [it] is'" (PO 111–12). Then she turns on the stove. "Steam rose in a hot, moist vapor, tainting the air with a nauseating stench ..." (PO 113).

She lets the bones cook for over a hundred pages and tries to gross out McGovern. She offers to take her to lunch, then says, "I have bones in a pot that need heating up. You can come with me, if you have a strong stomach" (PO 215). A little coroner humor? Even though Kay says a blessing over the steaming bones, this image still carries us into Jeffrey Dahmer territory.

Mutilation can be a means of redemption. In *Omens of the Millennium*, Harold Bloom sees identity fragmentation as an altered state of consciousness. Bloom presents the example of the resurrected Christ (140). "Though undergone in ecstasy, shamanistic initiation frequently involves death by mutilation, followed by a resurrection that reintegrates the body" (141).

Cornwell tries to use mutilation in that manner. However, Kay's psychic fragmentation is too profound. Cornwell's attempts to glue her back together fall short. The shootout scene between the two helicopters is ludicrous. The book's final pages are puzzling.

At Benton's funeral, Kay looks at Lucy's eyes through the helicopter bubble and says, "I gathered my splintered spirit into a core" (PO 355–56). Then she throws Benton's ashes into the ocean while Lucy whips up the water with the helicopter blades. Blowing away Benton's ashes is the ultimate indignity.

Literary Examiner's Conclusion: Kay Scarpetta, MD, died after nine books, of a mushy brain and a hardened heart with complications from apoplectic outbursts and stiff-necked jealousy.

And who murdered her? We have more clues. Newton Joyce pastes the faces on mannequins, exactly what a writer does to create characters. In his house are photographs of Joyce posing with his helicopter (PO 341). For the past two books, Cornwell herself has appeared in exactly this pose.

Perhaps in anticipation of Scarpetta's demise, Cornwell has begun another series, featuring Police Chief Hammer. *Hornet's Nest* and *Southern Cross* have earned mostly negative reviews. The book reviewer in Fort Lauderdale's *Sun-Sentinel* found *Southern Cross* to be contrived and loaded with stereotypes, an insult to the South (Cogdill E-3). Cornwell is no longer only a writer, but a commodity. A children's book and film of *From Potter's Field* were in development through 1999. Cornwell also has written a cookbook, *Kay Scarpetta's Winter Table* (1998). Published just in time for Christmas, it features recipes for meals that Kay whips up for Lucy or Marino. Fortunately, it does not include a recipe for cannibal soup.

If the quality of the Scarpetta series has declined this drastically, how do we explain the continuing high sales? John Cawelti notes, "Primarily it is a matter of psychology that addicts of a particular formula find some pleasure in any rendition of it, no matter how dully written or hackneyed" (106). The writer must recognize what the publishers do not, that the character's possibilities have played out. Even Kay tells us. Despite her new morgue, she has "no more room to evolve" (PO 102). Let us slide the drawer marked *Doctor Kay Scarpetta* back into the cabinet.

While this particular character may have flat-lined, Doctor Scarpetta has taught us well. She was one of the first protagonists, man or woman, who dared to look the murdered corpse full in the face. For Fairfield's Alex Cooper and Reichs's Temperance Brennan, Scarpetta led the way along dark morgue hallways. Cornwell has helped to define a new mystery type, forensics.

Narcissus sought in the river a sense of wholeness, a vision of a "bodiless dream." Through the many ways a body can be violated, forensic investigators in fiction seek with varying degrees of success the same vision.

CHAPTER 4

RELIGION IN MYSTERIES: OF THE ESSENCE

Holy men and women march in throngs through the chapels of mystery solving. The air is thick with chimes from time-tolling bells. G.K. Chesterton's Father Brown leads the pack at the beginning of the twentieth century. Begun in the 1970s, Harry Kemelman's series featuring Rabbi David Small guides us through the days of the week: *Monday the Rabbi Took Off* or *Friday the Rabbi Slept Late*.

A number of women authors have taken up the clock from Kemelman's mantle. Ellis Peters sets her mystery series featuring Brother Cadfael in medieval times, a complete displacement from the modern world. Former convent-dweller Christine Bennett Brooks solves murders themed to the holidays in the series by Lee Harris. Author Sister Carol Anne O'Marie includes references to the Church calendar in book and chapter titles featuring her sleuth Sister Mary Helen. These time markers transcend the days. Each season has its ordered celebrations and ceremonies. Each chapter takes the name of a church festival or Saint's Day. Order and routine are paramount.

A series by Michelle Blake features Lily Connor, an Episcopal priest who fills in "part-time" at various parishes. On many levels, Lily is still in the process of getting in touch with seasons of the Church. Adam Dalgliesh, the poet-detective created by P. D. James, is nearing retirement as a senior Inspector at Scotland Yard. While not officially connected with the Church, he is no stranger to sacred matters. He is the son of a rector and a veteran of several previous church-related murders. In *Death in Holy Orders* (2001), both his police background and a highly developed spiritual sense help him solve the case. Faye Kellerman, Rochelle Krich, and Winona Sullivan also march in this procession of mystery writers using religious themes.

Unless these women authors have merely expropriated Kemelman's time theme, something about the clerical mystery makes time a critical component. Is time in fiction an equivalent of a force from above?

Most murder-solving mysteries refer to time at least in passing. Detectives establish who last saw the victim, determine time of death, and coordinate alibis. The sleuth's intensified role in bringing the murderer to light also makes time relevant. When the killer is hidden, regular time slows down, and the community is in suspense. Once the murderer is unmasked, time can resume. The rhythms of life proceed.

In ecclesiastical mysteries, time plays a more complex role. Much about time evokes near-religious feelings of awe. Like God, it is all powerful and ultimately unknowable. Despite hyper-accurate wristwatches and atomic clocks, we cannot control it. We measure it and try to manage it, but Time wins in the end. Sometimes, when one character cuts short the life of another human being, Time wins in the middle.

A person murders, but Time is the ultimate killer. Solving Death is really an attempt to control and comprehend temporality. Time is Death in another guise. Time rolls toward inevitable change. This inexorable force of time moving forward shapes views of our own mortality and links us with images of an all-powerful Being. The well-ordered seasons of sacred life and long-standing traditions of the Church form a backdrop against which the cleric works out the solution to the mystery.

Time is a key to religious mysteries, and the sanctified space of the church building is essentially enclosed time, tradition in the form of a building.

A religious meeting place is in some ways no different from any other organization. In the church office behind the sanctuary, a church, temple, cathedral, convent, or monastery is run by a clearly defined hierarchy. Like most organizations, tensions among group members can spark ambition, greed, hatred, all common motives for murder. Churches hide secrets, and they make ideal hiding places. Mostly abandoned during the week, the large building is isolated. The murderer can leap from a shadowy pew or from behind the altar as easily as from a dark alley. Whatever the context, murder desecrates all life. However, murder in the cathedral is particularly despicable. All the moral and social restraints are in place, and they still fail. Blood lands on a sacred carpet.

People seek solace in a house of worship. Each person brings the naked self to the church to confront secret shortcomings. A church provides a setting for contemplating mortality, time, and the eternal. It's a psychological safe place where a person may risk an intense encounter with the inner life. A person at prayer is without defenses or social pretense. Murder in such a place violates individual as well as communal sanctity. A holy place is supposed to celebrate life and provide solace from death, not the other way around.

Mysteries set in a holy place emphasize a deep tearing of traditional social and moral fabric. The murder directly challenges moral values and absolute commandments in a way that mysteries with secular settings do not. For mysteries outside an explicitly sacred environment, it is enough that the murder is illegal. Murders in a sanctuary are immoral as well. They sin against life. Breaking the dictate "Thou Shalt Not Kill" is a human being's worst crime against a universe in which humanity is the most divine creation.

Where the man or woman of God travels, the house of worship is never far away. *The Thanksgiving Day Murder* (1995) shows us former nun Christine Bennett Brooks returning to the convent for a visit. As an orphaned child, Chris had gone to live at St. Stephen's Convent when she was fifteen. She is now thirty, and left St. Stephen's six months ago to marry Jack Brooks, a police detective: "There is always a rush of feeling when I see the roofs and spires in the distance. It was my home for fifteen wonderful years, and I left as a friend of the convent and a friend of every nun I had loved while I was there" (145). Chris is happy to return and receive advice from her mentor, Sister Joseph. She feels that the convent is her home.

From the Gothic conventions of abbey ruins and Poe's "Fall of the House of Usher," churches in mysteries are often crumbling, uncertain structures. Secluded and full of shadows, the church building evokes traditional values yet the pending murder shows these values under attack. From the outside, crumbling churches or cathedrals make effective symbols of death and decay. They imply a moral lesson, not only about a slide toward death but the decline of a social order.

As *Murder in Ordinary Time* (1991) begins, Sister Mary Helen is in a bleak mood. The Church reinforces this depression. Author Sister Carol Anne O'Marie paints the world of Mount St. Francis College in "gray-green" and "black": "Now that all the students were on semester break and just a skeleton crew [was] on hand, Mount St. Francis College seemed like a ghost college, high on a lonely hill, with the City below hidden in the overcast" (2). She sees her life there "in the ivory tower" as "deadly dull" (3). When she must travel into the City for a television interview, she sends a cheery hello to some friends, "a couple of nuns shivering on the corner by St. Bridget's Church ..." (11). The Church is not a particularly welcoming refuge. Sister Mary Helen enthusiastically trades the ivory tower for a TV studio, past for future.

Later, a storm threatens the convent. It is Martin Luther King, Jr.'s birthday. "Towering pines creaked and the branches of the elms slapped and scraped against the convent windows. Screeching gulls, signaling a storm, flew across the darkening sky" (62). Sister Therese enters and makes a fire to take the chill off, but Mary Helen is not warmed. "It would take more than that puny fire to lift my spirits, Mary Helen wanted to say; it would take at least a ten-ton crane" (63). The Church is subject to the same forces of violence as everywhere else.

Placed next to their churches, the two sleuths create a telling contrast. Christine is now out in the world as an extension of the convent, a successful "graduate." As a young but mature person with a basically sunny disposition, she moves certainly between sacred and secular worlds, her past in the convent and her future as a wife. The convent serves as a temporary retreat when the future seems unclear. Sister Mary Helen, on the other hand, has been in the Church for over half a century. She feels moribund in the institution and has a strong need to stir things up. The world out there is gloomy and possibly dangerous, but she has faith that she can deal with whatever leaps from the present fog.

Lily Connor's current faith is nowhere near as certain as Christine's or the good Sister Mary Helen's. Lily must prepare for the reality that a church's charming exterior may cover mysteries hidden within. Such is the case in *The Tentmaker* (1999) by Michelle Blake. The word "tentmaker" means a priest who maintains an occupation outside the church. Lily is a tentmaker, serving as an interim Episcopal priest at St. Mary's in Boston. Lily has not been at the church for long, but she quickly comprehends that all is not well there. The previous priest has died a mysterious death. Outside, the church virtually glistens.

> As she turned off Brimmer, Lily could see the graceful spire of St. Mary's rising above the church buildings on the corner of River and Lee. Lee Street was a single block of elegant private homes, their brick fronts facing directly onto the narrow lane. At the end of the street sat the church, a small gem in the crown of the diocese, famous for its intricately detailed stained-glass windows depicting the life of Mary and the side chapel with its miniature rose windows [15].

After Lily views this paragon of a church from afar, she ominously glimpses a "dark figure" using a key to slip inside. Inside, the church building holds a secret belied by its radiant exterior.

In P.D. James' *Death in Holy Orders*, Adam Dalgliesh has been summoned to investigate a death at Saint Anselm's Theological College. It is on a deserted stretch of England's east coast. A wealthy student was found buried on a rocky beach nearby. Local police had ruled the death a suicide, but the student's wealthy father receives a note raising suspicion that all was not as it seemed at the College. Nearing retirement, Adam takes particular interest in investigating the case. His own father had been a rector, and Adam lived at St. Anselm's for three summers when he was a boy.

James creates a scene of shambling decay that is both familiar to Dalgliesh yet changed over time. The road leading to the building is sunken and overgrown, a tangle of vegetation. Then the building looms before Adam:

> As he reached the cliff edge and turned north on the gritty coastal track, it came into distant view, a bizarre edifice of brick and layered stone looking as bright and unreal as a cardboard cut-out against the strengthening blue of the sky. It seemed to move towards him rather than he towards it, and it bore with it inexorably the images of adolescence and the half-remembered swinging moods of joy and pain, of uncertainty and shining hope [55].

The building is an image from a dream. It shimmers in Adam's present and his past.

Far from being an atmospheric set, the architecture of St. Anselm's is a kind of barometer of character. The beautiful Dr. Emma Lavenham, a literature professor from Cambridge, visits St. A's to present a seminar on metaphysical poets. Her specialty is George Herbert, but there are hints that she will soon take up the study of a living metaphysical poet currently employed at Scotland Yard. James shows us the building from Emma's point of view.

> And now St. Anselm's was clearly in sight, roofs, the tall chimney stacks, turrets, tower and cupola seeming visibly to darken with the dying of the light. In front the two ruined pillars of the long-demolished Elizabethan gatehouse gave out their silent, ambiguous messages: crude phallic symbols, indomitable sentinels against the steadily advancing enemy, obstinately enduring reminders of the house's inevitable end [101].

Despite being ravaged by time, Saint Anselm's represents youth and hope for Adam. He overcomes feeling old. By contrast, the church building represents decaying tradition, even waning masculinity to Emma. Through the varying perspectives, James achieves an effect similar to Monet's paintings of cathedrals. The church is changeable in different light and through different seasons. Still, it is a constant presence.

These characters, Christine Bennett Brooks, Sister Mary Helen, Lily Connor, and Adam Dalgliesh, show that they are particularly suited to solve murders. They understand the psychology of people under pressure. Death and life come as part of their job. These sleuths provide a redress for an individual's pain, a ritual balm necessary for healing, forgiveness, and mercy after the murder. The cleric's quest is not essentially personal but for spiritual and metaphysical fulfillment. The nuns, priest, and poet are shaman figures with specialized knowledge that raise them above other mortals. The murderer who stops time by taking a life has a more than equal adversary in these sanctified sleuths. Through sacraments of the Church or religious ritual, they wield the power of murder-solving rituals to mend the break in time.

In a lecture series presented at the University of Glasgow in 1990, George Steiner discussed the role of time in starting and structuring artistic creation. "It is no hyperbole to say that each work of art, music, and literature generates its own time-world, its own temporal space" (243). Steiner asserts that one book presents a whole temporal world, and from within that book can emerge various time environments. To characterize the many different time functions in ecclesiastical mysteries, we consider that smaller segments of Steiner's topographical metaphor of "time-world" could be called "timescapes."

Three distinct timescapes are useful in discussing the highly inflected versions of time in a religious mystery novel: mythic, linear, and forensic. For events on a mythic level, time has no meaning. The immensities of ocean or sky serve as parallels from a visual landscape. The character moves in a sacred, continual present. He soars into a state of becoming. A poem, artwork, or music lifts the character into a suspended, dreamlike state. This is the time when mind and spirit are ready to launch into creativity. This is the closest human experience comes to achieving immortality.

The linear timescape is horizontal, rooted to earth and to history. A path is an appropriate emblem. We can move forward and backward along a path, just as we can travel backward through memories. Linear time is historical. The person has a sense of time's duration, the progression of days, the calendar pages being ripped away.

Forensic time defines the third timescape. Its space is the blankness of the morgue. Official corpse handlers swoop in. The dead are isolated from the living. For this realm, there are only two relevant time points: before the murder and after. Time-rooted artifacts of the murder help the sleuth to re-enact the crime.

These timescapes layered one over the other create a textured narrative. When the murder occurs, it tears a hole through all these timescapes. Powers stronger than the sleuth have to mend this rift. Time serves as an immanent force, as if from above.

How do timescapes work in a novel? A scene from *Death in Holy Orders* illustrates.

The wealthy student found dead on the beach is only the beginning of unnatural deaths. After Adam's arrival, more disturbing events take place. A recurring nightmare of a bloody execution awakens Father Martin yet again.

4. Religion in Mysteries 73

An eerie windstorm howls outside. Father Martin is surprised to see a glimmer of light from the sanctuary. He makes his way to the church toward a shocking discovery. On the stone floor is a spreading pool of blood that matches his dream:

> The nightmare hadn't ended. He was still trapped in a place of horror, but one which he couldn't now escape by waking. That or he was mad. He shut his eyes and prayed, 'Dear God, help me.' Then his conscious mind took hold and he opened his eyes and willed himself to look again. The smashed skull; the Archdeacon's spectacles lying a little apart but unbroken; the two brass candlesticks placed one on each side of the body as if in an act of sacrilegious contempt ... [175].

This scene combines several timescapes. Father Martin's repeated nightmare already has cut a deep wound in him. The moment when Father Martin cannot distinguish dream life from waking life essentially makes time irrelevant. He is lifted from everyday life. The fact that the nightmare occurs while he is awake causes him to question his sanity. This lifting of time away from experience involves mythic time.

Once Father Martin shuts his eyes and prays, he descends to a spot separate from mythic time. He exists in history, on earth, in a time when prayer is necessary. This is a time of duration, causality, one moment following the other. This passage says something about Father Martin as a character, that in times of deep distress, he will call upon God.

A third timescape emerges through Father Martin's observation of the details of the murder. He summons consciousness and will to itemize the scene, the skull, the eyeglasses, and the candles. This inventory places him in forensic time, in which images and events have no meaning unless linked with the crime. The moment is "just after." In the passage, the shorter phrases list elements of the crime scene. They also speed up the action. Father Martin's reference to the candlesticks at once describes and draws a conclusion about the killer's design or intent. An implicit questioning links Father Martin to events. The pace of his curiosity contributes to the scene's existence in time. The rhythm created between questions posed by Father's Martin's mind, then the answers forthcoming or not from the scene, draw in the reader to create a decided suspense and vicarious fear. This is the time of the crime.

Time, then, is integral to character, plot, and theme in a religious mystery. Breaking the religious mysteries into timescapes enables us to see the sanctified power of the narrative. Sleuths who are agents of God do not merely faint or lose consciousness. Their altered psychological states provide the force for them to value and restore life. Scholes and Kellogg discuss the significance of myths as narratives:

The images in such narratives represent types of the god-like or the demonic more powerfully than types of the actual. They are esthetic images with a minimum representational or illustrative significance. Such esthetic fiction, historically, the unrationalized plots and motifs of sacred myth, is always a fruitful source of narrative structure, even in highly rational narrative traditions. Mythic archetypes, being the products, after all, of the human imagination, appeal powerfully to even the most empirically oriented audiences through their manifestation of universal psychic patterns [137].

Mircea Eliade's studies of myths among primitive cultures explain more fully what the stories say about deep experiences. The priest or shaman plays a prominent role.

> If we pay no attention to it, time does not exist ... although [life] takes place in time, [it] does not bear the burden of time, does not record time's irreversibility. Like the mystic, like the religious man in general, the primitive lives in the continual present. And it is in this sense that the religious man may be said to be a 'primitive;' he repeats the gestures of another and through this repetition, lives always in an atemporal present [*Eternal Return* 85–86].

By embodying a culture's deepest truths, myth erases time. If the story is meaningful enough, just saying it helps to counter death. Eliade's *The Eternal Return* lists numerous examples of stories possessing this force. Primitive man achieves power over death through a recitation of traditional words. Words said among Fijians "overcome and dispel darkness." Navajo singers recite creation myths over sickbeds as a way to withstand time's inevitable changes (81–83). Merely by speaking the myths, the sayer counteracts time. "Objects or acts acquire a value, and in so doing become real, because they participate, after one fashion or another, in a reality that transcends them" (3–4).

The repetition of ritual acts and gestures performed at special times are given meaning over time. Northrop Frye emphasizes the role of the church in achieving mythic states: "Creative repetition was represented by the sacraments of the church. A great deal of the measuring of time in this period was a by-product of religion, with clocks and bells marking the hours of worship or devotion" (Frye, *Myth and Metaphor* 160). In *The Myth of Eternal Return* Eliade notes how rituals leap over time. These are a way to recharge human experience by making everything new and setting events from the beginning.

> A sacrifice, for example, not only exactly reproduces the initial sacrifice revealed by a god *ab origine*, at the beginning of time, it also takes place at that same primordial mythical moment ... through

4. Religion in Mysteries 75

such imitation, man is projected into the mythical epoch in which the archetypes were first revealed [35].

Eliade's use of the words "projected into" suggests a forward progression or a lifting out of physical experience. The gesture happens all at once, in less than a moment.

Works of art, music, literature, and dance have a sacred power in primitive societies because they are ritual enactments of these same acts by the gods. They open pathways to the divine, according to Eliade (32). Literature and the arts achieve myth's timelessness by restoring humankind to paradise. Northrop Frye notes "everything that is genuinely good for man, that is in the largest sense of the term education, tends to raise him from ordinary experience a little nearer to the unfallen level that he was originally created to live on" (MM 160).

Through mythic power, the artists become the gods. As completed rituals, art, myths, actions, and story-telling give voices to the unsayable:

> the metaphysical concepts of the archaic world were not always formulated in theoretical language; but the symbol, the myth, the rite express on different planes and through the means proper to them, a complex system of coherent affirmations about the ultimate reality of things, a system that can be regarded as constituting a metaphysics [MER 3].

Mythic time, the *illo tempore*, or "that other time," provides an abiding comforting backdrop against which the terrors of linear time progress. Myth gives the sense of being alone in the world, at one only with the gods.

Author Lee Harris creates this mythic backdrop using a series with books titled after holidays. Connecting the murder with a holiday links the years for Christine, the former nun. Her daily activities of teaching are mostly forgotten in a blur of linear time, although she often teaches poetry, which keeps her in touch with the sacred. Her memories associated with holidays are clearer. She leaps backward in time from one holiday to another. This gives her memories that mythic quality of simultaneity, as they can all exist in the present. Harris integrates the mythic timelessness of holidays directly with the case in *The Thanksgiving Day Murder.*

Chris is now married to a police detective. She and her husband Jack attend a Thanksgiving Day dinner. A fellow guest, Sandy Gordon, approaches Chris with a story about his wife. Last year at the Macy's Thanksgiving Day parade, Sandy's wife Natalie said that she wanted to buy a balloon. She turned the corner and disappeared. Sandy says, "I pushed my way through the crowd to the corner and went around Seventy-fourth Street. It was empty. There were no people, there was no balloon man, there was no Natalie. I looked around, I looked up and there was one lone balloon rising into the sky" (8). Frustrated over the fact that official routes to find his wife had failed, Sandy wants to hire Chris to look into Natalie's disappearance.

While Christine empathizes with his frustration and fear, her own memory of another Thanksgiving Day long ago brings into focus a personal trauma.

> Now, as he spoke, the strangest thing happened to me. As if from the deepest part of my memory, I saw the parade. I was with my father, and we, too, stood on the street in front of a large apartment house, surrounded by throngs, adults and children, vendors selling food and balloons. How had I forgotten? How could I have let such a wonderful memory slip away into obscurity? [8].

She had forgotten for good reason: "there was a third person in the picture, a woman, and she was not my mother" (18).

Chris follows clues left by the missing Natalie and uncovers complex identity switches and murder. Just as importantly for her, the solution to Sandy Gordon's case parallels Chris's own mission to restore her own past. Christine essentially follows two missing women and ritually mends her own past by finding her mother's place in it. She ascends to the temporal plane of myth.

> Memory, therefore, is no longer the narrative of external adventures stretching along episodic time. It is itself the spiral movement that, through anecdotes and episodes, brings us back to the almost motionless constellation of potentialities that the narrative retrieves [Ricoeur 182].

For Christine, the Thanksgiving holiday leapfrogs back in time to past ritual celebrations. Its timeless dimension allows Chris to rearrange her memories into a life she could share with her yet-to-be children. For a woman who considers that her own life began when she was fifteen, this is no small gift.

Our sense of time is "a mixture of linear and cyclical movement" (Frye, MM 158). The linear timescape sets us back into time. The character's mind moves back and forth among memories or dreams. In this time dimension, time is sped up or slowed but never stopped. Its pace depends on the character's reaction to events. His thoughts and emotions pull him into mortality.

We may perceive linear time as tedium that seems to stretch. Time is duration. Without willing ourselves out of this state, there is not much to contemplate except the seconds, minutes, and hours chipping away at mortality. To contrast with mythic time of being in the world alone, linear time expresses being in the world with others.

4. Religion in Mysteries 77

Paul Ricoeur characterizes this dimension of narrative as a series of "nows" that all the characters share. In narrative this historical time "tends toward linearity due to its datable, public, and measurable nature and as a result of its dependence on points of reference in the world" (Ricoeur 166). But to consider the metaphor of a single line is somewhat misleading, because "the humblest narrative is always more than a chronological series of events" (Ricoeur 174). Linear time is mortal, but it is also changeable, according to dreams, memories, and hopes. We may think of linear time as moving according to the hours of the psyche.

As *Murder in Ordinary Time* opens, Sister Mary Helen is trapped in linear time. She is at odds with the seasons and her age.

> Ordinary time! Ugh! That was one of the few liturgical reforms set in motion by the Second Vatican Council that she totally opposed. Ordinary Time, indeed! Some liturgist with a sense of humor, which was rare in itself, had called it a "season without a reason."
>
> Why, in the old days — good grief, she was beginning to sound like a seventy-six year old — or was it seventy-eight? [1].

This church season upsets the Sister so much that even her own birthdays fail as time markers.

Mary Helen is destined to earn parole from her prison of linear time, however. Anchorwoman Christina Kelly will interview Sister Mary Helen about past cases on the "noon news." Distinct dividing lines of time, such as midday, noon, midnight, or the stroke of midnight on New Year's Eve stand apart as regular time delineations. Their repetitions give them ritual significance to signal a shift from one temporal plane to another.

After Sister Mary Helen arrives at the studio, Christina Kelly chokes and dies. A murder plunges the good Sister into mythic time. She experiences myth's power when her mind moves from the plane of everyday action and blends with all past moments. Mary Helen tries to compose herself.

> Had this really happened or was she dreaming? How quickly everything had changed. One moment Christina Kelly was alive, smiling, asking her a question, and the next, she was gone. Crazily, a snippet of poetry caught in her mind. "For brief as water falling will be death, and brief as flower falling, or a leaf..." The rest escaped her [34].

At this moment of shock, she recites poetry. Works of human art open pathways to the divine according to Eliade (32). In a narrative, poetry or description of an artwork gives the story a different texture. Action pauses. Poetry slows the pace of the word line. The author underscores the incomprehensibility of sudden nonexistence. "The time-honored way of dealing with problems we don't understand is to project them on God, who presumably does understand them" (Frye, MM 157).

By answering the call of death, the sleuth rouses out of everyday existence. "The unique, nameless, humdrum, 'sinful' events that occur in profane time, the succession of which constitutes 'history' in the modern sense, were annually destroyed in ritual death, purification, and rebirth" (Scholes and Kellogg, 134).

The sleuthing nun spends some brief moments recovering from the mythic shock of the murder. She then tumbles back into linear time. A telephone call from Inspector Gallagher wakes her and summons her back to the studio (39). There is much fuss over time and being late. The rhythm of the day resumes. On this timescape, characters experience duration and change. Mary Helen would call it "ordinary time," with a small *o*. This is the profane time, defined by Eliade as time "without meaning." It is the "modality of man, which is coupled with death" (Eliade 35–36).

The pace changes, however. Sister Mary Helen ascends to a mythic dimension once she begins solving the crime. From an odd smell in the studio, she concludes that the victim was poisoned with cyanide. "And anyone who reads as many murder mysteries as I do knows that cyanide works fast and smells like bitter almonds. Just smell for yourself, Inspector" (31–32). By repeating a ritual absorbed from a lifetime of nights spent thumbing through detective novels, Sister Mary Helen transcends what she feels as her own tedious life.

The Inspector's assistant, Kate Murphy reinforces the ritual when she says, "The case is almost too close to an Agatha Christie mystery to be true" (43). A former graduate of Saint Francis, Kate knows Sister Mary Helen from previous cases.

Along with other nuns, Sister Mary Helen attends Christina Kelly's funeral at an ornate San Francisco cathedral. The sublime setting includes many luminous icons lining the cathedral walls. Still, the light-filled beauty cannot disperse the significance of "the casket bearing the body of a murdered woman and the dark-clad, stooped shoulders of her family members huddled together in the front pews" (80).

The gathering after the funeral affords Mary Helen a chance to view a line-up of possible suspects. It also gives her a bad case of the jitters, thus beginning a transition to another timescape — forensic time. "Yet she could not shake the uncanny feeling that finding one murderer could lead to another murder. I've been reading too many murder mysteries, she chided herself" (87). Sister Mary Helen sees her fears as a negative side effect of ritual murder solving. Yet trembling and feeling unsettled are necessary accompaniments for the ritual dispersal of death's shadows.

All detective novels pose questions, but the mystery with a religious setting probes directly into the wound of our deepest fears. It presents an arduous test of faith. What message does unexpected death send to those still proceeding in the gradual march of time?

Does Sister Mary Helen fear being murdered? It appears not. "God and she had been friends for so long that the thought of meeting him face-to-face delighted her. Besides, He owed her a number of explanations" (47). What upsets her more is the idea that she could be a murderer. "At the thought of being a suspect, Mary Helen felt her stomach give a sharp lurch" (46). As a member of a possibly culpable community, Mary Helen is eager to cleanse the specter of guilt. She plunges ahead with the querying mode that marks forensic time.

For this "time of the crime," the sleuth asks questions which may or may not have answers. The sleuth holds a stopwatch but only up to murder-related events. Time of death, rigor mortis, alibis, all provide a sense of the characters co-existing in the same time as the crime. The sleuth pieces together bits of information so to re-create events leading up to the murder. In this re-creation, time becomes even more crucial. The re-enactment may be incomplete or inaccurate until the murderer is unmasked. Even then, the full replay may not occur.

Questions and answers mark Sister Mary Helen's entrance into forensic time. The pace of these questions reflects her nervousness. What story was Christina working on now? Was that the key? Could it be someone in her own network? Who had a reason and how did they do it? She is so assertive with her curiosity that Inspector Gallagher tells her to quit it. But the good nun is not to be deterred. She is curious, asks a question, finds an answer, stops, feels uneasy, recollects something new, asks another question, finds an answer, stops, feels uneasy, and so on. This variable pace is clearly different from both the stopped quality of myth and the steady rhythm of linear time.

Set in the presence of mighty forces, the religious mystery raises the issue of how a novel, which is after all merely words on a page, frightens a reader. Does the writer add uncontrollable powers of nature, like the windstorms in *Murder in Ordinary Time*? Place the protagonist in an upsetting situation? Christine Bennett Brooks learns that her personal history has been a lie. Does a writer compile images of unnatural death? *Death in Holy Orders* has not one but four murders as well as the mother of all windstorms. Place conflicting images together? The killer stalked by Adam Dalgliesh wears a monk's cowl through the halls of Saint Anselm's.

In a study of horror and the supernatural in literature, Noel Carroll partially addresses this issue of literary suspense. He develops a theory he calls "erotetic narration":

> ...scenes, situations, and events that appear earlier in the order of exposition in a story are related to later scenes, situations, and events in the story, as questions are related to answers.... Such narration,

> which is at the core of popular narration, proceeds by generating a series of questions that the plot then goes on to answer.
>
> In a mystery story, for example, a murder early on generates a question—whodunit?—to which later scenes contribute towards answering in the form of clues and which the final or penultimate scene—the summing up by the detective—conclusively answers [130].

Carroll's theory has relevance for the religious mystery. It describes mystery structure more flexibly than other existing "grammars" of the detective story. Through the repetition concept and question/answer equation of plot, the theory incorporates the unknown. However, Carroll does not explicitly address how these narrative repetitions affect the character's perceptions of time, and how this time generates fear. For these elements we can turn to ideas from Heidegger.

Heidegger's grand phenomenology developed in *History of the Concept of Time* covers much more than we need here, but the philosopher cites questioning as an essential part of the self (147–50). Heidegger discusses the uncanny as a preliminary questioning state (283–98). In examining flight and fear, Heidegger suggests gradations of being frightened: "All fear finds its ground in dread" (284). Detriment or threat from fear comes from a sudden apprehension at the last moment.

Being frightened, then, has to do with the rhythm that springs up between questions and answers. The questioner creeps ahead then recoils through the discovery of the answer. There are degrees of being afraid, as in the uncanny, then dread, then fear, then outright terror. These gradations of fear arise from curiosity, questions unformulated, then questions raised, posed, and answered. Or questions may not be answered, at least right away. This is a situation likely to evoke terror.

As Mary Helen asks more questions, her fear level increases. She characterizes events as "uncanny," feeling a nervous shiver (87). She does not fear the Lord, but she feels dread in not knowing whom to trust (167). After she finds an important cache of clues in the dead woman's briefcase, she takes the case home. In the night, Christina's case throws shadows. It seems like a tombstone or "a small, narrow open casket" (169). When Mary Helen calls Kate to inform her about the documents, Kate detects a glimmer of fear in the Sister's tone (173).

One murderer is found, but Mary Helen is not satisfied. She cannot stop herself from trembling.

> If I were in my right mind, I would be happy this is over, Mary Helen thought. But something in her mind was not right. She had lost her way. Not her way down the straight, wide boulevard, of course, but

in her own mind. Something was amiss; something she ought to sort out [202].

A combination of Mary Helen's emotional state and unsatisfactory answers builds suspense until she arrives at her revelation.

Two literary allusions, from Keats and the Bible, lend the sister's insight the force of an epiphany: "Of course! That was it! Mary Helen was as stunned as if she, like Saint Paul, had been thrown to the ground, a great light flashing from the sky. How had she missed it?" (220). Sister Mary Helen chases down her answer into a moment of timelessness. "The kitchen was deadly quiet. Mary Helen watched, horrified. It was like a scene from a nightmare with time standing still" (228).

Mary Helen has solved the case. Her sacrifices of fear give her the power to ascend to myth and roll time back for an accurate re-enactment of the crime. As Eliade notes, the human being's ritual sacrifice of feeling life in peril equates with original divine sacrifice.

Lily Connor, the protagonist of Michelle Blake's *The Tentmaker*, has difficulty in ascending to this mythic plane, although she senses it. She has already sacrificed much, nursing her terminally ill father until his death. Lily can briefly transcend her heartache through dreams or memories. Her problem, however, is that she cannot achieve this timelessness through the rituals of the church. She is a "part-time" priest in many ways.

Like Sister Mary Helen, Lily is stuck on a linear track, but she blames her ecclesiastic life. "Lily leaned back in the old-fashioned desk chair, closed her eyes, and prayed. She prayed for compassion, she prayed for insight, and she prayed, if it was anywhere in the scope of God's will, for release from this job, which was driving her crazy" (1). With the rhythm of three items and the repetition of "prayed," author Michelle Blake drops Lily into "ordinary time" with a thud.

Living in the rectory of the recently deceased Father Barnes forces Lily into the man's rigidly ordered, pseudo-historical framework.

> After a moment, she swiveled the chair to her right, toward one of the walls of books that lined the small office — theology, philosophy, church history, all predictable and all alphabetically arranged. So far, she had not found one out of place: Abelard, Anselm, Aquinas, Barth ... many of whom Lily had read in seminary, few of whom she still read. She had formed an opinion of her predecessor, the late Reverend Mr. Barnes, as a straight backed, tight-lipped conservative — that is, as the enemy. His obsessively alphabetized library only confirmed her suspicions [3–4].

The library represents for her the rigidity of the Church. Lily cannot yet truly feel a higher power. She views a frozen pond and deserted park. "But she could not view the scene without adding an overlay — like plastic transparencies in an encyclopedia — of spring tulips and daffodils" (34). She is still in the winter of her soul. Her name gives her a goal to strive for, of rebirth and spring.

Lily Connor has dreams, but they are often of her father on his deathbed. The Bible holds little solace, because the words set up an impossible standard for her spirit. "She still believed in prayer, in the Holy Spirit's power to move and change her. But now her beliefs made no difference; they only existed in her head" (35).

Lily Connor does not connect to detective books, like Sister Mary Helen, but films or books with other-worldly themes draw her in. She finds one especially compelling, about a woman whose lover dies and returns to her as a ghost. Lily stays "lost in the world of the movie" (72). The aesthetic experiences of these films pull her attention away from linear reality and toward a spirit world that substitutes for transcendence.

Still, her emotions are filled with longing for spiritual sustenance. One memory involves Christmas shopping with her father and seeing a crèche scene. She sees a plastic baby Jesus, with his arms out "as if he were begging to be held. Looking at him, she had felt sad, so sad that she kept her sadness a secret" (130).

The alphabetized system of Father Barnes sets the stage for Lily's forensic timescape. She comes upon a note in his pocket bearing letters and numbers in a type of code (23). Eventually she deciphers these to recognize that Roy Talbot, a young boy from the parish, is in trouble. Somehow the death of Father Barnes is related to Roy's difficulties. She visits the house of Roy's parents. The mother is drunk. When Roy's father comes home, Lily senses sadness in their desperate home situation. "She felt suspended in time, or out of time, caught in an instant of distortion in which she was witnessing the most private darkness of these peoples' lives" (88). On a positive note, her mission to find out about Roy begins to lift her from her troubles.

To locate the teen, Lily must navigate a maze or labyrinth through a run-down neighborhood. The one-way streets make no sense.

> At the end of the street, in the distance, an elevated garage stood, its skeletal beams and levels silhouetted against a starless sky. The streets were deserted, the cold forcing everyone inside; it was a moonscape. Lily wanted to stop, to go home, but she had no real home, and there was no stopping now [202].

Lily is stuck in what seems to her to be a time and community with no God. She feels inadequate to the task of her role, feels the forces of evil humanity massing against her, and has little understanding of how to summon her powers as a priest. She is only human, after all. Eventually she asks the right questions and finds Roy. As an explosion in the city intensifies the narrative, Lily finds herself reaching for the power of life to stop death. She knows she can do it, realizing that "God would work through her, if only she would get out of the way" (254). Lily fails to achieve an unambiguous transcendence, but she arrives at a resting point in linear time that gives her strength to move on.

Death in Holy Orders presents complex, nuanced timescapes. The title suggests time, with "orders" meaning not only religious organizations, but connoting rows, sequences, and the line coming from one and leading to another. The novel is segmented into four "books." These are "The Killing Sand," "Death of an Archdeacon," "Voices from the Past," and "An End and a Beginning." The "book" titles trace a temporal arc suggesting how creation and destruction play out against time's larger canvas. They also in a sense re-create four "seasons," each with its discrete mood.

James uses myth's timelessness to characterize Dalgliesh's creativity enhanced through literature and art. Visions of death soar into a mythic realm of timelessness. Working on a linear timescape, James knits together the materials of history, photographs, diaries, newspapers, and documents with personal memories of Dalgliesh to capture aging and gradual changes through time. The third-person perspective presents a very full forensic timescape as perceived through the eyes of Adam and his assistant, Inspector Kate Miskin. Reading this novel is like visiting an intriguing clock shop, with clocks ticking at difference cadences.

Technically, Adam is not a cleric but a rector's son and a poet. At home in the contemplative tradition, he is that rare sleuth, a law enforcement professional and a man of sacred words. Adam's past at St. A's gives James an opportunity to portray his memories and develop past-present comparisons. The book tackles the biggest mystery of all: the passage of time.

Adam's reason for visiting St. A's is to investigate the death of Ronald Treeves, the student who supposedly committed suicide. In his only encounter with Sir Alred, Treeves's father, Adam senses evil. Sir Alred is an excessively wealthy, powerful man who can pay for everything. He asks Adam about updating the Nicene Creed: "I don't look to the fourth century when I run my company. Why look to [the year] 325 for our understanding of God?" (22). Another example of evil comes from Archdeacon Crampton. He confronts the young man who tends the pigs at St. A's and berates him for not attending church: "you shouldn't think that you have a job here for life" (82–83). He also makes it clear what he thinks of the College as an institution. "St. Anselm's will be closed. It has served the past well, no doubt, but it is irrelevant to the present" (135). Both Sir Alred and the Archdeacon are interested only in the form of the religion, not the substance of it. To them, tradition is worn out, an old shell of feeling. Their lives in linear time have dead ends.

By ignoring time, the Archdeacon makes the past his enemy. James creates an intriguing victim profile through the Archdeacon's tortured memories. Like many others at the college, the Archdeacon mourns a death, that of his wife. Whenever her image floats up in his mind, he tamps down the memory. "He had consigned his first marriage to a dark oubliette of his mind and shot the bolt" (128). Other bits and pieces of narrative suggest that the Archbishop may have murdered his wife. When memories of his culpability in her death begin to flood him, he feels "caught between a dream and a nightmare" (165). In the "dream-time," he re-enacts what happened with his wife's death (166–67), and the stage is set for his own execution. The Archdeacon is himself a murderer of time.

Adam Dalgliesh is a man of the world, yet one who cherishes meditation. Without forcing the name symbolism, we can suggest that this Adam can hear the silence of Eden. Before he even arrives at St. A's, he takes a lunch break, shutting off his cell phone: "The small, almost indistinguishable sounds of the countryside came to him on the sweet-smelling air, a distant unidentifiable birdsong, the susurration of the breeze in the tall grasses, the creaking of a branch over his head" (54). Through his poetic sensibility which is at one with nature, Adam travels *illo tempore*, to that other time. "In the background are the still slower rhythms of nature, a nature which is not itself human, and yet contains something that complements human experience, where life and death assume different patterns and suggest different proportions" (Frye, MM 163–64). Once at St. A's, Adam carries a halo of mythic time around him. Adam's past shields him from the linearity of the murder case.

His memories propel him back to earlier times at the College, when he was fourteen and in love with Sadie. Adam had written the teenaged girl a poem. Sadie was impressed more by his death-defying dive into the sea. "It felt as if he were in the grasp of some uncontrollable force, as if strong hands were seizing him by the shoulders and forcing him backwards and under" (28). Though his words have little erotic force for Sadie, the fact of his nearly drowning wins her over. They spend many happy domestic moments under the wrecked hull of a ship (29).

The timelessness of poetry becomes a way of marking stages in the poet's life. After Adam settles in at St. A's, he visits Father Martin for more information about the death of Ronald Treeves. Father Martin gives Adam a piece of paper, a poem Adam had written when he was fourteen, which he had left there so long ago.

> The sight of the handwriting, familiar and yet strange to his eyes, despite the careful calligraphy, a little tentative and unformed, jolted

him back over the years more strongly than an old photograph, because it was more personal. It was difficult to believe that the boyish hand which had moved over this quarter-sheet of paper was the same as the hand that now held it [69].

Juxtaposing an old hand with a young one, James achieves a poignancy of aging. This section would be the same as the rest of Adam's St. A's experience, familiar and yet strange, but James elaborates even more on the sheet of paper, moving from the hand that wrote it to the words themselves. Adam recalls that his inspiration for the poem had been the image of his father presiding at a child's funeral.

Later, Adam writes another poem from his position in time now. Death is again the inspiration — his own. He thinks of his "self-imposed solitude since his wife's death" (285). He composes, or rather de-composes, a poem.

> **Epitaph for a Dead Poet**
> Buried at last who was so wise,
> Six foot by three in clay he lies
> Where no hands reach, where no lips move,
> Where no voice importunes his love.
> How odd he cannot know nor see
> This last fine self-sufficiency [286].

Adam needs to replenish his creative spirit. Solving the case is a crucial way for him to restore life to his own dying soul.

The case takes Adam away from poetry, back onto linear time. This corridor is like a hall of mirrors. Many of the characters reflect Adam's unresolved grief as a son and widower. Several lay residents at Saint Anselm's are also there to recover from the death of a loved one. One woman mourns her son who survived a war and lost his life in a political battle. A police official seeks refuge after a divorce. The first murder victim, Ronald Treeves, wanted to become a priest despite his father's wishes. Adam did not go into the clerical life, despite his father's hopes that he would. Similarly, we have the reflection of Eric and Karen Surtees, half-brother and sister, and lovers. On the forensic timescape, their relationship is a red-herring. They are innocent of the crime if not a taint of incest. However, as reflections of Adam's past, the two stand for Adam's unresolved relationship with Sadie, living like brother and sister but in the shadowy underside of the ship.

Caught in linear time, Dalgliesh fails to see above the rush of events. He cannot reconstruct motives or means for the death of Ronald Treeves. Clues left in a dead woman's diary provide a starting point to the investigation, but they yield no conclusive answers. The woman died while she was knitting, and the absence of a knitting pattern is significant. Dalgliesh finds no pattern (94). Adam explains the case to the College attorney.

"I can't see how it's relevant to the death of young Treeves."
Dalgleish said, "Nor can I at present" [123].

Adam's search takes him through materials of the historian, old photographs, letters, birth records, notes, and newspaper articles. With all the police resources at his disposal, leads trickle in. Until the death of the Archdeacon, the case is at a standstill.

Through the poetry of Dalgliesh, James provides an intensified dimension to life. She also uses visual art to mythologize death.

As Adam explores a motive for murder, he considers that possession of Saint Anselm's valuable artwork could have prompted the killing of Ronald Treeves. Among St. A's treasures are two striking paintings and an archaic papyrus. One painting hangs in Father Martin's office. It shows four young women in a sentimental, pastoral setting, "a beautiful romantic dream exuding the artist's famed light which never was on land or sea" (57). The other painting casts its gloom in the Church.

> The *Doom* could be illumined by a light fixed to a nearby pillar. Father Martin lifted his arm and the tenebrous, indecipherable scene sprang into life. They were facing a vivid depiction of the Last Judgment, painted on wood.... At the head was the seated figure of Christ in glory.... To his left, the Devil, with scaly tail and grinning lascivious jaws, the personification of horror, prepared to claim his prize [63].

James graphically describes the wicked falling into the pit.

Later, the Archdeacon is murdered before the *Doom*. As Dalgleish approaches the murder scene, he sees Father Martin and Emma frozen in time, standing over the body. Adam "stood transfixed by the tableau before him.... For a moment, disorientated [*sic*] he could almost imagine that the black devils had sprung from the *Doom* and were dancing round her head" (178–79). Dalgleish thinks the *Doom* painting has leaped to life. In a way, it has.

The paintings create opposing configurations. The first vision of the four girls depicts celestial, endless time, and the other splays out a demonic vision, the chaotic end of time. Because the *Doom* presides over the Archdeacon's death, it appears as if that painting holds the dominating power over the novel. However, another valuable in Saint Anselm's treasure trove is the famed papyrus.

Theoretically dating from the time of Pilate, the papyrus is "an order for the removal of the crucified body of a political troublemaker" (259). Father Martin considers that the papyrus is probably fraudulent, but the College hears requests to test its authenticity. James uses artwork to set up a celestial/demonic dichotomy to human nature. The author comes close to using the papyrus to reconcile these two visions. However, in the novel's closing pages, the artwork remains the ultimate "mystery." Father Martin removes the papyrus from scrutiny for good (414).

Forensic time proceeds like a fast forward or a rewind of a videotape. There is only before the murder and after. As "after" lengthens, the risk increases that the murder will be unsolved. Investigators will not be able to rewind the tape to re-enact the time before the murder, so the ritual to restore life will never be complete.

After the Archdeacon's death, the sped-up pace of forensic time infuses the narrative. The pathologist breezes in on a motorcycle (204). The speed contrasts with the abrupt ending of life. Dalgliesh's assistant Inspector Kate Miskin feels and nearly enjoys "this surge of adrenaline at the beginning of a murder inquiry" (211). A possible clue is secularized, as one member of the crime team holds the opinion of "It's only a palm print, it's not the Holy Grail" (225). The tape around the crime scene de-sanctifies the area by the altar. The priests hold a Roman rite to re-purify the sanctuary (242–43).

Nearly all the clues gathered by Adam's investigative team involve pinpointing time. Dalgliesh discovers disturbed dust in a pew. The time of a phone call to the Archdeacon, 9:28, is crucial. As clues pile up, the police investigators name their unknown murderer Cain (219–20). They use time to piece the murder together, and their re-enactment ritually follows the first murder under the watchful eye of Adam.

Alignment of alibis poses an intriguing challenge for the team. On the night of the murder, nearly all the suspects had attended the Compline prayer service. Initially, the investigators rejoice. This is an absolute time against which all the suspects' alibis are measured. Then the progression of rigor mortis supplants Compline as a natural clock. The time of death changes, shattering obvious alibis. No one can agree where they were at the crucial time. Dalgliesh himself had been between waking and sleeping on that unholy, stormy night. One young man wonders if he could have killed the Archdeacon and not known it. Watch out for false alibis, the investigators warn each other. "If Arbuthnot planned the murder for midnight, for example, he could easily murmur to Burkhurst when they settled down to sleep that it was after twelve o'clock" (250).

More questions give way to more time-keyed evidence. What time was a monk's cowl hung on a peg? Who started the laundry cycle of a clothes washer? What time was the cycle interrupted?

Through interviews with the murderer, evil expresses itself as a satisfaction with linear time. We see the killer as a person who cannot transcend, who has no awareness of mythic time. The killer remarks on two horrors of human life, "boredom and the knowledge that we die" (272). Frye associates this state of mind with demonic time: "The same things keep turning up, the same cycles of nature go round and round, life is involuntary and death invariable ..." (Frye 166). With this view, the killer is inches away from justifying murder. The murder happened only because all the events came together in linear time. All the characters' timelines synchronized, and the murderer took the opportunity to act. Life's end didn't matter to the victims, but it mattered to the killer. The killer displays the ultimate arrogance in taking control over someone else's time (407).

Over the course of the frantic investigation, Emma Lavenham drifts in and out of Adam's thoughts. Her beauty and presence of mind draw him to her. He realizes the impossibility of beginning a relationship with her, but as he says goodbye to his "self-imposed solitude," he is beginning to yield.

The concluding pages of all these religious mysteries form a core sample of the power of myth's renewal.

Christine Bennett Brooks goes with her husband to yet another Thanksgiving Day parade. She delights in the floats, buys a balloon, laughs, and cries. She says, "I will take my children someday and we will stand on that corner, and while they enjoy the moment, I will remember a time long ago, the happiness of being with my father, and a woman who wanted to make her peace" (Harris 245). Sister Mary Helen discovers that by asking the right question, she can perceive a motive that lies in "the incomprehensible bond of love between a mother and her child" (O'Marie 230).

When Lily Connor's adventure ends, she is still unable to lift herself into the power of myth. However, she is on the verge. She thinks about the ocean and how we cannot comprehend it all in one time, just as we cannot comprehend God. She remembers a line from William Blake: *To see Heaven in a grain of sand*. And eternity in an hour.

> We had to stand back to encompass the sense of vastness. To take it all in — We had to stand very far away, farther and farther up, on the tallest lighthouse of the world, and farther still, where the parallel lines of two truths, of the world and the spirit, of the church as it was and the church as it should have been ... these lines began to curve, to meet [Blake 265–76].

While she can explain the experience, she does not yet feel it.

The moment of confrontation when Adam grapples with the murderer on the edge of the cliff is interminable for Kate Miskin. "She had stood immobile, as if every muscle were locked, her eyes fixed on the two motionless figures" (398). James paints the scene as a timeless gesture of Adam against Cain. When Adam loses consciousness, he captures the life-filled moments with Sadie, renewing time through the promise of love with Emma. "The poetic or creative pulls in the opposite direction: its vision is always a renewal of the freshness and energy of man's view of nature. The next step is to realize that there are two powers in the consciousness, one analytic and the other synthetic, and that the latter is the poetic faculty, properly speaking" (Frye, MM 166). Through these closing scenes, James emphasizes the redemptive power of art. Adam finds an answer to life by ending his time of grief over his wife, and starting a new relationship with Emma. "For the poets Eros was another force that could raise man to a higher awareness of time" (Frye 161).

The three timescapes present the religious mystery as a series of time-linked rituals designed to counter death. In the narrative, these re-create the character's sensation of time transcended, historical time ended, and a community's time line restored. This focus on time also suggests a mechanism for assessing fear in a narrative by the degree of a character's emotion, rather than by events.

What is the connection between mythic and linear time? Ultimately, that is probably an unanswerable question. However, it is intriguing to think that the unsolved death in the middle of a narrative represents a nexus, a meeting point for myth's timelessness and history's limited vantage point.

"The art of storytelling is not so much a way of reflecting on time as a way of taking it for granted" (Ricoeur 171). A religious mystery never takes time for granted. On many levels, mystery novels are escapist fare, but religious mysteries bring the reader face to face with the meaning of murder. With death at the center, the novel becomes a temple of contemplation with death at the center, a body laid over the altar with all looking on. Religious mysteries make it obvious that the sleuth, whatever her occupation, carries out sacred rituals to repair disrupted time. By emerging ourselves in this action, we as readers can feel a similar experience of creative renewal.

CHAPTER 5

BLOOD DUES: RITES OF INITIATION IN CAREER THRILLERS

The 1990s gave us television's gavel-to-gavel coverage of high-profile trials. This comprehensive media treatment whipped up audience eagerness to view every shadowy courthouse corridor. The phenomenon netted even higher book sales for novelists like John Grisham, Scott Turow, and Steve Martini. If the story included a legal proceeding, it warranted the label of "legal thriller." Works highlighting lawyer protagonists and dramatizing issues of justice still mean very big business for the publishing world.

Many more women are trying the case in this subgenre of detective fiction. Instead of limiting proceedings to the courtroom, women writers show us sleuths testing the edge of justice in classroom and newsroom settings. In many ways, academics and journalists belong to the same category as lawyers. Mysteries featuring these protagonists follow a similar narrative pattern. As one strand of the narrative, the sleuth, who could be an academic or journalist as well as a lawyer, nails the wrong-doer/killer. As another accompanying story strand, this very smart, well-educated main character must go back to school. As she moves from not knowing to knowing about the killer's identity, she also understands more about herself.

To accommodate the various occupations of protagonists, the label "legal thriller" could be changed to "career thriller." The object of the quest is somewhat different depending on the sleuth's job, but the narrative structure for all is the same. The plots of these thrillers rest on rites of initiation. To be allowed entry into these select secrets, the sleuth pays a very high dues—heartache, loss of a loved one, professional failure, or sometimes even a literal wound resulting in spilled blood.

The searcher is a professional in a high-pressure career. In addition to solving the murder or crime, she seeks a Grail of idealistic perfection through her profession. The ritual action of passing tests and finding herself worthy plays out repeatedly over the narrative. This protagonist, already a well-educated practitioner in a highly specialized occupation, must re-learn her profession from the inside.

To complete a successful run of the initiation gauntlet, the main character confronts a series of difficult, even painful challenges. The professor becomes a student. The journalist writes her own story. The lawyer experiences guilt. To move from innocence to experience, the questing professional measures the distance between the world perceived as ideal and the world as it is.

Career thrillers provide a high degree of realistic backdrop for the crime. Most of the authors have extensive resumes in the same occupation as the sleuth. Carolyn Heilbrun has for many years been a professor at Columbia University. Edna Buchanan and Elaine Viets are professional journalists. Lisa Scottoline held clerkships at state and federal levels and worked as a trial lawyer. Barbara Parker began her professional life as a prosecutor with the state attorney's office in Miami-Dade County, Florida.

The world of the professional mystery is representational, but it is also metaphysical. The quest for transcendence takes the searcher through a tense struggle between and through opposites. Joseph Campbell amplifies the Grail search in *Transformations of Myth Through Time*.

To illustrate this concept of "going beyond," Campbell calls upon medieval Grail legend tradition and Percival or Parzival, one of the Knights of the Round Table. The name "Parzival" is emblematic of the direction that the search for the Ideal takes. Campbell notes that the name is related to the French, "*perce a val*, the one piercing through the middle of the valley, going between the pair of opposites" (TMOT 247). Despite the searcher's capability and professional expertise, she approaches this configured mystery as a neophyte.

Ritual initiation gives proof to the human experience that education of the spirit continues throughout life. The purpose of painful suffering is that suffering and falling short reveals secrets. It gives the protagonists "the courage to be at one in their wanting and their doing, their knowing and their telling" (Campbell, *Creative Mythology*, 85).

As professionals, these candidates sleuthing toward initiation already belong to an exclusive club. The ones who do not pass have already been burned away. The searcher must survive tests toward wisdom, truth, and justice. "Heroes emerge from their Ordeals to be recognized as special and different, part of a select few who have outwitted death" (Vogler 186). Through the typically reversed logic of myth, the expert becomes a learner.

"Initiation" usually refers to an individual's change from childhood to adulthood. Some psychologists have used the concept to explain physical and psychological development well into adulthood, as in Gail Sheehy's *Passages* (1976) and the more recent *New Passages: Mapping Your Life Across Time* (with Joelle Delbourgo, 1996). In fact, organized initiation appears in numerous facets of American public life. In the political realm, voter primaries serve as concentric rings of initiation, with the Presidency as the highly coveted prize at the center. The currently popular television show *Survivor* illustrates the same process in action. Thousands of potential contestants submit applications for the show. These applicants are winnowed down to people who actually appear on the episodes. Then the show presents viewers with an intensified view of the final tests.

Inevitably, the contestants endure failures. Again, through the reverse logic of myth, one achieves success only through failure and facing limits. The structure of overcoming obstacles and moving ever closer to a prized goal is deeply etched in our collective experience.

As she passes each test, the searcher is incrementally rewarded. New perceptions, the ability to pierce the veil of deception, and clairvoyance comprise this reward package (Vogler 187). The searcher finds clues, locates missing witnesses, or breaks free from being captured. Through this process, the searcher finds the murderer, but she also finds an inside truth. With this realization, the searcher becomes worthy of proceeding in her profession.

What makes professional life so amenable to a mystery novel plot? Every person's life is a journey in its own way. Bureaucracies on the job make modern employment more complex. Campbell mentions that in the past the purpose of mythology was to stamp the individual with the values of the group. Now professional organizations have evolved into "an increasingly officious array of ostensibly permissive, but actually coercive, demythologized secular institutions" (CM 86). Educational preparation for these professions encourages individuality but may fail to alert students to more restrictive conditions on the job.

Fiction about unsolved death fits these professions in particular for several reasons. Academe, journalism, and law sit atop a solid tradition of possibly ambiguous linguistic constructions. They are also professions in flux. Academe is changing in terms of more claims on the time of students, concepts of students as education consumers, and online delivery systems. Today's newsrooms deal with high production costs, changes in readership, internet competition of news coverage, and publishing monopolies. The law likewise is changing in terms of publicity and an ever-shifting balance of power between defender and defended.

Start with an intractable tradition, add the impulse toward sweeping change, mix with a dose of interpretation, and stand back. The outcome is bound to be an uncontrollable situation for which mystery fiction poses an appealing forum for resolution.

Through a series of harrowing tests the protagonist relearns the profession. The process, ultimately, is what is important. The detective sleuth stretches the bounds of experience by rediscovering what caused her to become a professor, journalist, or lawyer in the first place. The experience leads the sleuth to recommit to the profession and reaffirm ideals.

Dorothy Sayers's *Gaudy Night* (1935), in which Harriet Vane uncovers skullduggery at Oxford, is among the earliest novels in this genre. Since then, there has been open admission on academic mysteries. Even a partial list of authors with academics or retired academics as sleuths forms a lengthy roster.

The academic world is a prime setting for crime. College life proceeds in a closed, regulated community, but conflicts and human frailties abound. The professor, teacher, or student sleuth possesses the highly refined skills of observation and cognition to draw conclusions others miss.

Our highly alert sleuth looks for the murderer in residence halls, classroom buildings, graduate seminars, and along campus walkways. In some ways, academe is on a different calendar from the rest of the world. The entire university community subscribes to the same schedule. Professors have office hours and regular class times. Students live mostly in a communal setting, with set schedules. The clock on the ivy-covered hall helps investigators keeps close tabs on alibis.

A university sets an environment ripe for murder. By definition, it is a place where people from different social and educational levels clash. Academics often have meetings with students or peers in high-pressure situations. These meetings provide an opportunity for embarrassment, humiliation, and worse. Frequently, the person killed is a horrible professor, student, or administrator exerting power inappropriately. We don't shed tears for the victim and may even sympathize with the murderer. With tenure and fatly endowed research positions in short supply, academe is a hotbed of greed, politics, and ambition. Where ambition builds, motives for murder soon follow. Despite the passion of the crime, the murder often occurs in a context of the system ridding itself of evil.

A university can perpetuate the disparity between a searcher's outer world and inner reality. Campbell pinpoints a few reasons for the toppling of the ivory tower.

> There is no time, no place, no permission — let alone encouragement — for experience. And to make things even worse, along now come

> those possessed socio-political maniacs with their campus rallies, picket-line slogans, journalistic ballyhoo, and summonses to action in the name of causes of which their callow flocks had scarcely heard six months before — and even those marginal hours that might have been left from study for inward growth are invaded, wrecked, and strewn with daily rubbish [CM 374].

A university must blend polarized goals. It has traditions to uphold while at the same time fostering independent inquiry. The result can be a split between experience and inner truth.

Academic mysteries highlight the sleuth's method of investigation. Critics have drawn lengthy comparisons between the research skills of an academic and the skills of the murder investigator. "Research skills make good sleuths" (Leonardi 113). The process of locating and combining evidence to formulate theories parallels more general paths toward knowledge. Israeli author Batya Gur teaches literature in Jerusalem. The homicide investigator for most of her mysteries is Michael Ohayon. Ohayon has an historian's background.

In Gur's *Saturday Morning Murder* (1988), Dr. Eva Neidorf, renowned psychologist, professor, and lecturer has been found shot in the head at an office in Jerusalem's Psychoanalytic Institute. Ohayon lays out his method for interviewing a witness. He needs to "get onto the wavelength of the person sitting opposite him and pick up on those ostensibly trivial things, the things people said between the lines and sometimes never said at all, that in the last analysis provided the master key to solving the mystery" (Gur 51). Ohayon gains his best clues from silences in between words.

Ohayon also uses his keen interest in history to re-construct the crime and determine motive.

> And there was also what he privately referred to as "my historical need." In other words, the historian's need to obtain a full picture, to see everything concerning human beings as part of an overall process, like a historical process processing laws of its own, which — he never tired of explaining — if only we are able to grasp their meaning, provide us with the tools for going right to the heart of the problem [Gur 51].

Here Gur presents the mystery as a larger objective reality that lies ahead of Ohayon. Being an astute detective and researcher, he digs out the information necessary to reach the correct conclusion. The words themselves are only tools, signs pointing beyond themselves to a meaning out there.

Like Gur, author Carolyn Heilbrun (*aka* Amanda Cross) is herself an academic. Cross's sleuth is literature professor Kate Fansler. Kate is a crusader, but

5. Blood Dues

inevitably, Cross arranges the quest so that the development of Kate's personal life parallels the mystery's solution. Because Cross so often places the reader in Kate's head, the most deeply scored line of the narrative involves Professor Fansler's own education.

For *Death in a Tenured Position* (1982), Cross structures the narrative so Kate's investigation into her colleague's suicide mirrors the sleuth's own indecision over whether she should become more involved with Reed. To marry would give away her ideals. For her, the marriage could be her own death in a "tenured position." The permanence of tenure is similar to being a wife. She runs the risk of losing herself. Why should she marry Reed? She is already married to Reading.

In *The Puzzled Heart* (1998), Cross sets up a similar "dual track" narrative. The case challenges Kate on a personal level. Reed is now Kate's husband, and he has been kidnapped. Kate receives an unusual ransom note. The note asks for no money, but it is blackmail, nonetheless. To obey it, Kate must undergo a drastic personality change: "publicly recant your insane feminist position" (12). This request upsets Kate almost as much as if Reed were threatened with bodily harm. As she sees it, the worst that could happen to Reed is that the kidnappers will "try to brainwash him and make him see the point of view of his captors" (26). This is basically the same threat the kidnappers hold against Kate. What she fears most for herself is that she could be forced to consider another point of view as valid. This order tests Kate's principles as an educator, her strength of mind, concepts of learning and being fair, and achieving Wisdom.

The first note about Reed's kidnapping knocks Kate sideways, and she needs strong tea to bring her out of the shock. She takes the second note more in stride. The note reads, "Neither the police nor any government agency must be contacted" (14). Here she remembers who she is and summons her superior knowledge of language to counter the unseen villains. "'I hate people who use *contact* as a verb,' Kate said" (15).

Despite her considerable sleuthing experience, Kate is too emotionally involved with this case to work it by herself. To pass the first hurdle, she calls in professional help, her friend and retired law professor Harriet.

The professional quester is essentially alone in undergoing rites of initiation. Still, kind souls along the way serve as guides. In *The Hero with a Thousand Faces*, Campbell describes the "wise guide," a mentor "whose words assist the hero through the trials and terrors to the weird adventure. He is the one who appears and points to the magic shining sword that will kill the dragon-terror" (8–9).

Although still new at this detective biz, Harriet is Kate's wise guide. Her age is a plus in the detective agency, because she is so unlikely a P. I. Like the wise old man, Harriet is enlisted to "conduct people across those difficult thresholds of transformation that demand a change in the patterns not only of conscious but also of unconscious life" (HTF 9). She attempts to ease Kate's mind by telling a humorous anecdote about the first time she used a gun.

Kate's next obstacle is meeting with Harriet's partner at the detective agency to formulate a plan. This encounter lends Kate's interaction with the agency a more official status. Thanks to Harriet, Kate's meeting with Toni happens in a setting completely familiar to Kate, her office. Toni comes in undercover as one of the students. Having student conferences is a usual part of Kate's job. Only this time, the student conference ritual is turned on its head, because a student educates Kate, not the other way around.

Kate is more used to giving tests than taking them, but she has more to pass. Her third test involves the dog that Harriet and Toni have arranged to give Kate a cover story for contacting a suspect, owner of a kennel. The idea throws her for a loop. "She realized that for the first time she felt her life to be completely out of her control. That she might have a dog foisted on her seemed as likely as anything else that had been happening" (32–33).

The dog is a Saint Bernard puppy, well suited to her role as a rescuer. The dog is named "Banny," after Anne Bancroft. The sudden changes in Kate's life render her nearly speechless. Named after an Award-winning actress, the puppy exudes more articulate expression than Kate.

The professor is so tied to her schedule, she cannot imagine getting out to interview people outside the university. Banny's rescue of Kate comes just in time. The dog uses Kate's hall as a bathroom and refuses to stay in the car's backseat. Banny represents the uncontrolled, natural world, a world not defined by books or reading.

Kate is amazed by the next move Harriet and Tony suggest. To move closer to the suspect, Kate has to enroll in a dog training class. She is aghast by the way the desks are turned. Not only does the class expose the professor's ignorance, but Dorothy the kennel owner finds Kate's academic curiosity wanting. Dorothy says, "'You have not asked a single question, intelligent or not.' 'I'm an observer,' Kate said, rather defensively" (42).

Dorothy, the key to Reed's kidnappers, sees through Kate right away. Placed in this role as a student, Kate questions her own skills as a researcher and amateur detective. Her very identity as an assertive professional is at stake. "She had never felt so powerless and devoid of personality in her life" (44). However, little by little, she is drawn by the woman's knowledge and becomes capable of new insights. "I am certainly learning something about the dog world I wouldn't have dreamed of knowing a few days ago, Kate thought" (47). She even comes to admire Dorothy. If she were paying attention to her detective's instincts, she would certainly know better. However, a reverence for knowledge wins out. "Kate thought how nice it must be to know absolutely everything there was to know about one subject, even dogs" (48).

5. Blood Dues

This segment in the dog training class tests Kate's willingness to be a student and revives her spirit of theorizing. She wakes up about her own passivity as she's waiting in line to pay the toll to cross the Henry Hudson Bridge (53).

> "I know you said not to call," Kate explained to an outraged Harriet, "but that is an order I've decided not to obey. You are working for me, you and Toni, and I want to see you tonight. Here. I don't care if someone is watching me, or if they see you visiting, or if they wonder whether you're visiting as friends or detectives. We've got to talk" [54–55].

Thus, she lays out her theory of who could have kidnapped Reed and why.

Before long, Kate and Banny rescue Reed, and he walks away from his kidnappers suffering few ill effects. His first words upon seeing Banny are "And where's the brandy?" (71). But Kate has yet to identify the reason for the kidnapping.

Who could have the most vengeful feelings for her? She finds the answer in her family's past and in her professional life. Kate's efforts to forestall yet another marriage ceremony turns out to be the motive of hatred against her. Kate arrives at a conclusion about herself.

> Her life had held, it seemed to her, fewer turmoils than most. What had threatened her, if indeed she had ever felt truly threatened, had been not violent emotions, but from time to time a sense of the purposelessness of existence, of the lack of reason for much that occurred. It was a sin of the spirit, she knew: a failure of faith in the rightness of the universe — of God, in short [175].

Another failed exam involves a "student" who turns on Kate. "They lie in wait sometimes..." (204). The student figure emerges first as a savior, then as a double agent. It is the worst humiliation for Kate as an educator. She cannot see the student's attempts for what they were, manipulation and a false education. Kate takes her failing grade to heart, imagining all kinds of hellish punishments.

> "I am simply going to die or to become a fugitive like Lord Jim, lurking about in hot climates. I hate hot climates. Oh, God!" It was a cry worthy of someone without faith actually calling upon an exalted deity [251].

The phrase "Puzzled Heart" comes from a poem by Emily Dickinson, which Cross uses as an opening epigram for the book: "to contemplate the journey with an unpuzzled heart." By the novel's end, Kate has clearly fallen short of this view of the journey. Her heart remains frustrated and troubled by life. But it appears that Cross looks askance at the unpuzzled heart. The most evil woman at the center of this mystery proceeds without puzzlement or question. This figure of evil has the certainty of a zealot, living in an ambiguous world with an unambiguous agenda. Cross gives Harriet the last word about what the puzzled hearts of the world can do in the face of such certainty: "We mustn't give up" (257).

Like the academic, the journalist detective absorbs clues and attempts to forge new meaning. Instead of reaching the Holy Grail of Wisdom, the journalist wields the Word. The journalist dwells in a landscape where words and meanings are separated. People are the story. Through an accurate re-creation of these stories, the journalist enacts change for good and unifies inner and outer worlds. She has spoken the Word Beyond Words.

"Word" as a word carries several potent meanings. The original Old English "wyrd" is connected to fate, which is Shakespeare's meaning for the "three weird sisters" in *Macbeth*. It also is a form of the verb "to be," and related to "worth," as in the Old English "weorth" (Moore and Knott). Speaking the Word Beyond Words is a very powerful secret, connected with destiny and worthiness. It has value beyond measure.

> And so, proceeding, we come to the problem of communication: the opening, that is to say, of one's own truth and depth to the depth and truth of another in such as way as to establish an authentic community of existence [Campbell, CM 84].

Edna Buchanan's journalist sleuth Britt Montero learns the worth of this elusive word. As police reporter for the *Miami Times*, Britt walks the sun-steamed sidewalks of Miami. She has many opportunities for reporting that makes a difference. In *Contents Under Pressure* (1992), Britt has an in-box crammed with stories: a hostage crisis defused outside an elementary school and a former pro football player dead of a car accident due to a police chase. After Miami boils over from simmering tensions, Britt has the chance to write the story of her career, but she learns a more valuable lesson.

The elementary school story ends happily. Britt sounds more than a bit cynical as she writes it up: "A hero, a satisfying ending, readers happy at getting their money's worth from a dedicated public servant, cops happy at getting good press.... What more could a reporter ask for?" (10).

In the past, Britt has expected more from herself as a professional. A luncheon with her mother brings out the old idealism. Fed up with her mother's constant carping, Britt re-articulates what drives her as a journalist. "'Mom, you know how I feel about my job.' My stomach was beginning to churn.

'The world is full of poverty, ignorance, crime, and corruption. I do what I do because I think I can help change things'" (49).

The usual stories that run across the police blotter will not help change things, but Britt re-traces the cop chase of the pro football player. She uncovers a story of double-dealing and abuse of power. This story could indeed make a difference. Britt passes the first series of tests. She is willing to risk everything to write these words. She is threatened, stalked, and wounded, but she refuses to back down. She watches a good friend die in her arms. When tropical paradise explodes into a confusing nightmare, Britt nearly loses her own life. Still she navigates through broken glass and Molotov cocktails to live the complete story. She is not the only one proud of the effort.

> As we pieced together the stories of destruction, terror, and confusion, the managing editor emerged from his carpeted office in shirt-sleeves, smiled at me, nodded and said, "Good work, Britt."
> I sat there numb as he walked away but his words stayed with me. Exhaustion, deadlines, and breaking stories suppressed my conflicting emotions and guilt for a time [282].

Unfortunately, these words from her editor are the only reward she has. Due to the editors' decision to spare the city more violence, the story Britt writes about evil in the top ranks of the police department fails to make it into print.

> As soon as the riot coverage ended and the city was under control, I began putting together my story about the truth, what really happened. I worked hard on it, for two days. It explained everything. It was never published [284].

Britt knows that her story can never exist on its own. It has to fit into the context of everything else that happened in the city. "The best things cannot be told" (Campbell, CM 84). The most Britt can achieve is to understand the secret about truth — that she can never tell it. She has reached the Word Beyond Words.

Elaine Viets's mystery series headlines journalist Francesca Vierling. Set in St. Louis, the series features Francesca's story-writing as an instrument of social justice and her wise-cracking wit as editorial cartoons that keep the creeps at bay. Francesca's rites of initiation also end with her entrance to an important secret territory. She comprehends the limits of the word in reporting the depths of human experience.

In *Doc in the Box* (2000), Francesca has to pass many tests. She is without love, having broken up with her long-term squeeze Lyle. She learns that her dear friend and professional mentor Georgia has breast cancer. These two trials end in the worst conviction of all for a reporter. She is having a hard time writing.

Francesca can handle her balding managing editor, Charlie of the bad comb-over and petty power plays. He assigns her to write a human interest story about a stripper's life. Francesca opts for a male stripper, Leo D. Nardo, a major drawstring at the Heart's Desire club.

Not so easy is knowing her own heart's desire. Deep down, Francesca suffers without Lyle. Even Leo D. Nardo's well-oiled, sculpted body pales by comparison. "The only book Leo had opened since he flunked out of school was the Yellow Pages. I liked my men smart. Like Lyle" (9).

Both love and writing leave Francesca's world. Her descent into the realm of male strippers essentially strips her. The next day at the newsroom brings a crisis of self-confidence:

> Something was wrong with my column, the one in today's paper. I knew it. I just didn't know what it was. Had I misspelled a name? Misquoted someone? Gotten some obvious fact wrong? Did someone call the paper and complain? [17].

Something is indeed wrong with her column. Charlie has replaced it.

Francesca has difficulty recapturing her usual breeziness. Her promise to be a "model columnist" doesn't last long. When she sits down to pound out the article on Leo, she realizes that she forgot to ask him two key questions (32). There among the hard bodies, her interview skills dissolved. She cannot finish the story, because Leo, like her column, has also vanished.

At this point, Francesca can barely manage the rough draft of a recipe. Charlie presses her to contribute to a St. Louis recipe collection. The non-cooking journalist contemplates giving him "Francesca's Top Five Food Delivery Numbers" (43).

Francesca passes a crucial test, however, when she makes a correct choice. She knows that her loss of writing ability takes a back seat to serious illness. Francesca helps transport Georgia to the hospital for treatment. Cancer and chemo are bad enough. Slick hospital floors and greasy cafeteria food add insult to injury. First Francesca summons all her word power to buoy up Georgia. She jokes that God is God "because he couldn't get into medical school" (29). Then she stops a huffy receptionist with her own patented South Side glare. Francesca chants, "I am a witch, and I curse you and your curse is that you will be treated the same way you treat these cancer patients" (31).

While the two wait in Radiation Oncology, an intruder shoots a receptionist and a doctor in an adjacent office. It's as if Francesca's word power has summoned strength and taken action of its own accord. Then the journalist learns that Doc in the Box, an office building crammed with physicians, is also on the killer's list. More doctors die. One kindly doctor victim is Dr. Jolley. The murdered doctors represent revenge for all the patients they rob of love, joy, and humor. The murders, then, are not random aberrations, but logical necessities. The narrative follows the reverse logic of rites of passage. The doctors, ordinarily healers and life-givers, must die to bring the dead to life.

The pressure is on Francesca to prevent more murders, but is she really trying? Given the pain Georgia has endured at the hands of the medical community, Francesca takes more than a little perverse satisfaction in the killing spree. She shocks her fellow journalist Tina by admitting aloud that "I've always wanted to give the killer a list of people who should be shot" (113). The murderer is only doing a public service, which is a refracted image of the journalist. Francesca's friend Valerie the chemo nurse has a theory reinforcing this tie. She tells Francesca, "For all I know, you're doing it. You could be using Georgia as a cover to get in these doctors' offices" (120). Could it be?

Like the murderer, Francesca seeks revenge as a way to regain love and creativity. She still whips out her trademark snappy comebacks. She deflects one slimy creep with "If I spent six months in a lighthouse, I wouldn't call you" (86). She admires the widow of one murdered doctor: "She was as tough as a two-dollar sirloin" (106). But part of the difficulty of initiation is following its reverse logic. Francesca thinks that by writing an award-winning story, she can regain her stride. "I wanted that prize. I wanted it like a lover. In place of the lover I'd lost" (114). She does not yet fathom the secret that only failure is winning.

Francesca can still speak truth, but she can't write it. Searching through words should be a journalist's forte. In hunting the doctor killer, Francesca must pore over medical files. In better days, she could have invented some way to track these clues herself. We understand the depth of Francesca's impotence when her friend, pathologist "Cut up Katie," becomes a surrogate search engine (154).

Francesca's personal and professional sorrows continue to mute her responses to the world. She has no personal life (139). She senses her distance from the world of light and love (140). She has a hard time writing even the simplest 50th wedding anniversary story.

The couple had courted, half-a century ago, at a famous St. Louis landmark, the Whispering Arch. The semicircle holds the secret that whatever is whispered at one end can be heard very far away at the other. With Francesca looking on, the couple exchanges loving words through the Arch.

When Francesca interviews the "bride," she admires the woman's courage and finds herself lacking. "'If you don't take chances, you don't live,' she said. Her words were like an ice pick in my heart" (149). Francesca goes through the same ritual of listening at the Whispering Arch. Instead of words of love, she hears something else. "Die, bitch, die!" (150).

By the reverse logic of initiation rites, Francesca will find life only by searching the land of the dead. Down is up, and vice versa. In a final test, Francesca chases the murderer up the Down ramp of a parking garage.

> Our pursuit took on a dreamlike quality, one of those dreams where you run and run and nothing happens. I saw a constantly shifting collage of car fenders and hoods and brake lights, heard my own hard breathing and the drivers' furious honking. Then suddenly, we were in blinding sunlight on the open upper deck [220].

Only by falling through the looking glass can Francesca land before the door to the Word Beyond Words. She hears the killer's story "in the long silence" (237) that she can never completely write. Only after suffering comes the promise of love and life. The Heart's Desire club, Leo's employer, sits at the end of a road to a St. Louis chemical plant. She wades through the toxic puddles to reach it.

Both Britt and Francesca complete their initiation rites toward the Word Beyond Words. Telling the story the best way, interviewing the witness closest to the scene are techniques each reporter hopes will have an impact on the world. But each journalist must earn her stripes by discovering the Holy Grail in a truth that can't be written.

To say and understand The Word Beyond Words is to discern the difference between life and death. As Joseph Campbell points out, the concept as articulated by religions and mythologies around the world and through the ages is contained in the syllable *AUM*. This utterance is sometimes written as the *Om* of chanting rituals or the *Amen* of prayers and hymns. *AUM* has been called the quintessential sacred word, because it contains the building blocks of all words. To say it is to vocalize all sounds, from the open sound in the back of the throat to the *mmm* sound ending with the lips coming together. All vowels are contained in *AUM* (Campbell *Power of Myth* 230–31).

In addition, *AUM* stands for one other concept. Campbell says, "*AUM* is called the 'four-element syllable.' *A-U-M*— and what is the fourth element? The silence out of which *AUM* arises, and back into which it goes, and which underlies it" (PM 231). All the words a person says over a lifetime can be summed up in AUM, but its silence represents the eternal. So *AUM* combines the mortal, all sounds, with the immortal, silence. Being able to understand this Word Beyond Words is to distinguish between the "mortal aspect and the immortal aspect of one's own existence" (PM 231).

How does *AUM* fit into the sleuthing professional's quest for the Ideal? The sleuth sees, feels, and is shaken by the recognition of what lasts and what doesn't, what is mortal and what is immortal. Britt Montero comes to find value in the story that is not written. Francesca listens to the silence of her love for Lyle.

> It's been said that poetry consists of letting the word be heard beyond words.... But when you really realize the sound, "AUM" the sound of the mystery of the word everywhere, then you don't have to go out and die for anything because it's right there all around [Campbell, PM 230].

The final sentence of *Doc in the Box* shows that Francesca understands *AUM*. She declares her love for Lyle. "The words that had been so hard to say slipped out so easily now." Then she, the perpetual word-generating machine, is finally silent. "For once, I listened to my editor" (Viets 243).

Law is another intense profession that lends itself to mystery. Legal thrillers generally feature a trial. A classic work such as *To Kill a Mockingbird* sets the premise. Atticus Finch is a moral wise attorney. He fights for forces of good, defending the underdog and attempting to bring justice to a corrupt land. As we know, the efforts of Atticus are less than successful. "But the fact that Atticus cannot single-handedly defeat racism in no way detracts from his hero status" (Denvir 150). Atticus is Good, through and through.

Today's legal thriller has evolved into a new phase. The lawyer sleuth also seeks to close the gap between what may be legal and what is right. Unlike Atticus Finch, the protagonist may be forced to stand outside the "prosecution versus defense" structure of the courtroom drama to question the very premises that make that structure possible. At the same time, the sleuth questions himself and his ideals. This model adds the very human need for retribution and revenge onto the scales of Lady Justice. From this perspective, the world is a complicated place. It poses a series of tests to shape the character's belief in Ethos, a fairness and morality beyond technical justice.

In an article examining the success of legal thrillers, John Grisham summarizes the basis for plots in his books: "You throw an innocent person in there, get 'em caught up in a conspiracy, and you get 'em out" (1992). While Grisham's formula captures the idea of the character moving from one dilemma to the next, it fails to address how these changes affect the character. How does the lawyer progress from initial innocence to experience?

Grisham's *The Firm* (1991) sets a model for this narrative type. The title contrasts the decidedly "unfirm," even immoral, law partnership with "the firm" ideals of the young attorney who will test them and himself.

The idealistic hero fresh out of law school rockets to the top of his profession. For a brief time, he feels that he has it made, only to discover to his horror that the very organization he had idealized is itself corrupt. The young professional works his way through hidden motives of his colleagues, double-dealings, and his own temptations toward that same corruption. Often he finds that the corruption comes very close to home. For instance, in *The Firm*, Mitch's wife had been his mainstay, the one person he could trust. However, she too yields to temptation, being seduced by one of Mitch's senior colleagues. After a series of setbacks, the protagonist begins to fight back. He uses the same chicanery or semi-legal maneuvers to turn the tables on the evildoers. He pushes to a point where his need for retribution places him on the same moral level as the corrupt members of The Firm. Should he sink to their level?

In the end, he fights for a just resolution. This generally occurs in a different arena, a different version of the institution he had originally imagined. Even as Mitch learns that The Firm is anything but, the value of the overall prize has been ratcheted up several degrees. This justice is better because it has been hard-won. He takes steps to unify outer reality with his renewed inner awareness of what justice, or Ethos, really means. The way to this insight is not easy.

Greek mythology presents several stories of humanity discovering the difficulty in deciding between what is right and what is just. The tale of Orestes dramatizes the cycle of retribution and the human cost of yielding to it.

Agamemnon and his wife Clytemnestra have three children, two daughters and a son. To win favorable winds from the gods so he can sail to Troy, Agamemnon sacrifices one of his daughters, Iphigenia. "A father's hands/Stained with dark streams flowing/From blood of a girl/Slaughtered before the altar" (Hamilton 182). Agamemnon returns home ten years later, triumphant from war, but a spirit of vengeance is in the air: "every sin causes fresh sin; every wrong brings another in its train" (Hamilton 241).

That night, the warriors hear their leader cry out. His wife Clytemnestra comes out into the square streaked with blood. She is strangely calm. Hamilton says of her demeanor, "She saw no reason to explain the act or excuse it. She was not a murderer in her own eyes, she was an executioner. She had punished a murderer, the murderer of his own child" (243).

Young blood comes onto the scene. Orestes, son of Agamemnon, brother of the slain girl, has a dilemma. He hears Apollo's order that he must act "to appease the angry dead." In addition, his surviving sister, Electra, has a request: "Electra frequently reminded her brother by messengers of the duty of avenging his father's death..." (Bulfinch 186).

Orestes is torn. If he lets his mother live, his father's murderer goes free. "But yet—but yet/The deed is to be done and I must do it" (Hamilton 245). Orestes kills his mother. "Atone for death by death./Shed blood for old blood shed (244).

He emerges from the murder seeing hallucinations of women whose eyes

5. Blood Dues

drip blood. They are dressed in black, with hair like snakes. These are the Furies, spirits of Vengeance sent by his murdered mother. He wanders the world but the Furies never leave him. "I have been taught by misery," he says. After many years "the black stain of his guilt had grown fainter and fainter through his years of lonely wandering and pain" (246).

Orestes asks for a trial, at which he takes sole responsibility for the murder. Athena releases Orestes from his suffering. She persuades the avenging goddesses also to accept it. "From the Furies of frightful aspect they became the Benignant Ones, the Eumenides, protectors of the suppliant. They acquitted Orestes. And with the words of acquittal the spirit of evil which had haunted his house for so long was banished." (248)

Orestes pays a high price for his law degree, his knowledge of justice. Through long suffering, he achieves the strength to accept responsibility. This step of transcendence has a valuable reward in ending a cycle of retribution. Lisa Scottoline and Barbara Parker write about women lawyers searching to solve both professional and personal dilemmas. The legal tangle is resolved on one level. The evildoer is captured or identified and either killed or punished through the system. Yet on the character's personal level, Oresteian suffering over paying the blood dues of initiation comes into play.

Scottoline's protagonists work in an all-female law firm, Rosato and Associates. Parker's sleuth Gail Connor is in corporate law. The characters are drawn into a cycle of murder and retribution, an eye for an eye. They move through increasingly intensified initiation rites from innocence to understanding. They must then renounce sharing the motives of hatred that drive a murderer to seek retribution. Frequently, the narrative arc draws up short before the characters' complete redemption. Ostensibly this occurs so the series may continue with these characters. But at the end of each novel, the lawyer protagonist perceives the duality of weak against strong, unfairness against fairness, to enter the sphere of merciful law and forgiveness celebrated by the myth of Orestes.

Scottoline's *Rough Justice* (1997) features defense attorney Marta Richter. Marta is wealthy, high-profile and knows her way around a courtroom. As the novel begins, she is bringing a murder trial to what she had thought to be a successful close. She worked to free her client Elliot Steere. She had even bragged to the press: *"I just win boys. I leave the details to you"* (6). Now with the jury in deliberations, Marta's client drops the mask of Mister Nice Guy. Marta realizes that her client is indeed guilty of murdering a homeless man. To forestall Marta taking action, Steere sends a hit man to take out Marta. In turn, Marta becomes a hit woman and must unearth, literally, evidence that will send her client to prison.

Marta wants to report Steere to authorities, not from any altruistic motives, but out of hatred for him. Steere had manipulated her with an unstated promise of seduction. Marta goes after him as a woman scorned.

> In the split second she realized it, Marta's fury became unreasoning. She could have sworn he wanted her. He'd given every signal. He'd lean too close at counsel table, look too long at her legs. Once he'd touched her knee ... and her response had been so immediate it surprised even her. The memory made her feel crazy, unhinged. Unleashed. "I'm going to Judge Rudolph with this," she said [6].

At this point, Steere's role in the murder bothers her less than the fact that Steere had played her for a sap.

Later, Marta has the opportunity to wield the same technique. She capitalizes on sexual vibes from a member of the jury. During the blizzard delaying the jury's verdict, she sweet-talks her way into the man's hotel room. She needs Christopher's help in proving Steere guilty before the snow lets up. Christopher makes an open plea to her. Does she have feelings for him? Will she also use sex to manipulate, falling to the same level as Steere?

> Every instinct told her to lead him on, lie to him, even take him to bed if it got her what she wanted. Marta couldn't imagine telling the truth with the stakes this high. Then she looked at Christopher's rugged, open face and couldn't imagine not. He was a decent, kind man, and she was asking him to do something that could get him thrown in prison. He deserved a straight answer. "No. Not at all," she answered [201].

Marta later becomes a killer, essentially guilty of the same crime as Steere. The murder is a ritual acted out in the hot-blood of self defense. Still, from that act, she comes to understand guilt from the inside and knows that despite being tested, her value system has emerged intact.

Scottoline's *Moment of Truth* (2000) directly addresses the death of Honor, both literally and as a symbol. Main character defense attorney Mary DiNunzio searches for Ethos, the meaning of truth. Like Marta, Mary works in the all-female law practice of Rosato and Associates. Mary's search is cast in terms of an initiation. The values of the justice system are overturned, and Mary's task is to right them again.

Jack Newlin is head attorney for estates and trusts at Tribe & Wright, a high-profile Philadelphia law firm. He confesses to the murder of his wife, Honor. The problem is that Jack's confession is a lie. Jack's motive in getting himself arrested for murder is to shield his daughter, Paige, who he believes actually did have a hand in the murder.

As an attorney, Jack knows what the police will ask, so he arranges his story to fit the facts. Prosecutor Dwight Davis plans to ask for the death penalty.

5. Blood Dues

> Davis scowled. A lawyer, killing for money. It brought shame on all of them. Davis had always been proud of his profession and hated Newlin for his crime. On his own behalf, and on behalf of the people for the Commonwealth. There was only justice to protect all of us. It sounded corny, but anything worth believing in ultimately sounded corny. Davis believed in justice; Newlin believed in money [91–92].

Davis makes the words sound good to himself. The dreadful fact is that the prosecutor knows Newlin is lying, and he does not care. He is really the one who believes in money. He sees this case as a way to advance his own reputation. Again, Scottoline reveals the hollowness at the core of people in the justice system.

The initiation narrative kickstarts with Jack's choice of an attorney, Mary DiNunzio. As a contrast to Jack and Marta, Mary is decidedly low-profile. "I don't have much experience with homicide cases, not as much as Bennie Rosato or lots of other lawyers in town" (29). Basically, this is why Jack has chosen her. He expects her to fail.

Mary is an alumna of Catholic parochial school. Her beliefs are formed but untested. She thinks of herself as a lapsed Catholic. Although convinced of her own venial sins that disappointed the nuns, she is basically innocent. She has a prim way of seeing the world, a way some would call "old-fashioned." Basically, Mary believes in her job and has faith that the cards of truth and justice will fall the right way. Her faith is soon put on trial.

Mary has an insight about Jack's fatherly sacrifice, because Mary's own father, Mariano, says he also would take a murder rap for his daughter. Mary is impressed with Jack's sense of duty. He will follow the correct path. After all, Jack is a member of Tribe & Wright. The name of the law firm carries connotations that Jack will do what's "right" according to the "tribe," or morality derived from the group. Still, Mary's values will be challenged. After interviewing her client, she tells Jack not to worry, "without understanding why" (34). She carries around only a shell of morality.

Mary clings to her world because it is seemingly fixed and impermeable. When she visits her home, she revels in its permanence. "The DiNunzios still used a percolator to make coffee, its bottom dent the only signs of wear in thirty-odd years. Progress was something that came to other households. Thank God" (81). But change is coming. Mariano suffers constant back pain. He puts on a brave front, but he brings deception into Mary's life and worse, a foreshadowing of death. Through a series of tests, she must move herself to a deeper understanding of the ambiguous choices necessary to reach Ethos.

Mary faces her first tough challenge when she informs Paige, Jack's daughter, that Honor is dead, and Jack has confessed to the killing. Mary questions her own career choice. "She needed a job with less emotional involvement. Emergency room doctor perhaps. Or child cancer specialist" (45).

As Mary toughens, she finds ways to combine her training from the nuns with her newly acquired skepticism. She suspects that Jack is shielding Paige because something about the girl is wrong. Jack's daughter is so offhand, nervous, and impolite. Her fellow lawyer, the more worldly Judy, tries to set her straight. "Bad manners aren't against the law" (132). However, as Mary proceeds with the case, she finds more evidence for her theory. Her eyes open to a world that fails to conform to her original ideas of truth and justice.

Professor Kate Fansler has Harriet the law professor as a wise guide. Mary's mentor on this quest is Lou, a retired investigator sometimes hired by Rosato and Associates. While Scottoline presents him as a comic figure at times, he sums up some useful thoughts about moral lapses:

> Lou didn't get up from his chair, even though it was his chance to slip out of the place. He felt tired suddenly. He didn't know when kids had changed, but they had, in his lifetime. They got to be empty inside; they didn't care about anything ... they collected guns and shot each other ... it had happened to Paige Newlin, too. There was something missing at her heart, and Lou worried that there was nothing in the world that could set it right [184].

At one point, Lou's world-weary ways help Mary overcome her squeamishness. Mary and Lou have been following Paige, Jack's daughter. They locate the sixteen-year-old and her boyfriend at a motel. Mary has a strong reaction.

> Her mouth dropped open. She didn't know she was such a prude. Well, she kind of did. "They tried to get a room together?"
> "No, separate," Lou snorted. "Of course, together."
> "That's disgusting. They're way too young for that."
> "Not possible. Anyway, the hotel was booked and they didn't have a reservation. The room is beside the point, anyway."
> "It is? Why?"
> "Because they're having sex in the cloakroom" [158].

Mary eventually overcomes her disdain for Paige. They are both, after all, daughters of honorable men, and Mary is finding Jack more honorable by the minute. Her personal attachment to him is another assault against her professional ethics. Mary's next challenge involves saving Paige from a masked gunman. The faceless threat sends the two women on a long chase down an alley. "She ran straight for the door with Paige, threw open the screen, and darted inside, fumbling for the main door and slamming it closed behind them" (283).

By saving Paige the daughter, Mary adds another dimension to herself as a worthy daughter, as a woman with love to give, and as a lawyer. Mary's willingness to place everything on the line for Paige wins her passage to the next level.

The final challenge remains. To prepare for battle, Mary visits the shadows of her church and finds light and tears of renewal. She thinks of the permanence of prayer. She is nearly to the Word Beyond Words, her own Moment of Truth. "The words summoned themselves from a place in her brain she didn't know existed ... The words were the same as they always had been, as were their rhythms, falling softly on her ears" (336–37).

Armed with a strengthened sense of her own values, Mary confronts the source of evil, where it dwells among the offices of Tribe & Wright. There she faces the masked gunman, and for Mary, he wears the face of her own mortality. "Mary stiffened with terror. She couldn't speak. She didn't know who he was. She didn't know what to do. She couldn't believe it was happening. She didn't want to die" (341). In a frantic rush to escape, Mary flees down the stairwell of the skyscraper containing Tribe & Wright. She cries for help, "but even she couldn't hear it over the din" (345).

Like Francesca the journalist, Mary's confrontation with evil traces a symbolic path down the ladder at the center of established truth. With each of the floors passing in turn, she basically relives her initiation process. The descending floors represent a paring away of her various levels of ethical constructions. The process continues until she speaks into a realm where she can't hear her own voice. Then her descent ends. She lets go of light and drowns in the "sound of a siren that hadn't brought help" (344–45). She realizes that established order, represented by the siren, is of no value. She must find the way herself.

Mary's initiation ritual nearly kills her, but she reappears bedecked with flowers, a figure resurrected by her Moment of Truth.

Barbara Parker's series features attorney Gail Connor. All the novels present the image of a questing novice in search of fairness. Major players in this series include Gail, a divorced corporate attorney, and Gail's love interest, Anthony Quintana, a defense attorney from a well-established Cuban family. Gail's mother Irene is from an old Miami family and a bastion of WASP respectability. While the growing love affair between Gail and Anthony measures the strength of Gail's heart in balancing personal and professional ethics, she faces other tests. She is a pivotal character between ex-husband and daughter, between Irene and memories of her dead sister, and between the Cuban and Anglo communities in Miami.

The first book of the series, *Suspicion of Innocence* (1994), knocks justice off the bench. Gail's sister is found dead, and Gail is one of the suspects. She has faith that the system will exonerate her, but her release is long in coming. The accusation also launches Gail onto a quest of self-scrutiny. She examines all the ways she has been guilty or sought retribution. Final revelations about Renee's murder essentially destroy Gail's version of her own past and question the values of people shaping the city's entire legal system.

Suspicion of Betrayal (1999) conflates several themes in Gail's struggle to balance the scales of justice. The narrative takes on tones of a Gothic thriller in which Anthony is the dark figure Rochester and his home in Miami, surrounded by a fence with spikes, is both protective fortress and prison. This duality is not lost on Gail, as she imagines herself there as mistress of the manor.

A stalker theme reinforces the novel's Gothic cast. Gail keeps receiving threatening phone calls, hate mail, and death threats. Graphic photos suggest that her daughter Karen is in danger. These threats compound Gail's guilt from the past. She has regrets over her divorce from Dave, the light-haired ex-husband, and over being a professional woman instead of a full-time mom.

This is only part of the story, however. Gail's struggle toward a sense of fairness lifts the novel out of the Gothic genre. Gail must prove herself worthy of being called a lawyer and she is not willing to compromise in this struggle.

Throughout the Gail Connor series, Parker uses houses to reflect Gail's inner life. In *Betrayal*, to escape influence from the Pedrosa homestead, Gail and Anthony buy a house together. It is on the "bad side" of Coconut Grove. This house needs new wiring, landscaping, and a major plan to encourage rat evacuation. Time, decay, and a horrible handyman nibble away at this house, as if at Gail's attempts at starting a new life. While problems with property are very real for a divorced woman, Gail herself needs a corporate lawyer to help her manage her own shifts in property. The house changes are reflective of Gail's psyche. She is certain in some areas and very confused about others.

One of Gail's initiation rites involves buying a dress for her wedding to Anthony. She meets with her prospective women in-laws at Lola Benitez's exclusive dress shop. The shop is so exclusive that even Gail's mother belongs to the inner circle of clients. The shop unites Irene with the Cuban women from Anthony's family. Karen, Gail's rebellious eleven-year old, feels comfortable with this group and finds a dress she likes at the shop.

The only one finding this whole process of feminine bonding unsatisfactory is Gail. In a sincere gesture, Anthony's relative Elena welcomes Gail to the family:

> "I just wanted to tell you how happy I am that you're going to be part of our family. I've sensed sometimes that you don't feel comfortable with us. I hope I'm wrong."

Gail turned her back to be zipped up. "I don't know why you should think that. I'm very fond of you all" [204].

Gail knows enough about shady dealings in Anthony's family to wonder if marriage to him would essentially mean being "married to the mob." The Cuban women represent a female chorus, affirming the values of marriage and traditional obedience to the husband's will. In response, Gail enacts a self-imposed exile from their group.

Parker sets up a complex moral universe, however. Gail is really in no position to judge the values of others, and she knows it. Her own ethics in dealing with clients are questionable. Financial shortfalls have prompted her to play fast and loose with a client's money, using it to finance her ex-husband's business deal. She tries to help a battered woman leave her husband. However, that woman continuously returns to her husband. Given Gail's rocky relationship with Anthony, she is hardly qualified to offer advice to smooth out a marital relationship.

Another case from Gail's past returns for retribution. Gail had played a central role in a house foreclosure. This is especially ironic, given her own difficulties with real estate deals. She knew at the time that the foreclosure was legally right, even if it was not fair or moral. The foreclosure has tragic consequences. The client returns bent on revenge. This woman, crazed with grief over losing her husband and children, reflects in some measure Gail's own situation. Through her clients, Gail comes face to face with the weaknesses of her own ethics.

In the myth of Orestes, the House of Atreus is cursed. Similarly, caught up in a cycle of retribution, the power of Anthony's family is on the wane. "The house of Pedrosa was falling" (419). Gail seeks a middle ground between her house in Coconut Grove and that of Anthony's family. Gail lands at her mother's home, where she had grown up. In doing so, Gail leads the spirit of retribution to the house of Irene.

Gail's own actions have set this revenge drama in motion. The murderer is indeed a kind of Fury. The spirit of vengeance stalks Gail as it did Orestes. The dead must be avenged.

The two are locked in a struggle, each condemning each other to hell, until the final demonic scene. The murderer prepares to kill Gail, and her mother and daughter, but the plan backfires. Murderer becomes victim.

> Orange tongues licked across her body, down her legs. Her eyes opened wide in agonized terror, and a scream tore from her lungs. Hair burned and crackled. Gail stood immobilized, horrified. The knife clanged on the terrace. Shimmering, dancing, the flames ate into the darkness and leapt up, outlining the aluminum frame supporting

the screen. The fire spun and beat at itself, mouth agape in a soundless cry. Its image flickered on the surface of the water. Then image and fire came together. Flesh hissed. Water surged upward and fell back [414].

Once the figure is extinguished in fire, the immediate danger is gone. Still, Gail's crime had its origin on paper. "Bits of curled, blackened paper floated on the surface" (414). The pieces are evidence of her guilt, a final recrimination.

In many ways, the figure in flames is Gail's double. Gail Connor has similarly demanded retribution against the unseen stalker, against Anthony, and many other wrongs. Gail must move, sometime, to that unstrained quality of mercy, but not yet. She is doomed to wander, like Orestes, an outcast from the human community.

At novel's end, Gail is away from most of the people she cares about. Her ex-husband and daughter take a sailing trip without her. Anthony, her future husband, is out of the country and has left strict instructions that he will accept nothing from her. Gail's pain over the trauma has started to fade, but it has not ended. As Gail and her mother prune trees, Irene asks about her plans. Gail asserts that without Anthony, she feels truly free, but she shows little joy in the discovery. She has fallen short of experience. "Don't I even get to have *my* life, imperfect as it may be? That's all I want" (422).

In *Suspicion of Malice* (2000), the fifth novel of Parker's "Suspicion" series, attorney Gail Connor is drawn yet again into a murder investigation. During the case, she travels farther along the halls of justice as she is more successful in blending personal and professional values for an inner Truth. However, she has a way to go. "Unfortunately for the truth, too much of it would remain with the dead" (340).

So far in the "Suspicion" series, Connor has not yet reached the point in her Orestean saga where the Furies wield power as Beneficent Ones. That may change with the publication of *Suspicion of Vengeance* (2001), which promises an in-depth exploration of retribution and forgiveness.

Vengeance focuses on the death penalty. Anthony Quintana takes on the case of death row inmate Kenny Ray Clark. Clark plans to appeal his conviction with new evidence through DNA testing available through the Innocence Project. Familiar with the community originally shaken by the murder, Gail approaches this case with a cynicism about the justice system's power to right past wrongs. In a sense, the entire "Suspicion" series has been Gail's own Innocence Project. However, it is possible that in this adventure she will move to another plane in her understanding of Justice, with a capital "J."

Charles Rosenberg, law professor and a frequent television commentator during the O. J. Simpson criminal trial, writes, "The stone structures of ancient Greece are mostly dust. Even the Parthenon lies in near-ruin. Greek dramatic structures, by contrast, are alive and well and living in your television set" (Jarvis and Joseph ix). For "your television set," we might substitute "the pages of mystery fiction." Many mystery novels work out a conflict between people doing good and people committing crimes. "Where you have opposites of good and evil, you are simply in the field of ethics." (Campbell, *Transformations* 247). The more intense novels do not stop there. Like the Greeks, detective writers combine moral drama with the main character's struggle to understand the meaning of the drama, to solve a spiritual mystery. Its solution demands a high price. To learn this secret, the questing protagonist must "seek beyond the tumult of the state, in the silences of earth and sea and the silence of his heart, the Word beyond words of the mystery of nature and his own potentiality" (Campbell, CM 88). The reward is that the reader along with the sleuth has the opportunity to feel the spark of genuine experience.

CHAPTER 6

TRACING THE RAZOR'S EDGE

When will the beast leap out of the darkness? This central question of most suspense drives detective fiction. The confrontation between detective and monster draws much reader attention. We focus on the actual attack. If the detective loses, the confrontation plays out as a kidnapping, wounding, or loss of consciousness. When the sleuth has the upper hand as aggressor, we learn much more about her pursuit of the beast, the killer in a human being's clothing.

To structure the chase, mystery writers may use pre-set patterns. Examples from poetry clarify how this technique works. In the seventeenth century, metaphysical poets helped to shape a literary form called "topographical poetry." Samuel Johnson defined this category as verse in which "the fundamental subject is some particular landscape" (Harmon and Holman 520).

"Shape" is the operative word here, as the verse conforms to a pattern from nature. Sometimes the lines themselves even fall into the pattern. Various environments, such as hills, rivers, or caves, serve as landscape metaphors called *topoi*. These metaphors intensify the meaning of the verse. For instance, Henry Vaughan's "The Water-Fall" shows us the design of a geographical drop of a river, but it also conveys an allegory of death and rebirth.

The common pass
Where, clear as glass

6. Tracing the Razor's Edge

> All must descend
> Not to an end
> But quickened by this deep and rocky grave
> Rise to a longer course more bright and brave.
> [White *et al.*, ed., ll. 7–12]

The *topoi* are more than metaphors. They show both the mark of human consciousness on the land and the land as it affects consciousness.

Detective fiction uses a similar correspondence of meanings. In fiction, the configuration is much more complex. The mythico-geographical patterns unify action and character with meaning. The pattern is apparent in the wilderness adventures of Anna Pigeon, a ranger with the National Park Service. Not so obvious are the spatially patterned metaphors appearing in private investigator searches by Julie Smith and Linda Barnes. These *topoi* are traced out through the detectives' searches in cyberspace.

While on the solitary quest, the detective must tread carefully along the established trail. One or two steps to the side can mean the difference between life and death. Joseph Campbell quotes from Hindu literature:

> *A sharpened edge of a razor, hard to traverse,*
> *A difficult path is this—poets declare!* [*Creative Mythology* 22].

The Razor's Edge is a pattern traced over a wilderness that is both real and mythic in the mystery novels of Nevada Barr. Setting here becomes much more than local color. This series features Anna Pigeon, employee of the National Park Service. Anna's quest for the killer, the adventure that tests her mettle, is often inscribed visually as a map on the book's frontispiece. This image geographically represents much of the plot. But the map often serves as a kind of *topoi*, a metaphor for the mystery along with Anna's feelings about her job and life.

In the series' early books, Anna Pigeon works in the American West. The landscape she traces rolls out over rugged terrain in *Track of the Cat* (1993). *Superior Death* (1994) plunges Anna into a shipwreck and murder below the surface of Lake Superior. *Ill Wind* (1995) and *Firestorm* (1996) return her to the Southwest. The design of *Blind Descent* (1998) picks up and strengthens the *topoi* of The Cave. Anna must rescue a seriously injured friend from the claustrophobic, uncharted tunnels of Carlsbad Caverns.

Liberty Falling (1999) circumscribes Anna's mystery to islands off Manhattan Island. She values this transfer because her sister, Molly the psychologist, lies in a coma at a New York City hospital. In addition, Anna has to endure the knowledge that Frederick, her lover from the FBI, and Molly have fallen in love. Her dying sister has stolen her boyfriend. Anna takes solace in alcohol. The victim's fall from the Statue of Liberty mirrors Anna's fall in fortunes. This book is so far the weakest in the series. Even a trash-strewn island becomes unequal to the task of depicting Anna's littered inner world. The purity of her quest requires a broad territory for her to roam.

In *Deep South* (2000), author Barr is back on track with a fresh *topoi* of Anna's adventure. This time the pattern takes on a configuration similar to a Cretan labyrinth. This maze lacks a beast in the center. It is more obviously spiritual. This labyrinth is a "pathway to the center with the special quality of doubling back on itself without crossing any lines" (Pollack 149). The searcher may discover the way in, but the razor's edge out is lined with deceptive passageways and false sidetrips.

As Anna assesses her future with the Park Service, she worries about job security. Taking a management position is one way to secure her spot in government service. She takes the first opening that comes up. Nomadic Anna has been transferred to the Natchez Trace in Mississippi. The Trace has been worn down from centuries of mule wagons and trade routes from Memphis to the mouth of the Mississippi. In this book the *topoi* is a deep straight line cut through a maze of surrounding wilderness.

Anna investigates a camper's report of kids making a ruckus on the edge of the campground. As she penetrates the wilderness, she at first welcomes the rich night aromas. She moves toward the center. Then danger moves in:

> The ground beneath her inclined. Cobwebs stuck and tickled on her face and arms. Faint sounds echoed her passage in the woods to either side. The skittering of small creatures foraging, the scuttle of a tiny night beast alarmed by her presence. Subtly the smell of the forest altered. An earthy odor permeated the air, and, almost imperceptibly the nature of darkness changed.... Because of the thick curtain of trees to either side, the Natchez Trace created an illusion of isolation, wilderness. In reality, civilization in the form of roads, houses and fields pressed close on both sides [48].

In fact, this geographical landscape mirrors Anna's inner psychology. The natural world holds no fears for her. Civilization is what poses the perils. First, Anna is unhappy, as she has to spend too much time in her car. Secondly, the career track is straight, but she is surrounded by a wilderness of "good old boy" masculine hostility and tidbits of Southern culture that she does not comprehend. Her mission of investigating the death of a young girl gives Anna a serious purpose. However, the danger directed at her brings her deeper into a human landscape thickly vegetated with distrust. She falls victim to a deadly prank when an alligator trapped under her car lashes out. Even travel by car is not safe from human creatures with malicious intentions.

6. Tracing the Razor's Edge 117

Anna intuits the center, heads for it, and reaches it. Still, her way back is troubled. Anna is in peril from her excessive drinking. By staying "on the wagon," she must travel the implied razor's edge out of the labyrinth.

The *topoi* also depicts Anna's love life. When Anna falls for a mysterious man, at first the way to romance seems as pure and uncomplicated as the straight-shot road through the trace. With Paul, she will walk the "straight and narrow," avoiding lapses into abuses of alcohol: "Paul tapped on the door twice. Once he offered to bring her wine. She refused and knew she'd quit drinking. Again. Maybe for good this time" (351). However, as the book draws to a close, Barr implies that Anna's route back, if she travels with this man, will be overgrown with complications and ambiguities.

Barr's most recent book of the series, *Blood Lure* (2001), returns Anna to her beloved mountains in Glacier National Park. Again, the path follows large whorls along mountaintop trails. But Anna's assignment in Glacier is only temporary. If the series follows the hints dropped so far, this detective will find herself back in the Deep South, having to extricate herself from a deep swampland. Barr's so-called "ecological thrillers" are less about nature per se and more a mythic landscape for human nature. Northrop Frye notes that "mythology does not, except incidentally, make statements about the natural environment. It is a structure of human concern, and is built out of human hopes and fears and rumors and anxieties..." (MM 119).

A mythic *topoi* extends from the wilds of human nature to technology. Some mysteries trace out the design of the plot in the context of cyberspace. For today's fictional detectives, the phrase "to carry hardware" is just as likely to refer to a Pentium III processor as a Smith & Wesson .38. And why not? More police departments and crime-fighters in the actual world are online. We should expect that mystery protagonists would also use computers as sophisticated search tools. Computerized searches help sleuths to find clues in online chat rooms, websites, and encrypted file folders. In addition, mystery writers are likely to use cyber clues in other ways, as sterile counters to the human community or as metaphors for the dark side of human nature. What effect does downloading have on a PI's hunt for the murderer?

Linda Barnes and Julie Smith are two mystery writers with much urban landscape to explore. Linda Barnes's PI Carlotta Carlyle is a part-time cab driver traveling the winding, pot-holed streets of Boston. To crack a case in New Orleans, Julie Smith's rangy homicide detective Skip Langdon roams many a fetid back alley. Skip takes statements in musty houses shadowed with Spanish moss and chases perps through colorful masked revels at Mardi Gras. These authors use the cyberworld as an additional dimension to map the psychological growth of their detectives. But these uses are less a futuristic shift in the detective formula and more an upgrade in the detective hero's mythic journey.

In this narrative pattern, the hero must walk the line exactly or all is lost.

The Razor's Edge also explains how an apparently new twist in mysteries, cybercrime, or clues hidden in programs or hard drives, falls into a mythic pattern. Computer use or word processing duplicates the heroic journey. One step to either side, such as tapping a key out of sequence, or failing to hit "save" at the crucial time, can lead the searcher off the edge, and all is lost.

The story of Daedalus and Icarus is well known. Daedalus fashions wax wings so he and his son can escape from King Minos. Icarus flies too close to the sun and falls into the sea. Less known is what happens to the father.

Daedalus escapes to Sicily. King Minos is infuriated that the master craftsman has slipped from his grasp. The King sends out a challenge to lure Daedalus out of exile. The trap is an intricate seashell, and King Minos offers a reward if anyone can pass a thread through it. Daedalus cannot resist the challenge. He cuts a hole in one end of the shell, ties a thread to an ant, and waits for the ant to crawl out the other end, successfully trailing the thread. When Minos hears of this solution, he knows that he has found Daedalus (Hamilton 140).

Today the seashell is molded plastic and instead of an ant, the thread is tied to a "mouse," but the meaning is the same. As any Windows user can attest, negotiating software programs is indeed like threading the labyrinth. Tapping a key out of sequence or failing to hit "save" at the crucial time can lead the searcher into a dark maze.

Hard drives in the modern mystery tell us less about *2001, A Space Odyssey* and more about the mythic power of hidden recesses and inner journeys. Plenty of mysterious factors in cybercrime make it appealing to mystery novelists. As with break-ins, rapes, fraud, robbery, cyber crime represents a violation of privacy. The identity of the perpetrator is unknown. The evil is a shape-changer, lacking a human face.

Why compare these mysteries to narrative patterns of myths? The myth of the labyrinth presents a narrative pattern unifying the external and psychological struggle of the sleuth struggling to maintain order.

The labyrinth shapes Carlotta Carlyle's path in Linda Barnes's *Hardware* (1995). This novel internalizes the detective's journey by developing her pursuit of evil through a cyberscape of evidence. Barnes's detective, former cop and part-time cab driver Carlotta Carlyle, works for the Green & White Cab Company. The business is run by Carlotta's good friend Gloria. When organized crime attempts to muscle in on the Green & White, Carlotta decides that she needs some new equipment. She needs to upgrade her detection tools, but she is not totally happy about it.

> Computers have arrived. There it is. Pretty soon there'll be a different kind of cop show on TV. Uniforms'll sit around and punch keyboards and discover — gasp — who checked out porno tapes from Video-

smith today. I wish I could get *into* computers, but they have a level of abstraction that doesn't make me tingle [Barnes 59].

To add a tingle factor, Carlotta asks her lover Sam Gianelli for computer shopping advice. Sam belongs to a crime family but he is not part of *the* family, or so he says. He is a kind of Michael Corleone, twelve years younger than the eldest son, and adamant about staying out of the family business. Sam fends off any questions Carlotta asks, so she learns not to ask any. When Sam controls her access into computer territory, she is mildly agitated at first. She insists that she can deal with computer salesmen on her own. "'Sam,' I said, 'you know you don't need to come along to translate computer talk for me. I've done my homework. I'm not dumb'" (44). Later, she is glad for his translating ability.

Their way to the shady computer dealer in Mattapan is labyrinthine. Carlotta mentions repeatedly that the weather is nasty, filled with "mush" and slush (45, 51, 61) that makes driving and walking slippery, like a quagmire. "While we spoke, [Sam] was driving a twisty, turning path, but he couldn't fool me.... Few areas of the city retain their secrets. Mattapan holds more than most" (49).

Barnes makes their journey to Mattapan an impenetrable way not just by describing the curving route, but by explaining the city's history of forced integration, emphasizing the racial tensions. "The closest most whites get to Mattapan is the Franklin Park Zoo, a mile or so away, and most suburbanites are scared to go there" (50).

Their destination is one of three boarded up houses, with rotting wood, peeling paint and a "spongy porch" (51). Carlotta thinks at first that the address is a crack house. Their entrance requires a secret knock known only to Sam (51–52).

Sam introduces Carlotta to "Frank," a hopped up hermit living with lawn furniture in "cross between a computer warehouse and a junk shop" (52). Carlotta compares Frank to a "caged animal" (52). Later, she elaborates on Frank, continuing with the minotaur-motif: "If Frank reminded me of an animal pacing his lair, the beast was wolf-like" (56).

Frank's speech is like another language. "He spoke in initials and put his phrases together so oddly, with no apparent punctuation, that I didn't understand half of what he said" (60). Their purchase ends abruptly when a black van does a drive-by, guns blazing.

Armed with the new equipment from Frank, Carlotta has access to the dark side. She uses her new PC to tap databases inaccessible to people not in law enforcement. "I ran through my almost nonexistent caseload. Two skip-traces that would be speeded up by the acquisition of the computer. One inconclusive store surveillance, possible clerk theft" (67). She does background checks on suspects in the taxicab case.

Although Carlotta attempts to navigate the perils of the computer on her own, she is at a loss: "With manuals in hand, cursing whoever had laboriously translated them from the Taiwanese, I managed to hook up my computer, only to find it utterly useless without Frank's promised software" (75). Later, Frank breaks into her apartment and replaces the computer, but his methods are in hieroglyphs, signs that she cannot read. The labyrinth that began in her mind goes with her through the city. Although she had traveled to the center to meet the monster with Sam, she has difficulty making it back.

Carlotta searches for Gloria's brother. The trail takes her to Franklin Park, in "the heart" of the city. She is literally bogged down in a quagmire:

> The incline was far steeper than I'd estimated from a quick flashlit sweep. I started down too fast, following a muddy rut, and fell. Sat, cursing silently. My next attempt was more cautious. Oblique. I hung close to a scraggly line of trees, trying to dig my heels into the mud. The undergrowth snared my feet. My boots kept slipping in the mire. The second time I fell, twisting my ankle sharply on a hidden root, I made a desperate grab for a sapling, missed, and slid the entire length of the grade ... [this] silence is so deep you can imagine yourself in the wilderness, in some far-off wolf-inhabited woods [83–84].

This urban setting even manages to include a beast.

Eventually, Carlotta learns that "Frank" is not real. His identity is concocted from documents of a deceased child. She also thinks she discovers many things about Sam. Either his recent trips add up to another woman, an increased role in organized crime, or his preparation to testify against the mob in a Senate Subcommittee. The ambiguity of "Frank's" evil begins to affect Carlotta. The ambiguity over Sam finishes her off.

After Sam is injured, the pressure is on Carlotta to discover "Frank's" true identity. She begins with Sam's apartment.

> I moved into the study. Computer, laser printer, fax, copier. The sheer amount of hardware was daunting. So streamlined, automated. Clean. Unrevealing.
> I ignored the machinery and started with the desk, a massive rosewood block with eight hefty drawers. Slips of paper, business cards ... I found them reassuringly human [226].

She takes some of Sam's diskettes and tries to read them on her computer. She is hesitant. "What I didn't know about computer compatibility could fill volumes. Would I be able to bring up his files on my screen? What were my chances of destroying them in the process" (259)? In this case, her fears over computer incompatibility express doubts over her relationship with Sam. She fears destroying its most valuable parts.

Along with these revelations, Carlotta faces her ultimate evil beast in the form of the computer genius who offers her the world. He can hack into any account for her and give her ultimate power (305–06). "Used to be you could access hundreds of dark-side files. How to make your own weapons. How to kill somebody's credit rating. You want revenge, there's no better way" (310). She turns him down. Carlotta forces him at gunpoint to erase his access code and write out a confession.

In Barnes's work, the computer is a new-fangled tool that Carlotta renounces. Eventually the rangy PI eschews the computer and clings to the human touch. Still her submersion in the poisoned cauldron helps her to understand her unwillingness to commit to Sam and to live her own life more fully.

Cyberclues are really primitive myths in futuristic dress. Detectives distrust the machine, consider it a kind of fraud, and regard it with a certain amount of guilt. The mystery writer, however, uses the cyberworld to characterize aberrant personalities and to reflect psychological states of the protagonist. The cyberworld is another territory for the sleuth to search, to act out a conflict, and maintain balance. In solving whodunit in an emblematic landscape, the PI is essentially answering questions about the human heart.

When mystery author Julie Smith brings the information highway to Bourbon Street, its direction points not to the twenty-first century but to a distant past. Julie Smith has made a conscious effort to use myths to structure her books. In an April, 1999 discussion with this writer, Ms. Smith acknowledged that her novel *House of Blues* (1995) was patterned after myths of the House of Atreus. She also mentioned plans for a future work based on Demeter and Persephone, a myth we later use to examine *82 Desire*. Smith does not see high-tech as the latest trend in mystery writing. Instead, she holds more with the concept that we may try to escape our weaknesses, but murder dot com only upgrades the same human failings captured in timeless myths.

The Big Easy comes alive on the page through more than vivid description. Its mythic geography radiates meaning by tracing the hopes and frustrations of the sleuth protagonist. Smith's dynamic urbanscape expresses the book's forward motion through both the actions and psyche of the hero. In interviewing suspects and double-checking clues, Skip Langdon walks or drives the terrain. She traces a line on the earth, and each successive episode in the narrative advances Skip further into the labyrinth.

In *New Orleans Beat* (1994), Homicide Detective Skip Langdon investigates what appears to be an accident. A young man is dead after falling from a ladder. The deceased is Geoff Kavanaugh, thirty-one years old, employed at a video store but still residing in his mother's home. The neighborhood's shabby homes lead Skip to think that the people there are neglectful and depressed, or worse, alcoholic and crazy. After visiting the young man's room, Skip feels that she knows Geoff, "the very personification of 'nerd,' a bright young man turned inward, poorly socialized, who thought of that secret, dreamy place his computer took her to as cyberspace ... a place more real than his own life" (NOB 12). She is somewhat haughty about Geoff's cyber-life.

Skip travels vomitous back alleys interviewing Geoff's co-workers and acquaintances. She takes statements in musty houses shadowed with Spanish moss. Before long, Skip must rethink her assumptions about Geoff and her entire investigation. Geoff had belonged to a virtual community called "The TOWN," an acronym for "The Original Worldwide Network," like AOL. Skip thinks it's a type of bulletin board, but she has much to learn.

One witness tells her that TOWN is "More like a religion. Or maybe a real town. He'd talk about all these things going on in the TOWN, just like, you know, they were really happenin'" (NOB 17).

From another acquaintance of the victim, Skip learns that one TOWN discussion has opened old secrets. In a chat session, Geoff told about his dream. He came home to find his father dead on the floor, shot with his own gun. According to Skip's witness, Geoff continued to have flashbacks about the incident, and his attempts to learn the truth about that night may have led to his murder (NOB 26). Skip discovers that Geoff's dream had indeed been real. Her investigation of Geoff's death becomes intertwined with another death, over twenty years earlier.

Smith uses the virtual TOWN in a number of ways. First, TOWN expands on the character of Geoff, the victim. We come to see him as more than an antisocial, computer geek. We understand his addiction to a cyber-world. One informant tells Skip, "A strange kind of reality kicks in once you get on the TOWN ... The actual illusion is that you know people intimately when all you see is a few words on the screen" (NOB 29).

Geoff's TOWN presents a variant on the locked room mystery. The virtual community members are the equivalent of guests in a manor house mystery. All subscribers to the TOWN knew about Geoff's confession; not all had a motive to kill him. How much can they hide? Does an Instant Message window carry the privileged communication status of a confessional?

Smith achieves her deftest sleight of hand as The TOWN gradually enlists Skip as its newest member. At first, Detective Langdon scoffs at the virtual community and tries to keep herself apart from its artifice. For instance, just before she discovers more about the cyber world, Skip soaks up the palpable reality of New Orleans.

She approaches the Quarter, just off Dauphine. She appreciates the "tree-lined center divider" and calls the outside image "breathtakingly beautiful," even though she knows that drug deals and prostitution go on inside the houses. Just before she meets with her TOWN informant, she stops and jokes with an old black man sitting on the steps:

> It wasn't that funny, but she and the man shared a big laugh, pals for a moment—the sort of moment you didn't get in every city, she thought, when she liked New Orleans, which she did right then [NOB 21].

Skip is very definitely an outsider to the virtual community and proud of it. The problem is, she also starts to blend illusion and reality. She overreacts when she learns that the cyber citizens of TOWN knew the details of Geoff's story before she did. Several times she feels the case "spinning out of orbit," and notes that she hates the feeling of being out of control (NOB 23, 25). At one point, even her lover Steve Steinman knows more about Geoff than she does. Skip responds, "I'm asleep; I'm dreaming. This isn't really happening to me" (NOB 34).

At first, Skip needs help making the transition from solid ground into cyberspace. Asking to see one informant's computer, she says, "You might as well show me what the monster looks like" (NOB 28).

She soon learns that the real monster is that part of herself that covers self-doubts with a façade of superiority. Skip's investigation traces a labyrinthine path across the city that mirrors Geoff's involvement in cyberspace. Like Theseus, Skip sets out on a torturous route to slay inner demons.

When Theseus enters the maze, he uses sacrificial wine to give him courage. He carries Ariadne's thread as a link with the outside world (Grimal 59). After slaying the minotaur, he follows the thread back out (Grant 338–39).

The Cretan labyrinth is not a fortress-type maze, but a single path leading, as Joseph Campbell would say, "directly to the center of our own existence" (HTF 25). This is not an external task but an inward one. Like the slightly drunken Theseus preparing to enter the labyrinth, Skip also experiences an unreality, as if she is dreaming her life. She had made fun of Geoff's involvement with cyberspace, yet the hidden space has power to draw her in:

> Skip found, as always, that once logged on it was difficult to get off. It wasn't that she was fascinated—in fact, she was more or less bored—but there were so many choices, so many possibilities ... Who could resist checking a few of them out? [NOB 100].

Skip enters the computer's decision tree, a metaphor for how she weighs suspect's motives and alibis. She discovers too that the chief system administrator has the user name "Big Easy" (NOB 30). She pursues the investigation with a passion that surprises her. The more she investigates, the more she feels the pull of the New Orleans cults that make up the fabric of her actual community.

Geoff's girlfriend runs a boutique called Stringalong. It sells "jet beads, carved beads, beads in every color and beads of pristine clarity, about enough beads to fill up a shoe box" (NOB 18). They are her lifeline, like Ariadne's thread to the outside. When she visits one of her women informants, she hears eerie chanting, and watches in terror through a window. The women enact an ancient ritual. She sees

> some kind of small round plate with a star engraved on it — *Pentacle*, she thought, not quite knowing where the word came from. A large ceramic chalice was filled with some kind of dark liquid — *red*, she thought. *Or am I crazy?* [NOB 98].

In the logic of the labyrinth, Skip has to lose one part of herself to find another. Later, she follows a suspect and ends up observing a fuller enactment of the women's ritual, complete with costumes, more chanting, and talk of a child sacrifice (NOB 177–84). "She was unnerved at her reaction. She loved the thing" (NOB 185).

As Skip traces a labyrinth to psychic wholeness, she arrives at many realizations. She sees that she is not as involved with her community as she had thought. She lives in a little house, originally a slave quarters, apart from the main house, her family, and other women (NOB 2–3). She wears isolation as obviously as her badge. In the rhythm of her community, she is off the New Orleans beat.

The line she had drawn between herself and the bad guys is also not as distinct as she would like:

> It was only after she got home that Skip could really think about what had happened, and the thing that chilled her, the thing that absolutely paralyzed her, was not how close she had come to death but how close she'd come to killing... [334–35].

After traveling to the center of Geoff's TOWN and her own, Skip has a revelation that questions her intuitions about a case, indeed her entire world view. An image from the beginning of the book prophesied her entire transformation:

> But as she entered the jungle, she saw that there was a certain pattern to its wildness, an artfulness, a cultivation of the inherent drama of the thing — in fact, the jungle was an illusion, only a tangle at the front of the yard. Past that was a neatly mowed lawn and some beautifully tended beds [4].

6. Tracing the Razor's Edge

She learns the value of penetrating to the heart of the thing and casting off old illusions. As a result of her travels through cyberspace, Skip Langdon comes to a new understanding of the human community and her place in it.

The myth of the labyrinth is but one pattern that highlights cyber clues. Another is the myth of Demeter and Persephone, which some commentators have called the myth of enclosure.

Persephone is in the countryside picking flowers when the surface of the earth opens up and Hades, lord of the underworld, emerges and steals her away in his terrifying chariot pulled by dark horses. Persephone cries out, but her mother hears only the echo of her cry. In her grief, a disguised Demeter goes into exile. Then Demeter becomes involved in family life at the village of Eleusis. Her grief over Persephone causes the fields to go barren:

> That year was dreadful and cruel for mankind over all the earth. Nothing grew; no seed sprang up; in vain the oxen drew the plowshare through the furrows. It seemed the whole race of men would die of famine. At last Zeus saw that he must take the matter in hand [Hamilton 52].

Zeus instructs Hades to release Persephone. Before Hades does so, he forces her to eat a pomegranate seed. This ensures her return to the underworld. Demeter's joy at her reunion with her daughter restores life to the fields. The crops are plentiful. Demeter knows that her grief over being parted will return. "She did indeed rise from the dead every spring, but she brought with her the memory where she had come from" (Hamilton 54).

Aside from being trotted out as an explanation of the changing seasons in a farming culture, how does this myth connect to computers?

Although Hamilton does not emphasize this facet, Hades's kidnapping of Persephone connotes a rape. It emphasizes defilement and entrapment, being shut away from human socialization. Similarly, the computer is a dark, enclosed space. Dwelling in cyberspace can represent a total disembodiment of the self, a seemingly unnatural removal from the human community. The sacred cup of the Eleusian ritual is a symbol of nurturing and abundance. When Persephone ascends to Demeter, fertility is restored to the land. Her return is celebrated with the cup of the Eleusian mystery rites.

The myth of enclosed space is a kind of poisoned cauldron that has the capacity to change into an overflowing cup of nurturing or a golden bowl. The myth's fundamental meaning is that the two images must go together. Without seasons of fallow fields, there are no abundant harvests. This is the mystery of how death and awareness of loss validates life.

Smith's *82 Desire* (1998) presents a changed New Orleans beat for Skip. Her urban landscape is in drastic need of renewal. "82 Desire" is the name of the wheezing, broken down bus that has replaced Tennessee Williams's original streetcar. It hardly lives up to its namesake.

Skip's Homicide Division, like police districts in other parts of the country, has been decentralized. The streets are too controlled. Skip liked the old system, where anything could happen. When Skip discovers a corpse, her reaction is jaded. We see the dead man:

> His mouth was open slightly, almost in an *O*, and his eyes were wide open, staring in perennial amazement. A parade of bugs marched in them. Rusty-looking stuff—the man's blood—spattered the floor and his clothes. *Okay, fine, one corpse. Human. Male* [39].

The body, dead as it is, shows more liveliness than our sleuth.

Skip's home life, by contrast, is crammed with too many living people, too much chaos. Her relationship with Steve Steinman is beginning to wear. "Life was complicated. The whole place was in an uproar, not just her own space" (ED 34). Clearly, something has to give.

What gives is that Skip must learn the value of working for a cause larger than the self, restoring the broken human circle. "This person then takes off on a series of adventures beyond the ordinary, either to recover what has been lost or to discover some life-giving elixir" (PM 123). In a mystery, what's lost, of course, is life, the victim's and the sleuth's.

As in *New Orleans Beat*, author Smith sends Skip on a labyrinth-style journey to find renewal through her investigation. Her way is not a "big easy."

> She had the feeling of walking in quicksand—she really had no idea where solid ground might be after a great snowball of a weekend that had led, so far, to nothing ... and then the weekend was over and she was up to her knees in quicksand [77–78].

As Joseph Campbell notes, the hero may be ambivalent about his direction, but he suddenly finds himself in a transformed realm, a landscape that most addresses his weaknesses. Campbell reiterates that the hero gets the landscape he deserves. "You leave the world you're in and go into a depth or into a distance or up to a height. There you come to what was missing in your consciousness in the world you formerly inhabited" (PM 129).

What Skip lacks is excitement on the trail, satisfaction with life. She finds it while going out to interview a Mr. Newman. Skip notes that Mr. Newman's address is

> reached by taking the Mississippi River Bridge (aka the Crescent City Connection), and driving through quite a few miles of McDonald's and Dairy Queens, and finally coming to, of all things, the same river

you have just crossed. Because of an exceptionally kinky meander, you actually run into the Mississippi again [220].

Essentially she ends up where she started, but she has the information from "New-man," a name suggesting Skip's rejuvenation. The joy is back in the chase, and she asks Steve Steinman along to make a fun weekend out of it (ED 286-91).

The answer to whodunit in this book is a bit anticlimactic. The actual crime involves oil leases and out-of-control corporate types having fun putting one over on decent folks. The real heat in the plot comes from answering the basic question of how to sustain joy in life. Along with Skip, other characters, an executive, a reporter, a politician, face the same dilemma of staying interested in what they do. All the characters seek renewal. Author Smith overcomes stereotyped characters caught by a mid-life crisis. She repeats the labyrinth pattern as each character works out the way to restored life. This whole fictional universe of labyrinths is presided over by Smith's inspired creation, Talba Wallis, also known, mostly to herself, as the Baroness de Pontalba.

The Baroness is the original African queen. Sometimes she dresses in blue skirts and white blouses; sometimes in scarves and headdresses of African tribal colors. The contrast in styles exemplify that Talba is a rare combination, computer technician and poet. Talba lives with her mother, Miz Clara, who wears a pair of worn blue slippers and acts like a little old lady, although she is only forty-seven. Miz Clara despairs because Talba is too wild, goes with the wrong men, and doesn't make enough money.

We see Talba as the Baroness at her first public poetry reading. Her poem sizzles with rage. She seeks revenge against the doctor, or Pill Man, who suggested that Miz Clara name her infant daughter Urethra. Talba's poem starts a legend growing. The people at her reading ask, Is it true or an urban myth? Later Talba tells a friend that Urethra was in fact the name on her birth certificate: "It makes you feel shitty to have a name like that. Like you don't deserve any better" (ED 186).

Talba, computer expert/poet, is clearly a Persephone figure. She carries the pomegranate seed of despair and revenge around with her. She first learned computer skills so she could locate the Pill Man and expose him. We even have a Demeter figure in the shriveled and bossy Miz Clara. When Talba finally finds a man worthy of her, Miz Clara sheds her blue slippers to become years younger (DOB 335-36).

Smith weaves a computer subplot around the compelling Talba. A seedy private investigator enlists Talba's services to snoop on a missing oil company executive. She can do this easily:

And sure enough, it was the piece of cake she'd predicted. She sneaked back in, brought up the 'Find' command, typed in one of the names, clicked the 'Find Now' button, and kept doing it until she had nearly all the names — and all in a single file, called 'Skinacat,' which she copied onto a disk. She sneaked a peek before she copied it, but it was about as sexy as a sock drawer — just names and numbers, as far as she could see [61–62].

Then the PI shows up dead. He is Skip's victim, with a trail of insects on his face. The file he wanted is now hot evidence. Talba's efforts to refind the files are thwarted at first, but she finally gets another shot. "She clicked the 'Find Now' button, and murmured, 'Come to Mama.' The status line read, '0 Files found'" (ED 164). With yet a third try, she discovers the encrypted names (ED 228–29).

In this case, Talba's computer skills make her appreciate her talent for poetry. Her art earns her no money, yet she has to do it: "it was the most important thing in her life — in a long-term sense" (ED 53). In her Baroness persona, Talba appears before a high-school class telling them about the value of creation. "What I'm talking about is work that always makes you feel fine. And good about yourself. And happy" (ED 126).

Like Persephone, Talba's poetry releases her from computer entrapment. She rises away from the flickering monitor and comes to the earth's surface through her transcendent imagination. She rides that broken down bus and begins thinking not just of a poem, but a whole volume of poems and a special name to go with it. As Smith has done already, Talba will entitle the whole book *82 Desire*. "It had to be the most poetic damn bus in the world" (ED 208). Talba's poetic sensibility transforms the blasted urban landscape into something brilliant and gleaming with life.

The computer's enclosed space is a barren, artificial world of "0 files found." The novel ends with victory. The Baroness illustrates her joyful immersion into words and creativity before an actual community. She gives a poetry reading which nearly all the characters attend. She comes to grips with the Pill Man's pomegranate seed, her terrible name, and sheds her revenge like a shroud. Instead, she revels in the joy of creation. Her last poem includes these lines:

> *And when you think about where that old Urethra is,*
> *And how The Baroness myself is a poet of some renown,*
> *Doesn't that just make you want to elbow fate right in the ribs?* [337].

Cyberclues are really time-honored labyrinth and fertility myths on an eighteen-inch monitor.

Regardless of eco-scape settings or searches for high-tech computer villains, the detective's mission of restoring life is intricately bound with the human community. Through emblematic patterns and timeless myths, the sleuth finds the answer of how to restore a dead self to life. Nature and the cyber world present varied territories for the sleuth to search, but ultimately they merely point the many ways to reach the human heart.

CHAPTER 7

V. I. AND KINSEY: DEATH AND RENEWAL

> That corpse you planted last year in the garden,
> Has it begun to sprout? Will it bloom this year?
> Or has the sudden frost disturbed its bed?
> T.S. Eliot, "The Waste Land" (ll. 71–73)

If Marcia Muller is the mother of the woman private eye novel, then Sara Paretsky and Sue Grafton are its older sisters. Their careful storytelling and creations of idiosyncratic, yet engaging characters began the flood of fiction featuring women private eyes. In an important critical study *Detective Agency: Women Rewriting the Hard-Boiled Tradition* (1999), Walton and Jones examine reasons for the proliferation of this subgenre:

> The female private eye genre as it evolved in the 1980s was also fueled by a nostalgia for the idealistic social action of the 1960s and early 1970s, when the women's movement (and activism more generally) seemed to hold so much promise for changing both society as a whole and individual lives [34].

From the beginning, the woman private eye has searched mostly in the public arena for solving the mystery. Her search continues to fascinate a reading public eager to identify with a woman establishing control on her own terms. Protagonists in the latest best novels continue to be hard-driving private eyes. So the legacy of Paretsky and Grafton is unquestioned. However, after nearly two decades of solving tough cases, where are V. I. and Kinsey now?

Paretsky's most recent V. I. Warshawski adventure, *Hard Time*, was published in 1999. Grafton continues to erase her way through letters of the alphabet. *"P" Is for Peril* (2001) rocketed to the *New York Times* best-seller list the first week it was out. It is still there, and as of this writing has been on the shelves for barely a month.

The questing private detective conforms most closely to the "hero on the mission" myth. She faces the mystery on its most basic conflict level, which is to solve death and restore life. For all the similarities between Vic and Kinsey, authors Paretsky and Grafton have conceptualized the quest of each character quite differently. While Vic is bogged down in the "solve death" aspect of the equation, Grafton has opened up Kinsey to "restore life" in a radical way.

Vic and Kinsey work hard for the money. They are paid for their work, but solving the case is more than a job for them. Each woman is so fully invested in the case that her personal life gets short shrift. This does not mean that the authors skip over developing a personal side to the characters. We see many details of their non-crime solving lives. We are well acquainted with Vic's Mr. Conteras and Lotty, about Kinsey's baking landlord Henry and Rosie. Occasionally, a person from a past case drops by, a police contact or a former, always former, lover. However, the authors let the case express the inner life of the sleuth. By solving the case, the P.I. restores some unfinished part of herself.

Like Ishmael, Huck Finn, Isabel Archer, and hundreds of other enduring characters on the American literary landscape, V. I. and Kinsey have no families. They are essentially orphans, having to reinvent or revive cultural values for themselves. Each woman is alone, yet each has chosen a different route to rectify the situation.

V. I. seeks to merge with a family. Restoring lost children or patching broken family relationships is how Vic attempts to restore her life. The problem is that the quest is heavy indeed. V. I. is exhausted. Kinsey strives for enforced solitude and tries to stay above the fray. Each case, especially the most recent *"P" Is for Peril*, merits a different approach that hones Kinsey's creativity. Paretsky gives us the P. I. as social reformer; Grafton's version is the detective as artist. A close look at the most recent books by these writers reveals a crucial difference in each character's development and the shade of myths each author uses to pattern the narrative.

V. I. faces a crisis of creative vision in Paretsky's previous book *Tunnel Vision* (1995). In this saga, Vic's building suffers a power failure, and in some ways, for Vic the power of her creative self never comes back on. A homeless family huddling in the building's basement sets the emblem for the narrative. With V. I. to lead them to the light, the family will be whole again. Unfortunately, that particular group disappears, and the same situation crops up in another, more sumptuously appointed home.

When Deirdre Messenger, wife of a philanthropist and mother of three, is murdered, Vic takes on the mother's role. To save the children, she leads them through the tunnels under Chicago. She also nurtures the poetry writing of Emily, who had been caring for her two younger siblings. Vic tells her, "Keep a journal. Write more poems. Your poems will tell you the right thing to do" (418).

By saving this family, Vic is saving herself and her own creative vision, which is in need of clarity. Her dreams are unsettling. She awakes "feverish from interrupted sleep to a world encased in ice" (32). She has a nightmare of being "trapped in a steel coffin" (324). Crumbling and rat-infested, the cityscape of Chicago is exhausted of promise and life. Burrowing into the tunnels, Vic digs beneath the blasted surface to an older city and still fails to find a rejuvenating vision. The only image she summons up depicts a cycle of abuse: "When I thought about all the men beating on women, beating on their own daughters, beating on each other, I couldn't imagine my own efforts to intervene as anything but futile" (331). The burden of all the world's woes sits heavily on Vic's shoulders.

Even her memories are blurry and limiting. In a chapter entitled "Down the Shaft," she carries stolen files that help prove political payoffs. She digs deep for strength. She recalls a time during her childhood, returning home from school in a blizzard:

> Gabriella always put a lamp in the living room for my father on stormy nights. I knew she would set it out for me. As the balloon of snow encased me I peered up at the shadowy bulks of buildings, looking for the light [371].

Although V. I. experiences being a mother figure for Deirdre's children, she still lacks a creative vision. The tunnels represent escape and discovery, but they are closed in and without light. At the novel's close, Vic plans a trip. Mr. Contreras gives her a going away present, a repaired picture of the Uffizi that her mother had owned (432). For Vic, the future journey to Italy represents her mother, a revitalized imagination, and restoration of life.

V.I.'s treks through the underworld of Chicago attempting to revive a poetic impulse call up the myth of Orpheus. This myth shows the artist being given a second chance and losing it. Orpheus, we remember, was an extraordinary musician. His talent with the lyre calmed even wild beasts. His songs "moved the rocks on the hillside and turned the courses of the rivers"

(Hamilton 103). After the death of his beloved Eurydice, Orpheus "sang his grief to all who breathed the upper air" (Bulfinch 151).

Taking pity on the musician, the King and Queen of Hades allow him to travel to the Underworld to bring Eurydice back to life. The one condition they set was that he could not look back at his beloved. Orpheus descends to the Underworld and crawls back toward the mortal world with Eurydice following.

The two are about to emerge into light. Orpheus has to check that Eurydice is indeed behind him. He looks back. Just as the gods had warned, Eurydice faints and her soul is spirited back among the dead. Orpheus makes another attempt to retrieve her, but his way to Hades is barred (Bulfinch 151–53).

This myth emphasizes how suffering and loss fuel artistic inspiration. A more emphatic message involves acknowledging mortality. Orpheus can never bring back the dead Eurydice. Vic's immersion in lost causes is noble, but repeating what she cannot do keeps her immersed in that fatal moment of failure. Symbolic rebirth lies in transcending that moment to emerge into light.

After *Tunnel Vision*, Paretsky did not write a Warshawski novel for four years. *Hard Time* (1999) chronicles V.I.'s return to the blighted landscape. This time, the search is on again for family members. Memories of her father accompany Vic as she essentially undergoes a ritual death as a daughter figure. The detective stays above ground in this book, but her darkened vision from the tunnel lingers. V. I. is reading "a history of the Jews in Italy, trying to understand something of my mother's past" (159). If she did make a pilgrimage to Italy, the journey had no lasting effects of comprehension or renewal of spirit.

Hard Time continues the previous book's theme of thwarted creation and takes it a step further. Images of decay and corruption hover over a blasted, bleak landscape. The weather is humid, with the "oppressive mugginess of midsummer" (29). Even a sunset holds no life-affirming poetry: "The last dregs of light were staining the western sky pink..." (92).

Paretsky wipes out hope so completely that the landscape of *Hard Time* re-creates The Waste Land, "the land where the myth is patterned by authority, not emergent from life; where there is no poet's eye to see, no adventure to be lived, where all is set for all and forever" (CM 373). In this book of unforgiving time, V. I. will consider her search successful if she lands in Coolis prison. Her reward is a perfect emblem of the Waste Land.

> The prison stood two miles west of town; scraggly strip malls had grown up along the route.... Three layers of high fencing, with razor wire along the tops and current running through the outermost, separated us from the prison. It looked in some ways like a modern

industrial park, with its low white buildings laid out in a kind of campus — except that the windows were mere slits, like the arrow holes in a medieval castle. Also like a castle, watchtowers holding armed guards covered the perimeter. A kind of reverse castle, where the guards thought the enemy lay within rather than without [132].

The image combines medieval torture with high-tech business parks and even a hint of a university setting in the word "campus." Paretsky's prison stands for all dehumanizing institutions.

V.I.'s friend and reporter friend Murray has sold out his journalism to become a TV commentator. Murray's new boss is Global Enterprises, a corporate conglomerate. Murray seems unhappy in this new role.

If Murray were the chief character here, he could qualify as a "questing professional." The book might instead follow the pattern of an initiation rite to show Murray's progression from innocence to experience. But the story is Vic's and her quest is a set in a modernistic wasteland, impotent, corrupt, and incapable of being brought back to life. As the name suggests, Global Enterprises has corrupted not only Murray's journalism but the entire world. Vic's fellow artist crusader has aged. Murray's appearance is haggard. His beard had turned gray before he shaved it. Seeing his naked jaw disconcerts Vic (5). The visible outline of the bone shows both vulnerability and mortality.

The media is gathered around a young woman television star. She is not from a love story, soap opera, or sitcom, but of a romance-horror show. Lacey Dowell plays a popular television character, the Mad Virgin, who seems a combination of Madonna and Buffy the Vampire Slayer.

The program's premise is that the Mad Virgin died in medieval times defending her purity. She travels through time, wreaking vengeance on the man who killed her by preventing his ravishing other women, saving them in the nick of time. While the character is successful in defending honor, she also dies at the end of every show. That the show features vampirism rather than matters of the heart sets a tone for destruction and disintegration. Draining off bodily fluids, vampirism is a reversed image of sexuality.

Even more distressing is the reappearance of Emily Messenger, the young poet of *Tunnel Vision*. She has survived the ordeals of the previous book well enough to emerge here as a rabid fan of Lacey, the actress playing the Mad Virgin. Gone are any traces of her poetry writing days. Instead, she can barely contain her excitement over the possibility of obtaining Lacey's autograph. Emily has dressed for the occasion. "Emily was in Mad Virgin uniform: the black tank top, stretch pants, and platform shoes that were sold through the Virginwear label Global owned" (6). The Mad Virgin has co-opted the young poet.

7. V.I. and Kinsey

In some ways the Mad Virgin represents V.I. herself. The show's concept parallels the detective's efforts to restore what is right and good, to save purity. Throughout the novel, Vic sees her conflicts in medieval images. Vampirism is called up again, as Vic remembers her mother's death from uterine cancer. The trauma caused Vic to fear her own menstruation as a teen. She was terrified that she "would drain away from the inside" (182). Through a witches' brew metaphor, she depicts herself as anchorless and without hope.

> I badly needed help. This wasn't even an investigation. It was some kind of demon's cauldron I'd fallen into. I was bobbing around with the newts' eyes and bats' wings, and I wasn't going to have too much more time to figure out the brew before I drowned in it [192].

Despite these splashes of tortures from the Middle Ages, a more potent pattern of imagery dominates Vic's world — ruthless technology. On the way home from the Mad Virgin event, V. I. nearly drives over a girl's body in the street. The girl is almost dead, the apparent victim of a hit and run:

> In the light of my flash I could see that the woman was very young. She was dark, with thick black hair tumbled about a drawn face. Her breath came in bubbling, rasping sobs, as if her lungs were filled with fluid ... I pointed the light at her chest, as if I might be able to detect her lungs and recoiled in horror. The front of her dress was black with blood. It had oozed through the thin fabric, sticking it to her body like a large bandage. Dirt and blood streaked her arms; her left humerus poked through the skin like a knitting needle out of a skein of wool [13–14].

The girl later dies at the hospital.

The initial purpose of V.I.'s search is to discover the identity of the dead girl and ensure that her relatives can give the girl a proper burial. Vic learns the girl's name, Nicola Aguinaldo, and discovers that Nicola had died while attempting to attend her baby's funeral. Later, Vic learns that Nicola's grandmother never received the girl's body, never could hold a memorial service. The dead remained unburied.

Nicola's body has yet another meaning for Vic. The dying girl's breathing sounds familiar. Vic says, "I'd heard that kind of breathing when my father was dying of emphysema" (13). Vic again connects Nicola's body to her father in a disturbing dream:

> My father was lying in the road in the wasted final stage of his illness. He had left his oxygen tank on the curb and was gasping for breath. Before I could get into the street to pick him up, a squad car rounded

> the corner and ran over him. You killed him, you killed him, I tried to scream but no sound came out [17].

Later in the dream, Mallory, her father's best friend from the force, arrests her and seems not to recognize her. Vic's father is not only the source of her voiceless impotence but of anonymity. The sacrificial young victim lying in the street, a daughter, is essentially Vic herself.

V.I.'s dream conflates the accident with her own missed chances and lost opportunities. When her father died, Vic felt like the victim of a hit-and-run. Like Orpheus, happiness was grabbed from her. Her father's death thwarted her life.

> Emphysema had forced my father onto long-term disability when I was in law school. His illness affected everything about me then, from my decision to marry in the hopes I'd produce a grandchild for him before he died to my lack of interest in campus politics [29].

Vic's crusade to identify the dead body and find the family is her own ritual of burial. Along with the hand of the gods, her father had pulled her back from the land of the living. By tracing Nicola's route, she can finally put the pain to rest. She feels that she will gain a "family," a sense of herself as a fully integrated personality.

In the meantime, the image of the dead girl in the street launches a powerful pattern of motifs depicting human creativity destroyed by machines.

In *The Machine in the Garden* (1964), cultural historian Leo Marx discusses how technology has both enriched and corrupted ideas in American culture. Marx traces the relationship between pastoral ideals and industrialism from the early nineteenth century up until just before World War II. In an Epilogue entitled "A Garden of Ashes," Marx writes, "This recurrent metaphor of contradiction makes vivid, as no other figure does, the bearing of public events upon private lives" (Marx 364). Machines run over people. Vic does indeed take the burden of evil public events onto herself. This obsession is at once her saving grace and blindness toward that salvation.

The portrayal of technology as a counter to the life force continues in the person of Vic's antagonist, Robert Baladine. Baladine is CEO of a surveillance company called "Carniface." From the name alone, a combination of *carnivore* and *artifice*, we know that he is a predator.

While waiting in Baladine's posh office, V.I. first sees the man in photos: a "lean, tanned man with various sheiks and presidents and at the exhibits of memorabilia, ranging from a Presidential medal of Freedom to a mock-up of the women's correctional facility at Coolis" (86). A military veteran with a long resume in rapid-deployment weapons and prison surveillance, Baladine represents a destroyer of peace and freedom.

7. V.I. and Kinsey

Baladine's only redeeming factor, in Vic's eyes, is that he is a father. However, Baladine soon loses whatever credibility his parent status might lend him. He assures V.I. that he's never been an idealist or misplaced his trust. "Either about America's external enemies or her internal" (87). Baladine's grip of destruction reaches inward toward his own family, just as Vic's father's death had thwarted her. To save the promise of life and creativity, Vic gears up for all-out combat on a mythic battlefield. V.I.'s fight takes on the intense, sweeping quality of apocalyptic myths.

Mircea Eliade describes these tales of human and cosmic destruction. The stories are universal. From Judeo–Christian, Hindu, and Buddhist traditions, Eliade cites examples and note similarities among all cultures and major world religions. The story of Noah and the floods represents one apocalyptic tradition, although in other cultures, "The 'end of the world,' i.e. of a particular historical cycle, is not always occasioned by a deluge, but also arises through fire, heat..." (Eliade *Eternal Return* 66).

Corruption begins in the human heart. The evil festers and spreads on a global plane. Conflicting forces of good and evil grow until the souls of the dead visit the living in preparation for the "ritual combats between two opposing groups" (ER 53, 67–68). The groups remain locked in battle. Then the conflict explodes into "a magnificent apocalyptic vision, in which summer, with its scorching heat, is conceived as a return to chaos" (ER 66).

As a result of this final conflagration, "mountains will crumble and the earth become smooth, men will desire death and envy the dead ... [The blast] will absorb the whole universe in fire, thus permitting the birth of a new world, an eternal world of justice and happiness, not subject to astral influences and freed from the dominion of time" (MER 127). Although the end result is nothing, the good have nothing to fear. What remains are "the destruction of sinners, the resurrection of the dead, and the victory of eternity over time" (MER 129).

Eliade sees the patterns in these stories as laying a foundation for the philosophy of history (MER 60). One phase of history is wiped out to make room for the next. "In the last analysis, what we discover in all these rites and all these attitudes is the will to devaluate time" (ER 85). In these visions, no redemption is possible because there is no understanding of the past. Humankind drives itself to live on the crust of past mistakes.

Paretsky sees military, corporate, political power on one side and aesthetic idealism on the other. Vic meets Baladine's son Robbie, and she rapidly takes his measure: "Not the son for a manly man. Maybe he was swapped at birth with an artist's child" (88). The conflict continues to play out with technology pitted against creativity. The security company V.I. hires to do battle with Baladine's technology at Carniface is called the Unblinking Eye. Her security system is deified. It sees all, knows all. To counter the possible bugging of her apartment she puts on a Mozart or Bach CD (192, 215). Ironically, Vic cannot call on her old hacking buddy for help with a computer, because he is in the Peace Corps (239).

When Vic has car trouble, she brings it to Luke, another of her Mr. Fixit buddies. V. I. calls Luke "one of the few guys out there who still knows what a carburetor does, but he's so depressing I try to avoid him.... He identifies so totally with machines that it's hard for him to talk to people" (23). While she admires his skills, he too squelches human values. V.I. tries to establish their old rapport. "Luke cut me off, saying he didn't want to hear my tale of woe" (23). Her formerly stimulating conversation skills fail to take effect. The car she is forced to rent is hardly a chariot fit for a private eye; it's a Rustmobile, with no air-conditioning (145, 153, 191, 241). Later she refuses to have anything to do with the car, as she fears it could be rigged with a car bomb (236). The image is thoroughly in keeping with the book's symbolic structure. Machines kill.

A murderous technology affects even the sprightly Mr. Contreras, who usually revives V. I. with a pep talk or two. He regales her with a tale about a buddy who drove a Harley and ended up as "an eggplant for seven years before the good Lord was kind enough to pull the plug" (25–26).

If Mr. Contreras fails to cheer her up, V. I. takes some solace on the romance front from reporter C. L. Morrell. She has her first view of him, as she does with Baladine, from a photo, only this photo is on the back jacket of Morrell's book, *Vanishing into Silence*. The book documents Morrell's investigation into the disappearance of South American political prisoners. Unlike Baladine, whose photos are self-serving, Morrell mocks himself while posing for the photograph (127).

After V.I. ends up in bed with Morrell, she wonders about his initials, C. and L. She wonders if his parents had "named him for name brands, like Clorox and Lysol" (195). This is not a bad guess. Morrell provides a few light moments for Vic, a kind of surface disinfectant. Ultimately, he has no power to reach the dirt clogging her spirit.

In an interview with the *New York Times* ("Writers on Writing," 9/25/00), author Sara Paretsky says, "I'm a storyteller, I'm an entertainer, but the stories that come to me are almost always those of voiceless people, not those of the powerful."

She began writing out of a "desperate need to start writing down the lives of people without voices." Her writing focused on "ordinary people whose lives, like mine were filled with the anomie that comes from having no voice, no power. Even then, I still felt so voiceless myself that it was another twelve years before I tried to sell my work."

When Paretsky imprisons her detective, she strives for the ultimate horror. For Vic, the night holds only the terrors of being without a voice. The

7. V.I. and Kinsey

system is as corrupt as V. I. is empty of creativity. Like the title of Morrell's book, V.I.'s voice threatens to vanish into silence. As she struggles to figure out Nicola's case, Vic's own identity is at stake: "If I could only get the story together, narrative would come together on Nicola's frail body" (248).

This is a narrative beyond *noir*. The evil is widespread and runs deep. Vic characterizes the entire state as a system of political corruption.

> Illinois seems like a large place when you look at a map ... but it's really just a cozy little hometown, where everybody knows everybody else and nobody tells secrets outside the family. Businesses pay money to politicians to get even greater amounts of money pumped back to them via state contracts, and while some of it may be skuzzy, none of it's illegal — because the guys who have their hands in one another's pockets are writing the laws [132].

What hope does Vic's crusader have against a system of evil endemic to life?

More than a few times, V. I. refers to Dante's *Inferno*. She is trapped into the hell of Coolis prison through a Dante-esque series of concentric circles. First she visits the prison with Mr. Contreras and the dogs. Although they try to make a picnic out of the excursion, the prison's contagion and toxicity are clear. "Behind it ran Smallpox Creek, flowing northwest to the Mississippi..." (133).

During this visit, Mr. Contreras and Vic are undercover, trying to find out more about Nicola's death. As Vic draws closer to the circle of hell called Coolis, she continues to build a shell around herself. Finally after she attempts to save Robbie Baladine from his oppressive family she is arrested, on a kidnapping charge (256). She finally gets her wish to go to prison.

Life in Coolis is hell, and V.I.'s choice to remain a prisoner there is so extreme that we either question her sanity or applaud her altruism. The arresting police officer is Lemour. The name is close enough to *l'amour* to suggest that love is the reason for Vic's imprisonment. Lotty accuses her of wanting to follow Joan of Arc into the flames (181). The comparison is apt in that both carry a destructive end.

The book's title throws a klieg light on Vic's prison experience. *Hard Time* evokes Professor Gradgrind and a Dickensian view of poverty and industrialization.

The title also connotes the difficulty of understanding time and penetrating the veil of history to the past. Given the prevalence of images involving entrapment, encasement, and being frozen in *Tunnel Vision*, the phrase characterizes frozen time or time stopped. This is not the timelessness of myth, but the erasure of time through death.

Time essentially does stop for Vic in the prison. She trades in her reverence of the past, her father's watch, for a mechanized means of capturing the present. Morrell gives her the watch that is really a video camera to document the prison guards' brutality (296). Vic spends some frantic moments wondering if she has lost her father's watch (320).

The phrase *Hard Time* captures the prisoner's argot in describing long prison sentences. It suggests the intransigence and unforgiving quality of time that moves at its own pace, not of our wishes. Vic is in prison for four weeks, she tells us, not a month (284). She counts the days, essentially crossing them off as in a prison movie.

This quality of living life as an unending walk through hard time goes a long way toward portraying Vic's Waste Land. Northrup Frye describes this category of time:

> At the furthest pole from the mind of God, where time is an eternal now, is demonic time, time experienced as simply one clock-tick after another, an unending duration without direction or purpose, of which we know nothing except that it annihilates everything, including us [MM 157–158].

With the sweep of an apocalyptic foot, Coolis kicks the props out from under Vic's life re-generating powers. Roaches cover her as if she were already dead. She loses her identity and even her name. The guards know her only as "Washki" (290). Some of her fellow inmates are members of a gang called the West Side Iscariots, betrayers, traitors, exiles from the human community.

They are The Voiceless, with no freedom of speech. If an inmate speaks, she gives the guards "license to kill" (268). Once V. I. makes it to the inner circle of sewing machines, she witnesses that the restriction on speech is yet more oppressive. A woman speaking gives the guards an excuse to launch a blackmail threat: "We know where your little boys are" (311).

Because they cannot speak, however, V. I. speaks for them. She puts on paper their thoughts to sons, lawyers, and parents. "It was my letter writing that really saved my hide in Coolis" (292). In a sense, V. I. carries out the function Paretsky claims for her own fiction, giving voice to the voiceless. Still, the letter writing continues to drain Vic's own creativity. Even though hearing the women's voices allows her to ask questions, thus advancing her search for Nicola's story, her writing is derivative. She takes dictation from the women. She hides her "book" in a copy of *Cosmo*. Her art is without meaning, as she sees only the "shape of my words on the page without being able to read them" (315). She commits an author's cardinal sin by mailing the letter without reading it over (316).

V. I. has to silence her own voice to grow closer to Nicola. Only by holding her tongue can she access the inner circle of the sewing machines. Her arrival is hardly a rewarding goal. Once she arrives, the first words out of her mouth are "Puttana machina!" (307). The curse merely repeats what the book has said all along, that machines prostitute our souls. Machines kill.

Ultimately, Vic achieves the ritual death she seeks. She becomes more like Nicola, moving ever closer toward the beast at the center, technology. The stamping machines replicating the image of the Mad Virgin represent the mechanical replication that edges out life (310). Vic moves close enough so she can curse the machines and be victimized by them. She also undergoes the same punishment as Nicola (314). After re-tracing Nicola's route to death on the highway, Vic loses consciousness (318–21).

In mythic thinking, the ritual death of the god brings the blasted landscape to life. When Vic awakes, all she can afford is a brief *danse macabre*. Lotty brings flowers and a letter from Murray expressing regret over her near death: "I pinned one of the flowers to my blouse and danced around the Berman gardens with it" (331). Her friends' gifts are in essence funeral tributes. It is as if Vic is still dead. Healing and redemption have not been strong enough to banish the evil forces.

Widespread corruption requires a tremendous power of good to counter it. Does the legal system provide this power? Pictures from Vic's watch camera provide proof of wrongdoing at the prison. However, in the pictures, time fails to march forward. The pictures and Vic's presentation act out a ritual myth of repetition. This action presents a "supreme attempt toward the 'staticization' of becoming, toward annulling the irreversibility of time" (Eliade 123). Her watch camera keeps inhumanity in the eternal present. Images of degradation and brutalizing continue.

Does the church provide the necessary good for healing? Vic takes part in Father Lon's Mass. "I stood in the Lady Chapel of the enormous church and read from the book of Job about how God desires humans to see the light" (347). Even these ritual celebrations are not enough to bring light to the blasted Waste Land. Violence and corruption invade even this realm. The red tracer of a weapon follows Vic into the sanctuary (361). Shockingly, Father Lon at first tries to lie as a cover for the corrupt police (367).

Have V.I.'s efforts at prison reform made Coolis a better place? Ultimately, closing down the dehumanizing factory at Coolis makes no sense. Removed from their shackles, the women do not praise Vic. They are economically worse off, because they will not be paid as well in the kitchen (382).

Paretsky creates an order so corrupt that the usual methods for solving the crime fail. Truth does not prevail. This adds up to one embittered vision of humanity.

After the earth's final conflagration, Eliade tells us, the good have nothing to fear. The meaning of Vic's ritual death as Nicola is to understand that the good do have something to fear. Nicola was innocent, and she suffered at the hands of a machine-like brutality.

Perhaps redemption waits for Vic in her next adventure. Eliade discusses festivals celebrating a pre-apocalyptic happiness. People wear masks and ride horses, funerary animals, to show that "The dead come in procession to visit their families" (MER 67). When Vic gets a car back, it is a Mustang (383).

Her car and some money are the only positive results of the case. To match the rest of Vic's prison experience, this novel ends on despair. Vic fails in her quest to restore the land to life. She remains, like Nicola, a victim of a hit and run, with her father as the driver.

Eliade assesses the role of hopelessness in myths. "It is a despair provoked not by [humankind's] own human existentiality, but by his presence in a historical universe in which almost the whole of mankind lives pretty close to a continual terror (even if not always conscious of it)" (MER 162).

In the book's closing scene, Morrell attempts to comfort Vic. He tells her "You have to live in the world" (385). Although she has him as a "companion for her journey," she has seemingly learned nothing. Bloody and bruised, she's there again in bed with Pure Idealism. Next to Morrell, V. I. rests but with "images of terror" breaking into her dreams (385). It seems that Baladine is correct about one thing. The enemy does indeed lie within.

Vic does not understand herself or her desire to keep her eye on the Ideal.

> I could not
> Speak, and my eyes failed, I was neither
> Living nor dead, and I knew nothing,
> Looking into the heart of light, the silence.
> Eliot, "The Waste Land," ll. 38–41

For a while, it seemed as if *Hard Time* was the end of the road for V.I. Warshawski. Paretsky's next work, *Total Recall* is coming out in September 2001 (a few months as of this writing). The title suggests a certain wholeness of vision that might provide some redemption for Vic. However, given this last Orphic journey through a world devoid of creativity, total recall of that moment of loss is the last thing V. I. needs. In the meantime, V. I. Warshawski remains imprisoned in hard time.

Life comes from death. Eliot's corpse in the garden indeed has begun to bloom in the latest novel from Sue Grafton, *"P" Is for Peril* (2001).

Kinsey Millhone sprang to life in *"A" Is for Alibi* (1982). Her world is mapped out in *"G" Is for Grafton*. Authors Kaufman and Kay tell about Grafton's original conception of the alphabet-based series. "She was aware, she says, that publishers were very interested in series novels and she was deliberately looking for a device to signal that she was beginning a series." Another source of inspiration for the idea was, Grafton says, Edward Gorey's *The Gashleycrumb Tinies*, in which an alphabetical series of children are dispatched in various ways (Kaufman and Kay 327).

These two examples explain the source in terms of Grafton's experience, but her choice of the alphabet was more than a shrewd marketing strategy. As an understanding of myth shows, enduring patterns lie in the entire universe of words, waiting for the creative artist to carve them out. Robert Graves, author of *I, Claudius* and other works, had fueled his writing with an understanding of mythology. As part of extensive studies in classical literature and antiquity, he uncovered a concept similar to Grafton's in a Celtic-based system of myths called the "tree-alphabet."

This body of Celtic lore links a person's name and letter of the alphabet with a tree beginning with the first letter. For example, B is for Beth (Birch). "Each letter is named after a tree or shrub of which it is the initial." Graves's well considered opinion places the tree-alphabet as a "genuine relic of Druidism orally transmitted down the centuries" (Graves 165). The connection between the system of writing and organic nature is apparently very primal.

Graves provides a kind of dictionary or lexicon on the symbology of each tree. He writes, "I noticed almost at once that the consonants of this alphabet form a calendar of seasonal tree-magic, and that all the trees figure prominently in European folklore" (165). Starting with each letter, he tells how each tree fits in with the growing calendar, healing herbs, and Celtic story-telling. For instance, "the berries of the magical rowan in the Irish romance of Fraoth, guarded by a dragon, had the sustaining virtue of nine meals; they also healed the wounded and added a year to a man's life" (167). A potent metaphor for Celtic spiritual life, the tree-alphabet was very specialized, "used for divination only," providing expansive spiritual guidance for many facets of life for the Celts.

Sometimes a plant metaphor finds its way into Kinsey's cases. Who knew oleander was poisonous until Grafton pointed it out? Kinsey has encountered more than a few murder weapons fashioned from nature and horticulture.

This comparison does not suggest that Grafton's alphabet concept is in any way derivative. Rather, the similarity indicates that from the beginning, Grafton visualized Kinsey's story as proliferative, more than just one volume. To organize her work, she chose not an individual title, but an organic, life-generating list. With "A" as a seed, Grafton has all creation at her disposal.

A series entitled with symbols leaves a great deal of room for reinvention. Grafton's alphabet plan allows her to redraw meaning to create a new vocabulary or idiom for her protagonist. For each book, a letter represents an entire mode or thematic content from Kinsey's world. Kaufman and Kay remark on

Grafton's word play. The title letter continues with "supporting use of the alphabet for the locales and families involved in most cases" (326). However, the ramifications of this "play" are far-reaching. The whole series represents a process of becoming.

Grafton creates every book anew like individual leaves on Kinsey's family tree. Rather than viewing the works as separate letters in the alphabet, we can see Kinsey's adventures as an integrated saga. Kaufman and Kay also assume the organic nature of Grafton's work. They blend all of Kinsey's exploits into one "biography." Basically, *'G' Is for Grafton* presents the life of Kinsey Millhone as a still unfinished portrait of the artist.

Sue Grafton's series has never strayed very far from mythic images of creativity. Paretsky's *Hard Time* maps out a landscape of ashes surrounded with barbed wire. V.I. is in prison, while Kinsey is straining to break out. Her office is too small, her job is too small, and she is too small. In some ways, Grafton even suggests that the book is too small for the character. Using images from creation myths, Grafton has taken some innovative steps to deal with these constraints. Her most recent book builds a vibrant fictional world filled with images of rejuvenation and creation. Grafton's *"P" Is for Peril* places Kinsey Millhone in a fertile world of constant growth.

Backtracking a few letters before P shows Grafton treading a similar territory as Paretsky. Kinsey's searches involve family members. Inevitably, Kinsey identifies with the deceased. The case presents itself as an attempt of Kinsey to find herself a family.

In the same way that Vic merges her identity with Nicola Aguinaldo, *"K" Is for Killer* (1994) shows us Kinsey as victim-daughter. To determine who murdered Lorna Kepler, the detective traces the girl's steps, learns her habits, befriends the same people. Eventually, Kinsey discovers that Lorna was a respectable girl during the day, and a hooker by night. Events whirl upward forcing Kinsey to take an unexpected step. The interesting twist here is that along with becoming the deceased, Kinsey also identifies with the murderer. "K" stands for "Kinsey." In the end, Kinsey poses a question: "Having strayed into the shadows, can I find my way back?" (K 292).

In *"G" Is for Grafton*, the authors note that Grafton has previously used mythology to construct her works. In writing *"K" Is for Killer*, Grafton explored the mythological underworld. Grafton specifically wanted to associate her work with motifs from Jungian psychology. She was consciously applying some of these ideas to her fiction. "Because Grafton was also reading Joseph Campbell at the time, the novel reflects its author's growing interest in Jungian psychology and Greek myths" (Kaufman and Kay 308). Many themes of renewal through water find their way into this novel.

"L" Is for Lawless (1995) continues Jungian themes illustrating a search for a family. The centerpiece of this book features Kinsey on a road trip with

7. V.I. and Kinsey

amiable ex-con bank robber Ray Rawson and his very pregnant daughter, Laura Huckaby. In the car's backseat, Kinsey and Laura quarrel like jealous siblings on the cross-country trip. Ray never actually says "Don't make me come back there," but he very well could. Kinsey tries to behave, "especially for an honorary father who smelled as good as he did" (L 209).

Even though the three are essentially "on the lam," Ray takes time to point out sites of interest on the Kentucky/Tennessee border, Nolan River Lake and Mammoth Cave National Park. He regales his passengers with an unlikely comment, "That's another thing about Mammoth Cave. It smells like moss and wet rocks. Doesn't smell like sweat and testosterone. It smells like life before birth ... what's the word, primordial" (L 211). Eventually, they meet up with Ray's mother Helen.

Ray's remark about the cave is definitely out of character, but it shows Grafton's continuing experimentation with gender-related archetypes. Searches for locks and keys are important at the beginning and the end of the plot. With the story bookended by obvious Freudian symbols, the overall effect is somewhat less than successful. Still, *L* shows us a caper on one level and a mythic search for family on another.

The Epilogue provides a wedding picture of the nuptials between William and Rosie. Kinsey is lost in thought. "I stood there, thinking about Ray and Laura and Helen, wondering where they'd gone. I know it's absurd, but I found it painful they hadn't cared enough to stick around and see that I was okay. In some curious way, they'd become my family" (L 290).

The three books after *"L"* are variations on Freudian themes. The motifs are mixed and wandering. Is Grafton, like Kinsey, lost in the shadows?

"O" Is for Outlaw (1999) has a "stuck in time" feeling to it. In the opening scene, Kinsey pulls a unique breaking and entering job. Clad in overalls, she enters a home through a dog door. Unfortunately, the dog is still there, guarding the premises. She talks to him: "Listen, I hope you don't mind if I slide on in, because any minute your neighbor is going to look out the window and catch sight of my hineybumper hanging out the doggie door" (O 21). To keep the snarling beast at bay, Kinsey has to search the house on her hands and knees. "In my romper, I traversed the dining room" (O 22). It's as if she has returned to childhood, with the miniature door representing an incomplete rite of passage.

In a sense the entire book echoes this scene of Kinsey trapped in a passageway. Ostensibly the plot is about Kinsey's first marriage. New information about her then-husband prompts her to turn back the clock. Since Kinsey is forever in her mid-thirties, her history as a young woman is confusing. Anachronisms interfere with any themes of illusion versus reality, or "if I knew then what I know now" that Grafton might be after.

Compared to the other books, which appeared annually, *"P" Is for Peril* took longer to arrive, but it was worth the wait. Grafton presents an intriguing mystery for the perceptive reader eager to answer two questions: Where is Dow Purcell and where is Kinsey Millhone?

Compared to V.I.'s journey filled with terrors, Kinsey's vital imagination enables her to transcend most of the ugliness surrounding her. Grafton has refashioned the detective by giving her a power to affect events and an open-ended radiance.

The narrative begins straightforwardly. Kinsey is called in on a missing person's case. Dow Purcell has disappeared, and for the police, the trail has run cold. Dow's ex-wife Fiona hires Kinsey to heat up the search.

Kinsey feels uneasy with the rigid Fiona, who comes across as a Joan Crawford clone: "Her hair was dyed a dark brown, parted on one side, with puffy bags and clusters of artificially constructed curls pulled away from her face and secured with rhinestone combs" (5). In addition to a "Mommy Dearest" image, Fiona is associated with cloying or unpleasant odors, perfume, cigarettes, deodorant cream. To Kinsey, she smells of the past.

By contrast, Dow's current, younger spouse is rooted in the present. She is a former stripper but hardly a ditsy trophy wife. Crystal is balanced and in charge. She has her hands full with two children. One is a new baby with Dow. She also does daily battle with Leila, a rebellious teenaged daughter from her previous marriage to Lloyd. Crystal refuses to be intimidated by life, however. She has household help for the baby, a man who drifts in and out of the household to whisk the baby away during inconvenient moments. She also has help with Leila from Leila's school counselor, Anica. Crystal handles her awkward domestic situation with aplomb.

While tracking Dow Purcell, Kinsey feels restless in her current office. The space at Lonnie Kingman's has worked out so far, but Kingman probably intends to take over more space in the building. Kinsey also finds the other workers annoying, women she characterizes as Cinderella with her "spiteful stepsisters" (22). For a new office, Kinsey just needs room for a desk and a "tasteful executive potty" (20).

With help from landlord Henry, she answers an ad for a seemingly ideal space. She eagerly checks it out. Tommy, the brother of the landlord, is on the premises laying carpet. He asks impertinent questions about her dating situation and wonders if she likes her men "way too young for you or way too old" (65). She is put off but finds him attractive. She places a deposit on the office and feels a "sense of new beginnings" (129). Her enthusiasm is short-lived.

A very strange aspect to the plot is Kinsey's relationship with old folks. In the past, her landlord Henry, William, and countless other senior citizens have served a nurturing function. "Kinsey enthusiastically enjoys seniors who live their lives with gusto" (Kaufman and Kay 244). Here they let her down.

Their parts in the investigation fail miserably. At the nursing home, Kinsey buys Ruby, a lively resident, a hamburger, and asks her to keep a lookout. The episode ends with Kinsey's regret: "This was the last time I'd ask Ruby to man the lookout post" (258). When Tommy Hevener comes after Kinsey, Henry fends him off. However, the old gent makes the misstep of going against Kinsey's wishes by continuing the jewelry store fencing scam (238–43).

Later, problems with Tommy and his angry brother Richard cause her some anxious moments. The situation plunges her into financial and emotional peril. She has to cancel the rental deal, but not without some identity switches involving a gray-haired private investigator named Mariah.

With her usual persistence, Kinsey eventually clears up the mystery of Dow's disappearance. However, in many ways, the narrative presents knotty problems. Why is Kinsey so passive? How do those warring brothers tie into the plot? What's up with Mariah? What about that ending?

Grafton once said at a private-eye writers' convention that a fan had given her a terrific recommendation for a title: *"M" Is for Missing* (June, 1995, Milwaukee). Skip *M* and move to *O*, the fan suggested. She said that she was tempted. In *"P" Is for Peril*, it appears that Grafton has given in to the temptation. Someone is indeed missing — Kinsey.

Through all the meetings with clients and descriptions of house renovation, Kinsey is curiously absent. Crystal comes across as a more fully energized character. Far from being the tough talking, wise-cracking babe of previous books, Kinsey gathers the facts of the case with terse questions. "How so?" or "Why is that?" or "Because?" are typical.

She shows little of her old wit. During a fight between Crystal and Leila, for a few pages Kinsey does not talk at all (50–52). She also stays silent as Henry and William wrangle over items in the newspaper (57–58). Kinsey has never been chatty, but she is taciturn, even for her. The too-small office has cramped her language. She finds no room for conversational space.

Some commentators have seen Kinsey's speech as a weapon in her investigations. Scott Christianson calls Kinsey's patterns of speech strong evidence of a "gender-busting" feminism. Her conversation can lapse at any time into cursing or "talkin' trash." Basically, Kinsey proves a woman can curse like a man (Christianson 127–42).

That may have been true in the novels written up to 1995, but at the end of the twentieth century, Kinsey has changed. Her silence means that she sits back and lets the witnesses talk. Through most of the investigation, she seems almost to whisper. She makes one comment that vaguely recaptures her old spirit. When Crystal is angry at Fiona, Kinsey says, "Hey, babe ... if you're pissed off, take it up with her" (P 321). The comment blurts out like a sour note.

Many signs point to the absence of the old Kinsey. She parks where Dow had been that last night (141). Tommy asks, "Where'd you disappear to?" (146). We might at first ascribe a child's lightness of heart to her comment "I felt like skipping" (124). In light of other evidence, we cannot be sure.

Kinsey is drifty and moony. What is the reader to make of her frequent daydreams about childhood? She looks back wistfully at her time with Aunt Gin: munching on childhood "sammiches," skipping, fearing a booster shot, taking a nap in "kinnygarden," feeling abandoned at elementary school, having water in her ear, losing her teddy bear. A few anecdotes would be of interest, but here we have more than we care to know. She is stuck in time. This novel is set in 1986. She makes myriad references to herself as a child. Many events remind her of herself as a child. She goes back to get in touch with that self, because she doesn't have a self here. That Kinsey has only limited memories of her life is one of the perils of a series character. Even so, all the time of Kinsey's life post-adolescence would seem to be off-limits because these are stories told in previous books.

At the nursing home, Kinsey shows her P.I. license to obtain some records. "Merry squinted at my license, holding up the postage stamp-sized photo for comparison with my face-sized face" (74). In a sense, the adult woman's flashbacks to childhood dramatize this duality of Little Kinsey/Big Kinsey.

Another puzzle in the narrative has to do with that "potty." Along with Leopold Bloom, Kinsey Millhone is one of the few fictional characters to take a bathroom break. In fact, in this book, she takes several. It seems a part of her investigative technique: When in doubt, visit the bathroom. Perhaps Grafton is playing a joke, a little word game to hint what *P* actually stands for. This wordplay comes up in another way. When Kinsey places the baby Quentin in his playpen the child picks up a building block. He "banged the letter *P* against the plastic padding under him" (92).

The subplot with Tommy and Richard causes the narrative to take an abrupt swerve. To reveal their past, Grafton has to dig deep into a backstory that is never very clear. Mariah Talbot, who is investigating them, drifts in and out of the novel like a shade. She is identified mostly through her gray hair and wigs. Even Kinsey almost misses seeing her. "Unless you saw past the façade to the elegant bones of her face, she appeared frumpy and drab, not someone you'd notice in a crowd this size" (234). The denouement of this part of the plot involves name switches, deceptions, and mistaken identities. It is a loose end hastily tied up.

Kinsey makes several mistakes in this seemingly incidental narrative. She shows very bad judgment in being attracted to Tommy. Her initial attempt at romance starts with some sparks, but the potential affair is a disaster. "Jerk" is the operative word. Before they go out for their date, she thinks "With luck, he'd turn out to be a jerk ..." (130). Later as they meet, he tells her across the table, "You don't have to be a jerk. Lighten up" (147). Events spiral upward. She responds to his voice message on her machine. "I pressed Erase, wishing I could do the same with him" (233).

Along with the disaster caused by the brothers, Kinsey fails to piece together obvious clues or recognize obvious disguises. She is far from being the crackerjack investigator her years of experience warrant. Is this a more "human" dimension to Kinsey? Is she is more appealing and vulnerable when she makes mistakes?

Yet one more section of the book is anomalous compared to all other Millhone cases. *"P" Is for Peril* lacks an Epilogue. We have no last word framing Kinsey's case. Why? The answer to this and the other questions posed by the narrative may lie in Grafton's concept of the artist and artistic creation.

The many disparate sections of the narrative make sense when we place them across a very large canvas showing the universe being created. Landscape and weather, for instance, are more than atmospheric background. Kinsey surveys her domain from above. "Brunswick Lake fills the bottom of a geological bowl" (1). Land, sea, and clouds constitute the rest of the view, as Kinsey scans "the broad shimmering band of the Pacific Ocean stitched onto the shoreline" (2). This scene shows one of the few times the sky is clear. Dark clouds rush in, and rain pelts nearly every chapter. Precipitation intrudes onto the action as a force to be reckoned with: "The rain had picked up from the early morning lull and now pounded on my car roof with the staccato rattle of falling nails" (71).

At times, the weather serves as an ambiguous cloud from which the world eventually takes shape. There is no line between earth and sky. The rain clouds tear down. The setting is primeval, the earth before humanity, shapeless. At one point after the rain, a miniature world appears:

> The streets seemed to smoke, vapor rising in drifts. The sidewalks were still wet, water dripping from tree limbs as silently as snow. The gutters gurgled merrily, miniature rivers diverted by debris as the runoff traveled downstream into sewers to the sea. A fog began to accumulate, making the world seem hushed and dense [217–18].

Kinsey dwells in an amorphous, shifting universe. Grafton re-creates a natural world similar to that in cosmology myths or stories told about the origins of the world. One very common story relates to the idea of the Cosmic Egg.

We all know the nursery rhyme "Humpty Dumpty," with its essentially tragic outcome. It dwells on the limited powers of "all the king's horses and all the king's men." Humpty is in ruins. But imagine a story in which all the pieces of Humpty Dumpty *are* all the horses and men.

The myth of the Cosmic Egg is the obverse of "Humpty Dumpty." It is the "life principle ... undifferentiated totality" (Cooper 60). The beginning before time is represented by a sphere. The egg explodes and from the pieces all creation begins. The cosmologists' Big Bang theory on origins of the universe emphasizes this story. In some ways the Big Bang theory is the Cosmic Egg with numbers.

In Hindu cosmology, the *Rig Veda* emphasizes that in the time before humankind, there is neither land nor sea, neither day nor night (Bierling 37). Sky and earth are undifferentiated because this is a time before time, a realm before space. This is mythic time when humanity and gods were one.

The cosmic egg comes before the existence of Father Sky and Mother Earth. It takes a mighty force to tear them apart. "In most myths, it is a woman who accomplishes the great task" (Dundes 189). The earth is bigger than the sky and from the force of the Goddess, it contracts to create mountains and oceans.

In numerous images and motifs throughout the novel, Grafton re-styles Kinsey as a Creator Goddess. Kinsey is a variant of Joyce's Anna Livia Plurabelle, from *Finnegans Wake*, bringer of pluralities. Her figure is the one against which all other women are measured. The Goddess uses her powers of vision to break the universe wide open, releasing forces of destruction and creation at once. Kinsey is, in many ways, an archetype of the Goddess as Artist.

Even the name "Kinsey Millhone" signifies pure creation. Grafton tells how she picked her character's first name out of a newspaper birth announcement. She liked its androgynous quality and because it sounded "vaguely Southern" (Kaufman and Kay 277). A free association on the first name leads easily to "Kinsey Report," sexuality approached through rationality. Grafton settled on "Mill-hone," again, almost randomly: "Looking for a strong surname with a double or triple cadence, she researched the telephone directory until she found 'Millhone'" (277). Kinsey's last name likewise connotes creativity. It suggests the process of crafting raw material into shape. One mills wood and hones steel. We do not have to stretch too far to see a connection between this detective and a regenerating, creative artistry.

The Goddess is the source of all creativity. She is neither land nor sky but the force that separates and shapes them. She transcends time and culture, with its demands for money. She is neither old nor young. She is neither man nor woman.

The goddess is beyond space. Although Kinsey is tempted to leave the space of Lonnie Kingman or "King-man" and enter yet another space defined by the Hefeners, she drops the new rental. Space has never been all that important to her. Through all her daydreams, she defines space through her imagination.

The Goddess is beyond time. Kinsey first came to the reading public as the very image of a contemporary woman. Now she is trapped in a time warp. This *P* book is set, we learn early on, three years after she had moved from California Fidelity. Kinsey stays in 1986 (P 20). She is both young and old. She experiences youth through her numerous flashbacks and listens to William and Henry glooming over newspaper obituaries. "We all have to die of something," she hears them say (58).

Two concepts of time accompany her trip to the nursing home. "There was also a big clock with a clicking second hand I could hear from fifteen feet away." The other view comes across in capital letters. "One pillow had a saying embroidered across the face—YOU'RE ONLY AS OLD AS YOU FEEL" (73).

Despite the efforts of many commentators to promote the concept of goddess as a feminist cause, the Goddess as Creative Force is neither man nor woman. In the novel, Grafton sets up a symbology that is balanced between genders.

Two gender-connected creation myths show up in the book. One associated with masculine traits and the world of Dow, the missing man, concerns the so-called "Earth Diver" myth. As a balance to the Earth Diver are variations on the Mother archetype, which are explicitly feminine myths.

Anthropologist Elias Kongas has studied the Earth Diver myth extensively. It has widespread distribution among North American Indians. "A succession of animals dive into the primeval water, or flood of waters, to secure bits of mud or sand from which the earth is to be formed" (Kongas 334). In some stories, the hero himself is the Earth Diver, going down and coming up, over and over, bringing up mud to create land. American folklorist Alan Dundes calls the story of Noah and the flood an earth diver myth (Dundes 279). Noah's act of "creation" by collecting the animals minimizes the role of women in populating the work. Instead, the world thrives due to collecting and herding.

"P" Is for Peril includes several characters related to the meaning of this Earth Diver myth. One is Crystal's son Jordie, an infant who drowned (208). This is an odd episode, because Crystal mentions this traumatic event almost in passing. She seems particularly unconcerned about it, noting that the drowning had upset Leila more than herself. On one level, her apparent diffidence could explain later events; on another, Jordie is only the first of a series of earth divers.

Another one is Quentin, the screaming infant, who wields the *P* building block. When Kinsey tries to pick him up, he gives her a hard time: "He curled his body inward while he gathered his strength. Without warning, he flung himself outward like a diver in the midst of a back flip. He might have torn himself entirely out of my grasp if I hadn't grabbed him and swung him up from the floor" (92).

Dow, of course, is the most representative earth diver figure. What better name for the universe of compiling and hoarding property? From the beginning, Fiona speaks of Dow's waning potency and how in bed he "began to falter" (12–13). Dow took a downturn.

The results of Dow's ill-gotten gains, the money, are missing through most of the book, but from Kinsey's investigation, she assumes that Leila, forger of Dow's signature, now holds the key to her stepfather's collection. Found deep in the mud, his watch still ticking, Dow represents a civilized, though earth-founded life.

Tommy and Richard also belong to this universe of compulsive collecting. As feuding brothers, they are Cain and Abel. The spirit of greed divides the Earth Diver, and they appear in the Twin cycle of hero myths among the Winnebagos and other mythologies. The Twins complement each other: "One of them, Flesh, is acquiescent, mild, and without initiative; the other, Stump, is dynamic and rebellious ... they eventually sicken from their own abuse of power" (Henderson 113–14).

Throughout the book, Grafton is careful to distinguish Tommy and Richard through these opposite traits. Given how the two end up, their stories mirror the Earth Diver/Twin motif quite accurately.

Where does Kinsey fit into this pattern? Despite her forays into a masculine-dominated profession, her character has not taken on the shape of masculine myths. She keeps meticulous financial records, but after Dow is found, she seems above economic concerns. She is curious on the whereabouts of his missing thirty grand, and will stick with the case. "Not everything in this business is about the bucks" (260).

Dow Purcell, the father, the patriarchy, is dead and Kinsey is among the mourners. Unlike V. I. Warshawski, who can never bury the dead, Kinsey attends Dow's funeral, but she stays in a child's mindset. Her thoughts hover above the memorial service. She thinks back to the time she scandalized her Sunday-school teacher by reciting the "doctrine of conception according to Aunt Gin" (287–88). She is there at the funeral, but she dwells among thoughts of being a child thinking of a pre-natal self. Crystal holds a gathering after the funeral at her beach house. Kinsey "found a perch on the stairs, three steps down from the top, the perfect vantage point from which to view the gathering" (293). She sits there like a child watching a parents' adult party.

Neither is Kinsey's role synonymous with the Great Mother or Mother Earth. She is not like Goldy Bear. Kinsey is beyond images of woman as nurturer or provider of grains. She barely eats as an adult. She returns home to a refrigerator filled with fast food condiment packets and fuzzy vegetables. "A clever home economist could have whipped up a nourishing dish out of just such ingredients, but I confess I was stumped" (233) As a child, outside her body in her daydreams, she is ravenous while devouring tomato soup or snacks prepared by Aunt Gin. Kinsey is all appetite here. She is intake and excretion. We even hear about when her body responds to Tommy on their "date" (150). But of course they do not have a relationship.

As is well established in previous books, Kinsey and babies do not mix. She shares a scene with Crystal's baby, Griff. While Kinsey is captured by his appearance as a golden child, his language leaves her cold. She bids him "night-night," which she finds depressing. "This was worse than talking to a dog because at least there you really didn't anticipate a high-pitched voice in response. I wondered if we were going to conduct the rest of the conversation talking like Elmer Fudd" (54–55). To her, the child represents not growth and potential, but a throwback to animals and a deterioration of language.

Kinsey has another bad moment with Fiona's grandson, Quentin, the squirming earth diver. Fiona's fecund daughter Blanche must rush to another child's emergency outdoors. She leaves the toddler in Kinsey's care. Without his mother, the child is all set to scream, as they say, bloody murder. Kinsey's attempts to calm him are less than a success: "I tried jiggling him as she had, but that only made matters worse. Now I was not only a monster, but a Monster Baby Jiggler, intent on shaking him to death" (92).

Feminist critics admitted to being a bit "distressed" when in a 1989 interview Grafton essentially disowned some of her previous statements embracing feminism: "To me, writing is not about gender…. So what I prefer to do is to operate out of my own system…" (Walton 112).

Grafton's comment shows that the artist archetype is consistent with her own concept for her character. Grafton the author has readily shared that Kinsey is her alter-ego (Kaufman and Kay 276). Since creating is a significant part of Grafton's life, those same qualities are likely to find their way into Kinsey.

As part of Kinsey's job, she has to mediate between Fiona and Crystal, but that relationship works on a symbolic or iconic level as well. Windows appear in the narrative as a repeated motif. Kinsey first sees Fiona "through one of the two glass panels that flanked the door" (4). When she interviews Crystal, Kinsey again has a striking view. She sees Dow's younger wife through a skylight-style window in the ceiling lending a view upstairs through the floor. She watches Crystal "parade naked across my line of view" (42).

The three-part image of door and two windows at Fiona's sets out a kind of triptych, with Fiona on one side and Crystal on the other. As the source of all creation, Kinsey takes her place in the doorway. She is in the center, between the Dark Mother Fiona and the White Goddess Crystal.

Kinsey is beyond either of these traditionally feminine figures from myth, the crone or the virgin. Incorporating qualities of both man and woman, Kinsey represents the middle figure, "a fully matured" character, who understands all elements of humanity and "can bring any one of them into play at any time" (Pratt 370). Kinsey's own window on the world is an adjustable skylight. She can see out, but others cannot see in. She is a "private eye" in more than one sense.

A key function of the artist is to create anew, to bring visible and invisible together. Similarly, Kinsey demonstrates a powerful vision. Her sharp-eyed observation at first with the naked eye, then through the telescope answers the question about Dow's disappearance (199–201). She is all-seeing. Eventually she experiences a perfect moment of perception about the situation that prompted Dow's murder. In the book's closing pages, she has a revelation: "I suddenly understood what I'd been looking at all along" (352).

The process of transferring a self to the page is much more complex than relating autobiographical anecdotes. On the surface, most authors' lives are quite undramatic. This is not surprising since they spend so much of their lives wrestling with words, not people. To incorporate the concept of creative artistry to fiction, the androgynous artist figure is the most effective. These figures must stay free of human attachments to keep observation skills sharp. They understand all people. Tiresias in Greek mythology or Kokopelli in Native American myths are but two examples. Grafton shows us this same concept through Kinsey.

This private detective transcends gender. Just as Grafton is artist creator, so all the characters have no meaning except in relation to Kinsey's narrative of the case. All that she relates comes from a perspective behind the eye or 'I.' Monique Wittig discusses the significance of "I" in the creation of narrative:

> For when one becomes a locator, when one says 'I', and in so doing reappropriates language as a whole, proceeding from oneself alone, with the tremendous power to use all language, it is then and there, according to linguists and philosophers, that the supreme act of subjectivity, the advent of subjectivity into consciousness, occurs ... ungendered, universal, whole [80].

From Kinsey's "eye" and her story told from the "I" point of view come all characters, the earth diver men and the women representing a spectrum of types. There are the middle-aged horrors Fiona and Mariah, the California valley girls unreliable in the work place, such as Jennifer at Kingman's and Tiffany, head of her own "department" at the postal office (280). There are Crystal and Leila, Anica and Paulie, struggling to cope in proscribed roles. These women are all sources of information for Kinsey, but Kinsey the artist is a source for them. If she identifies with any of them, it is Leila. "I used to be just like you when I was your age" (194). Leila, whose whole life is geared toward rebellion and escape, is Kinsey's metaphoric daughter.

Grafton is working with a myth of all creation coming out of the body

7. V.I. and Kinsey 155

of the Goddess. We have ample, if fact more than ample, evidence of Kinsey's body, bodily functions, bodily needs. Her midnight excursion to the nursing home to retrieve proof of fraud provides a prime demonstration.

Because the Goddess precedes creation, she must create herself. At the nursing home, Kinsey is trapped under a desk while a night charge nurse and an unidentified member of the nursing home board engage in oral sex. Kinsey closes her eyes, "like a kid" (256). This entire sequence is set up so that Kinsey is in an almost pre-natal position, umbilical cord and all.

> I crossed to Merry's workstation, pulled out her rolling chair, and crawled into the kneehole space under her desk. I found myself sitting on a tangle of fat power cords, my head angled unnaturally to keep it from banging into the underside of Merry's pencil drawer.... They were about to play doctor and I was going to be stuck in the examining room! (255–56).

At first, Kinsey is horrified to be in the voyeur's position here, but eventually she imaginatively gets into the act. By the time the couple is finished, Kinsey has conceptualized her way into a *ménage a trois*. She has managed to make herself both conceived and conceiver. "All three of us fell back exhausted and I prayed we wouldn't have to pause for a post-coital smoke" (258).

In the myth of Adam and Eve, an already created part of the universe, that is, dust leads to human creation. However, in many other mythologies of the world, the universe is created from parts of the creator's body (Dundes 179–80). Other creation motifs present a world formed through struggle and robbery. The creator "shapes the world and gives it its character by Theft and Robbery of the sun, fire, or water" (Dundes 177–78). Another creation story from South Africa tells of the goddess splaying ashes from a wood fire across the sky to form the Milky Way (Ragan 359).

To prepare for her surreptitious mission, Kinsey carries a "flat flashlight the size of a playing card that fit[s] neatly in my bra" (248). She finds the records she needs and thinks about stealing them, but ends up making copies. She must leave the files intact for police evidence later. The light from the copy machine could give her away, so she presses herself against the machine. A bad thought chases across her mind. "I worried I was being permanently sterilized" (256).

She finishes the task in short order. "I straightened the stack of copies and slid those, still warm, back in my underpants" (256). The files themselves are documents about a dead person. She gives new heat to these paper corpses, creating a new order. As she draws closer to advance the case, light comes from between Kinsey's breasts and numbers and dollar figures come from her midsection. In the manner of myth, she uses her body to create.

Even more telling about this nursing home episode are the numerous metaphors about art, writing in particular. As Kinsey hunts frantically for the correct file, she bemoans the lack of a clear line through the piles of folders. She may reflect Grafton's own thoughts by saying she had hoped that the answer would lie in "an organizing principle as basic as A, B, C" (253). Her hope, of course, turns out to be false.

Kinsey pressing herself across the copier in the nursing home could be construed as an image of Grafton the writer. Kinsey suffers the perils of making copies of non-alphabetized files. Surely this is a deft metaphor for Grafton's own pressures about the reading public's expectations for an alphabet-based series. Also, in sticking with a series character for so long, what writer would not worry about repeating herself, producing "sterile" work as if from a copy machine?

Case-solving is to Kinsey as writing is to Grafton. From as far back as *A*, Kinsey's activity as an investigator paralleled the writer's craft. At various points in the case, she would write notes on index cards, tape them onto a bulletin board, and try to "sketch the story" (*"A" Is for Alibi* 221).

In several asides, Grafton casts Kinsey's investigative plans as metaphors of writing. Starting work on the case, Kinsey makes a "deeply symbolic doodle" while playing solitaire. She says, "It's not as though I didn't have a ton of other work to do, but I found myself distracted by the information circulating through my brain" (22).

Kinsey also perceives the problems of language's multi-layered meanings. She notes that in her line of work, "What looks good on the surface usually turns out to be crap underneath" (42). Another image refers to the inadequacy of language in capturing experience. In a passage describing the weather, the rain stops, leaving only fog. "Depths were flattened to two dimensions, bare branches no more than ink lines bleeding onto a page" (217–18).

"P" Is for Peril stands out in another striking way. This is the only book in the series from *A* to *O* that lacks an epilogue. No "last word" for Kinsey's written report. Because every book from Grafton links letters with concepts, the title "letter" refers to the narrative. The epilogue pressed the idea that the book we were reading was Kinsey's report of the case. The book's message on this abstract level was always something like this: The narrative starts with "O," refers to "O" throughout, with "O" sometimes pointing out a clue, then ends with the epilogue "respectfully submitted by Kinsey Millhone."

Up until now, the letter title emphasized, in post-modernist style, the self-referential nature of Kinsey's story. For *Peril*, however, the case begins with Kinsey being hired and ends when she turns over her final case report to Fiona. What are we to make of the remainder of the book? Grafton breaks with her own practice of seeing the book as synonymous with the case.

Throughout the series, Grafton has been inventive with Kinsey. The alphabet themes were new on the publishing scene when she started, but they have been constraining, too. Near the end of the book, Kinsey tracks down a clue involving house decoration. One ad catches her eye: "DON'T PAINT YOURSELF INTO A CORNER WHEN YOU CAN LET US DO IT. CHARLIE CORNER & SONS, PAINTING" (P 343).

The pressures of formula continue, yet Grafton explores new ways to keep the series fresh. With *Peril,* she has painted her way out of her own conventions. Instead, she has refashioned Kinsey into detective as artist in a mythic context.

Through this analogy, we may also find a clue on how to solve the puzzle of the missing epilogue. We can discuss the ending obliquely without giving away specifics of "whodunit."

As if we knew what those specifics were. In some ways, the closing raises more questions than it answers. In the half light beside the ocean, just past a landscape sharp with gravel, the characters gather. "We sat in the dark, just the three of us, sipping wine and chatting, listening to the surf rumble on the beach until Jonah arrived" (352).

Paretsky's *Hard Time* closes with V. I. taking but a pinched measure of comfort in solving the case. This ending, like the rest of the Grafton's book, carries a certain grandeur. Set against the ocean, the scene is open-ended.

The book's final scene is almost a Rorschach inkblot asking for the reader's interpretation. It invites us to join Kinsey in being a creator. Our realization of the last scene's meaning is simultaneous with hers. When Kinsey's "I" becomes "we," our perspective changes. The camera pulls back, and we cannot hear their conversation. We have an image of the three of them, there by the ocean, waiting.

Is this a fade out? Or a beginning scene for *Q*? The scene launches us both backward and forward with a Janus-like vision. *Peril* conflates *Perish* and *Purcell.* Is the title a clue? When all is said and done, what is in peril? The ending entices us by failing to say out loud what did, will, or should happen.

The missing Epilogue is yet one more example of how this series is a portrait in process. The book spills over from previously set outlines. Grafton bursts from not only her own conventions, but those of the women's private eye formula. The series has reached a point where the mystery story has changed its form. "Life streams upward from shapeless subjectivity into formative dream" (Spender 108). This book falls short of being poetry. Still, its emphasis on the myth-making imagination lends the narrative a poetic quality of truth that rises above convention.

After almost two decades of writing women's detective fiction, Paretsky and Grafton have created characters representing two ends of a spectrum. V. I. looks outward to fight wrongdoing in a public arena; Kinsey gazes inward to imagination. The work of both authors provides a ringing testimony to the vitality and inventiveness of women's detective fiction.

Though a good art work is bounded and unified, it also has these properties of transcending its boundaries, interacting with the consciousness of the viewer or audience, and overcoming the sense of distance. In this respect, art is also analogous to a living organism [Rothenberg 368].

The poetic imagination "does not invent myths, it experiences them" (Jung and Kerényi 73). As diverse as their visions have become, both Paretsky and Grafton show the artistry to select enduring myths to shape their detectives' experiences.

CHAPTER 8

LIFE RESTORED

The bloodstains have been washed, and the yellow tape rolled up from around the crime scene. Not only has evidence of death been whisked from the sight of the living, but the sleuth has nabbed the murderer and official measures to punish the guilty are underway. Lawyers have read the will without anyone fainting, and the estate of the deceased was parceled out. Now that the death rift in the human community has closed, at least for now, what lessons does women's detective fiction provide for readers and critics?

We cannot yet stamp "solved" on the file labeled "Women's Detective Fiction." You know what they say in the other departments, that the real causes for so many mysteries are rising crime rates and all the bad people out there. We need these sleuths and detectives to maintain law and order. They say that we might be off on a wild goose chase thinking that this detective fiction is an inside job. They say that throwing myth and ritual into the case maybe has thrown us off the scent, and that correlations to ancient stories and fairy tales only add up to circumstantial evidence. But as investigators know, the tiniest trace evidence has blown a case wide open more than once. Women's detective fiction may get off easy, with a charge of being "entertaining, escapist fare." Or it may be seriously implicated in the first-degree life and death matters at the heart of our investigation. In *The Triumph of Narrative*, Robert Fulford writes, "We know there is no such thing as 'just a story'" (Fulford 66).

Clues have begun to pile up almost as fast as bodies.

Edgar Allan Poe first tipped us off to this avenue of inquiry. The ongoing case covers more territory than even he imagined. If mystery writers "didn't see anything" during the murders and violence of ancient myths, why do they know so much about them? Are these writers just out for a breath of fresh air? We don't believe it. Do they think we were born yesterday? In 1957, Jung said, "We think that we are able to be born today and live in no myth, without history. That's a disease — absolutely abnormal — because man is not born everyday" (Berger and Segaller 147). These mystery writers know more than they are telling.

Perhaps we are only looking at the usual suspects. But we have grilled domestic mysteries, forensics, ecclesiastical sleuths, career thrillers, and private investigators. Their statements differ in the particulars, but basically, they all tell the same story. Detective fiction is involved in serious human experience up to its neck.

Mystery subgenres have all come out with important clues to the case. Under pressure, the suspects have squealed. They have let loose with dark tales of the psyche, the high costs of life restoration, and of learning to read valuable maps to clues about the crime. In some ways, these suspects are innocent; in others they know much more than they let on. The nuns, priest, and poet have tried to play us for time. We have them in a separate cell, but they are really no different from the rest of us. What about detectives climbing into caves or roaming around the mean streets of cyberspace? Are they just trying to chase down crime wherever they find it? Or is there something else that is "Most Wanted"? Are they looking to "touch anew that still point in this turning world" (Campbell, *Creative Mythology* 94)?

Those two experienced PIs told different versions of their roles in the case. Is it better to push back death through social reform or air it out with creativity? Shouldn't they get their stories straight? The suspense is killing us. Our investigation has uncovered many lies. Most importantly, we have heard our informants say the truth.

More suspects are out there to be rounded up in all these pages. Reporters have more to tell us. So do booksellers and librarians. Medical thrillers and police procedurals need to come clean about the seriousness of their themes. And we have not even begun to talk to the animals. Why do we keep running across them in this investigation? There are no coincidences. If this literary investigation opens additional inquiries, it has done its job.

The crime wave is not over. The tide of mysteries flooding the market is not likely to ebb any time soon:

> For the art of our time inclines toward a radical spiritualism, a solemnization of the secret transpersonal and suprapersonal forces of life and death, which surge up from within to compensate for the materialism dominating the outward picture of our times [Neumann 33].

8. Life Restored

Which is a fancy way of saying that mysteries are big business, but we like them because they are not about big business; they are about serious business. This is a heavy charge, but that's our story, and we'll stick with it.

For now, the weight of suspicion has settled upon two definite culprits. We like myth and ritual for this one. They know the truth in this case, and they have more to say. Let's listen.

Works Cited

Barnes, Linda. *Hardware*. New York: Delacorte Press, 1995.
Barr, Nevada. *Blind Descent*. New York: G. P. Putnam's Sons, 1998.
_____. *Blood Lure*. New York: G. P. Putnam's Sons, 2001.
_____. *Deep South*. New York: Berkley Books, 2001.
_____. *Liberty Falling*. New York: G. P. Putnam's Sons, 1999.
Berger, Merrill, and Stephen Segaller, eds. *The World of C. G. Jung: The Wisdom and the Dream*. New York: TV Books, 2000.
Bettelheim, Bruno. *The Uses of Enchantment: The Meaning and Importance of Fairy Tales*. New York: Vintage Books, 1989.
Bierlein, J. F. *Parallel Myths*. New York: Ballantine Publishing Group, 1994.
Blake, Michelle. *The Tentmaker*. New York: Berkley Prime Crime, 2000.
Bodkin, Maud. "Archetypal Patterns in Tragic Poetry." *Myths and Motifs in Literature*. Eds. David J. Burrows, Frederick R. Lapides, and John T. Shawcross. New York: The Free Press, 1973. 4–21.
Buchanan, Edna. *Contents Under Pressure*. New York: Avon Books, 1992.
Bulfinch, Thomas. *Bulfinch's Mythology: A Modern Abridgment by Edmund Fuller*. New York: Dell Publishing, 1959.
Campbell, Joseph. *Creative Mythology: The Masks of God*. New York: Penguin Books, 1968.
_____. *The Hero with a Thousand Faces*. 2nd ed. Princeton: Princeton UP, 1968.
_____. *Transformations of Myth Through Time*. New York: Harper Perennial, 1999.
Campbell, Joseph, with Bill Moyers. *The Power of Myth*. New York: Doubleday, 1988.
Carroll, Noel. *The Philosophy of Horror or Paradoxes of the Heart*. New York: Routledge, 1990.

Works Cited

Cassirer, Ernst. *Language and Myth*. Trans. Suzanne K. Langer. New York: Dover, 1946.

Cawelti, John G. *Adventure, Mystery, and Romance*. Chicago: University of Chicago Press, 1977.

Chernin, Kim. "The Underside of the Mother-Daughter Relationship." *Meeting the Shadow: The Hidden Power of the Dark Side of Human Nature*. Ed. Connie Zweig and Jeremiah Abrams. New York: Jeremy P. Tarcher/Putnam, 1991. 54–58.

Christianson, Scott. "Talkin' Trash and Kickin' Butt: Sue Grafton's Hard-Boiled Feminism." *Feminism in Women's Detective Fiction*. Ed. Glenwood Irons Toronto: University of Toronto Press, 1995. 127–147.

Cogdill, Oline. "Insulting the South." *Sun-Sentinel*. 17 January 1999, sec. E:3.

Cohen, Nancy J. *Permed to Death*. New York: Kensington Publishing, 1999.

Cooper, J. C. *An Illustrated Encyclopedia of Traditional Symbols*. London: Thames and Hudson, Ltd., 1978.

Cornwell, Patricia. *Cause of Death*. New York: Putnam's, 1996.

——. *From Potter's Field*. New York: Berkley, 1996.

——. *Point of Origin*. New York: Putnam's, 1998.

——. *Unnatural Exposure*. New York: Berkley, 1998.

Cross, Amanda. *Death in a Tenured Position*. New York: Ballantine Books, 1981.

——. *The Puzzled Heart*. New York: Ballantine Books, 1998.

Davidson, Diane Mott. *Catering to Nobody*. New York: Ballantine Books, 1990.

——. *Dying for Chocolate*. New York: Bantam, 1992.

Denvir, John. "Rumpole of the Bailey." *Prime Time Law*. Eds. Robert M. Jarvis and Paul R. Joseph. Durham, NC: Carolina Academic Press, 1998. 145–154.

Dickinson, Emily. "After Great Pain…" (No. 122) in *Final Harvest: Emily Dickinson's Poems*. Ed. Thomas Johnson. Boston: Little, Brown, 1961. 73.

Dilley, Kimberly J. *Busybodies, Meddlers, and Snoops: The Female Hero in Contemporary Women's Mysteries*. Westport, CT: Greenwood Press, 1998.

Dundes, Alan. "Earth-Diver: Creation of the Mythopoeic Male." *Sacred Narrative: Readings in the Theory of Myth*. Ed. Dundes. Berkeley: University of California Press, 1984. 270–294.

Eliade, Mircea. *Images and Symbols: Studies in Religious Symbolism*. Princeton: Princeton University Press, 1991.

——. *Myth and Reality*. Trans. Willard R. Trask. New York: Harper Colophon Books, 1975.

——. *The Myth of the Eternal Return, or Cosmos and History*. Trans. Willard R. Trask. New York: Princeton University Press, 1974.

Elias-Button, Karen. "Journey into an Archetype: The Dark Mother in Contemporary Women's Poetry." *Jungian Literary Criticism*. Ed. Richard P. Sugg. Evanston, Illinois: Northwestern UP, 1992. 355–366.

Eliot, Alexander. *The Universal Myths: Heroes, Gods, Tricksters, and Others*. New York: Penguin Putnam, 1990.

Fairstein, Linda. *Final Jeopardy*. New York: Pocket Books, 1997.

——. *Likely to Die*. New York: Pocket Books, 1998.

Frye, Northrop. *Anatomy of Criticism: Four Essays*. Princeton: Princeton University Press, 1971.

Works Cited

———. "The Archetypes of Literature." *The Kenyon Review* 12 (Winter 1951): 92–110. Rpt. in *Jungian Literary Criticism*. Ed. Richard P. Sugg. Evanston, Illinois: Northwestern University Press, 1992. 21–25.

———. *Myth and Metaphor: Selected Essays 1974–1988*. Ed. Robert D. Denham. Virginia: The University Press of Virginia, 1996. 3–17.

Fulford, Robert. *The Triumph of Narrative: Storytelling in the Age of Mass Culture*. New York: Broadway Books, 1999.

Grafton, Sue. *"A" Is for Alibi*. New York: Holt, Rinehart, and Winston, 1982.

———. *"K" Is for Killer*. New York: Henry Holt, 1994.

———. *"L" Is for Lawless*. New York: Henry Holt, 1995.

———. *"O" Is for Outlaw*. New York: Henry Holt, 1999.

———. *"P" Is for Peril*. New York: Penguin Putnam, 2001.

Grant, Michael. *Myths of the Greeks and Romans*. New York: Mentor Books, 1962.

Graves, Robert. *The White Goddess: A Historical Grammar of Poetic Myth*. New York: Farrar, Straus and Giroux, 1975.

Grimal, Pierre. *The Dictionary of Classical Mythology*. Trans. A. R. Maxwell-Hyslop. Blackwell Publishers Ltd., 1996.

Grisham, John. *The Firm*. New York: Doubleday, 1991.

———. "The Rise of the Legal Thriller: Why Lawyers Are Throwing the Books at Us." *New York Times*, Book Review Section, 33, Oct. 18, 1992.

Gur, Batya. *The Saturday Morning Murder: A Psychoanalytic Case*. New York: HarperPerennial, 1993.

Hamilton, Edith. *Mythology: Timeless Tales of Gods and Heroes*. New York: New American Library, 1969.

Harmon, William, and C. Hugh Holman. *A Handbook to Literature*, 7th ed. Upper Saddle River, NJ: Prentice-Hall, 1996. 520.

Harris, Lee. *The Thanksgiving Day Murder*. New York: Ballantine, 1995.

Hawthorne, Nathaniel. *The Complete Novels and Selected Tales of Nathaniel Hawthorne*. Ed. Norman Holmes Pearson. New York: Modern Library, 1965.

Heidegger, Martin. *History of the Concept of Time*. Trans. Theodore Kisiel. Bloomington: Indiana UP, 1992.

Heilbrun, Carolyn G. *Hamlet's Mother and Other Women*. New York: Ballantine Books, 1990.

Heising, Willetta L. *Detecting Women 3*. Dearborn, MI: Purple Moon Press, 2000.

Henderson, Joseph L. "Ancient Myths and Modern Man." *Man and His Symbols*. Eds. Carl G. Jung and M-L von Franz. New York: Doubleday, 1964. 104–157.

Homer. *The Odyssey*. Trans. W.H.D. Rouse. New York: New American Library, Mentor Classics, 1937.

Irons, Glenwood, ed. *Feminism in Women's Detective Fiction*. Toronto: University of Toronto Press, 1995.

James, P.D. *Death in Holy Orders*. New York: Alfred A. Knopf, 2001.

Jung, C.G. *Aspects of the Feminine*, Bollingen Series. Trans. R. F. C. Hull. Princeton University Press, 1982.

———. *Four Archetypes*, Bollingen Series. Trans. R. F. C. Hull. Princeton University Press, 1969.

Works Cited

Jung, C.G., and C. Kerenyi. *Essays on a Science of a Mythology: The Myth of the Divine Child and the Mysteries of Eleusis.* Trans. R. F. C. Hull. Princeton: Princeton University Press, 1963.

Jung, Carl G., and M-L von Franz, eds. *Man and His Symbols.* New York: Doubleday, 1964.

Kaufman, Natalie Hevenor, and Carol McGinnis Kay. *"G" Is for Grafton: The World of Kinsey Millhone.* New York: Henry Holt, 1997.

Klein, Kathleen Gregory, ed. *Women Times Three: Writers, Detectives, Readers.* Bowling Green: Bowling Green State University Popular Press, 1995.

_____. "Habeus Corpus: Feminism and Detective Fiction." Irons 171–189.

Kongas, Elli Kaija. "The Earth-Diver." *Ethnohistory* 7 (1960): 151–180.

Leitch, Vincent B. *American Literary Criticism from the Thirties to the Eighties.* New York: Columbia University Press, 1988.

Leonardi, Susan J. "Murders Academic: Women Professors and the Crimes of Gender." Irons 112–126.

Manson, Cynthia, ed. *Thou Shalt Not Kill.* New York: Signet Books, 1997.

Marx, Leo. *The Machine in the Garden: Technology and the Pastoral Ideal in America.* New York: Oxford University Press, 2000.

Moore, Samuel, and Thomas A. Knott. *The Elements of Old English.* Ann Arbor, MI: The George Wahr Publishing Co., 1972.

Murdock, Maureen. *The Heroine's Journey.* Boston: Shambhala, 1990.

Neumann, Erich. "Art and Time." *Man and Time*, Bollingen Series XXX. Ed. Joseph Campbell. Princeton: Princeton University Press, 1973. 3–37.

Oates, Joyce Carol. "The Simple Art of Murder: The Novels of Raymond Chandler." *New York Review of Books*, 1995. http://www.usis.usemb.se/sft/142/sf14213.htm.

O'Marie, Sister Carol Anne. *Murder in Ordinary Time.* New York: Dell Publishing, 1991.

Page, Katherine Hall. *The Body in the Belfrey.* New York: Avon Books, 1990.

Paretsky, Sara. "Eye of a Woman: An Introduction." *A Woman's Eye.* New York: Delacorte Press, 1991. vii–xiv.

_____. *Hard Time.* New York: Delacorte Press, 1999.

_____. *Tunnel Vision.* New York: Delacorte Press, 1994.

_____. "Writers on Writing." *New York Times.* Sept. 25, 2000.

Parker, Barbara. *Suspicion of Betrayal.* New York: Signet, 2000.

_____. *Suspicion of Innocence.* New York: Signet, 1994.

_____. *Suspicion of Malice.* New York: Dutton, 2000.

Pervushina, Lubya. "Amanda Cross Novels Link Women to Power." *Women in Higher Education.* Mar. 2000: 33.

Pollack, Rachel. *The Body of the Goddess: Sacred Wisdom in Myth, Landscape, and Culture.* Rockport, MA: Element Books, 1997.

Pratt, Annis V. "Archetypal Patterns in Women's Fiction." *Jungian Literary Criticism.* Ed. Richard P. Sugg, Evanston, IL: Northwestern UP, 1992. 367–375.

Propp, Vladimir. *Morphology of the Folktale.* Austin: University of Texas Press, 2nd rev. ed., 1996.

Ragan, Kathleen, ed. *Fearless Girls, Wise Women and Beloved Sisters: Heroines in Folktales from Around the World.* New York: W. W. Norton, 1998.

Reichs, Kathy. *Death DuJour*. New York: Jossey-Bass, 1999.
———. *Déjà Dead*. New York: Pocket Books, 1997.
Ricoeur, Paul, "Narrative Time." *On Narrative*. Ed. W.J.T. Mitchell. Chicago: University of Chicago Press, 1981. 165–86.
Rosenberg, Charles B. "Foreword" to *Prime Time Law*. Jarvis and Joseph ix–xii.
Rothenberg, Albert. *The Emerging Goddess: The Creative Process in Art, Science, and Other Fields*. Chicago: University of Chicago Press, 1979.
Samuels, Andrew, Bani Shorter, and Fred Plaut. "Archetype, Myth, Numinosum." *Jungian Literary Criticism*. Ed. Richard P. Sugg. Evanston, IL: Northwestern UP, 1992. 187–191.
Scholes, Robert, and Robert Kellogg. *The Nature of Narrative*. New York: Oxford UP, 1968.
Scottoline, Lisa. *Rough Justice*. New York: HarperCollins, 1997.
———. *Moment of Truth*. New York: HarperCollins, 2000.
Smith, Henry Nash. *Virgin Land: The American West as Symbol and Myth*. 2nd ed. Cambridge, MA: Harvard University Press, 1970.
Smith, Julie. *82 Desire*. New York: Ivy Books, 1998.
———. *New Orleans Beat*. New York: Ivy Books, 1994.
Spender, Stephen. *The Creative Element: A Study of Vision, Despair and Orthodoxy Among Some Modern Writers*. New York: Books for Libraries Press, 1953.
Steiner, George. *Grammar of Creation*. New Haven: Yale University Press, 2000.
Tome, Sandra. "Questing Women: The Feminist Mystery After Feminism." *Feminism in Women's Detective Fiction*. Ed. Glenwood Irons. Toronto: University of Toronto Press, 1995. 46–63.
Trocheck, Kathy Hogan. *Strange Brew*. New York: HarperPaperbacks, 1997.
Vaughan, Henry. "The Water-fall." *Seventeenth-Century Verse and Prose, Volume One: 1600–1660*, 2nd ed. Ed. Helen C. White, et al. New York: The Macmillan Company, 1971. 510.
Vickery, John. B., ed. *Myth and Literature*. Lincoln: University of Nebraska Press, 1966.
Viets, Elaine. *Doc in the Box*. New York: Dell Books, 2000.
Vogler, Christopher. *The Writer's Journey: Mythic Structure for Writers*, 2nd ed. Studio City, CA: Michael Wiese Productions, 1998.
Von Franz, Marie-Louise. *Archetypal Patterns in Fairy Tales*. Toronto: Inner City Books, 1997.
Walton, Priscilla L. " 'E' Is for En/Gendering Readings: Sue Grafton's Kinsey Millhone." Klein *Women Times Three* 101–115.
Walton, Priscilla L., and Manina Jones. *Detective Agency: Women Rewriting the Hard-Boiled Tradition*. Berkeley: University of California Press, 1999.
Wilson, Edmund. *The Edmund Wilson Reader*. Ed. Lewis Dabney. New York: Da Capo Press, 1997.
Wittig, Monique. *The Straight Mind and Other Essays*. Boston: Beacon, 1992.

INDEX

"A" Is for Alibi 142–143; *see also* Grafton, Sue; Millhone, Kinsey
academe 19, 90, 92–98, 134
Adam and Eve 155
Adventure, Mystery, and Romance 12, 18, 65–66; *see also* Cawelti, John G.
adornment 30, 38–41
Agamemnon 104
Agathodaemon 32
Albert, Susan Wittig 28; *see also* Bayles, China
alibis 68, 87, 93
alter-ego 53, 153; *see also* Döppelganger
amateur sleuths 10–11, 14, 27–44, 67–83
American Literary Criticism from the Thirties to the Eighties 6; *see also* Leitch, Vincent B.
anatomy of narrative structure 13–26
androgyny 3, 64, 154
animals in mysteries 11, 16, 36, 40–41, 96–97, 116, 119, 139, 142, 145
AOL 60, 122
apocalypse 137, 141–42
Apollo 104
Archer, Isabel 131
archetypes 7, 8, 47, 51
Archetypes 7, 23, 24; *see also* Frye, Northrop
Ariadne's thread 21, 123, 124
art, transcendent value 75, 86

Aspects of the Feminine 36; *see also* Jung, Carl G.
Athena 105
Atreus, House of 111, 121
AUM 102–03
autopsy 59; as metaphor for literary analysis 59–66
axis mundi 20; *see also* Eliade, Mircea; *Myth of the Eternal Return*; *Myth and Reality*

Bad Hair Day Mystery 38; *see also* Cohen, Nancy J.; Shore, Marla; *Permed to Death*
Barnes, Linda 19, 115, 117, 118–21; *see also* Carlyle, Carlotta; *Hardware*
Baroness de Pontalba, as Persephone figure 127; *see also* Wallis, Talba
Barr, Nevada 20, 115, 117; *see also* *Blind Descent*; *Blood Lure*; *Deep South*; *Liberty Falling*; Pigeon, Anna
Bayles, China 28; *see also* Albert, Susan Wittig
Bear, Goldy 29, 31–38, 152; *see also* Davidson, Diane Mott; *Catering to Nobody*; *Dying for Chocolate*
Berger, Merrill (and Stephen Segaller) 160; *see also* *The World of C. G. Jung*
Bettelheim, Bruno 27; on Cinderella 43; on Goldilocks 33; *see also* *Uses of Enchantment*
The Bible 82
Big Easy 121, 123

Index

black magic 37
Blair witch 31
Blake, Michelle 67, 70, 81–83, 88; *see also* Cannon, Lily; *The Tentmaker*
Blake, William 88
Blind Descent 20, 115; *see also* Barr, Nevada; Pigeon, Anna
Blood Lure 117; *see also* Barr, Nevada; Pigeon, Anna
The Body in the Belfry 28; *see also* Fairchild, Faith; Page, Katherine Hall
booksellers 160
Braun, Lillian Jackson 11
Brennan, Tempe 13, 55, 66; *see also Death DuJour; Déjà Dead*; Reichs, Kathy
Brooks, Christine Bennett 67, 69, 79, 88; as a nun 75; contrast to Sister Mary Helen 70, 88; *see also* Harris, Lee; *The Thanksgiving Day Murder*
Brother Cadfael 67; *see also* Peters, Ellis
Brown, Rita Mae 11
Buchanan, Edna 91, 98; *see also Contents Under Pressure*; Montero, Britt
Bulfinch's Mythology 39, 51, 104, 133

Cain 87, 88; and Abel 152
Calypso 3
Campbell, Joseph 7, 8, 13, 25; on academe 94; on Agathodaemon 32; on archetypes 8; on AUM 102–03; on bringing the self alive 56; on creative mythology 30; disjunct between inner and outer reality 32; ethics 113; Grail Legend 91; hero and landscape 20; journey 126; mythic monsters 24; on mythological healing 48; Parzival 41; suffering 17, 46, 91; the Waste Land 133; vision, inner and outer 46; wise guide 95; word beyond words 98, 113; *see also Creative Mythology; Hero with a Thousand Faces; The Masks of God; The Power of Myth; Transformations of Myth Through Time*
cancer 42, 99
career thriller 90
Carlyle, Carlotta 19, 118–121; *see also* Barnes, Linda; *Hardware*
Carroll, Noel 64; on erotetic narration 79–80; *see also The Philosophy of Horror*
Cassirer, Ernst 6; *see also Language and Myth*
castration 54, 57
Catering to Nobody 35; *see also* Bear, Goldy; Davidson, Diane Mott; *Dying for Chocolate*

Cawelti, John G. 12, 18, 65–66; *see also Adventure, Mystery, and Romance* 12
Celtic lore 143
chain bookstores 1, 10
Chandler, Raymond 14, 56
Chernin, Kim 47
Chesterton, G. K.: as pioneer of religious mysteries 67; on role of landscape 19
child, as metaphor 56
children, babies 146, 148; drowned 48, 151; lost 131; teenagers 146
Christianson, Scott 147
Christie, Agatha 10, 11–12, 27, 28
churches 68–70
Cinderella 30, 42, 146
Circe 3
Clytemnestra 104
Cogdill, Oline 65
Cohen, Nancy J. 25, 38–39, 47; *see also* Bad Hair Day series; Shore, Marla; *Permed to Death*
computer as metaphor 117, 123
confession, as ritual 15
Connor, Gail 109; *see also* Parker, Barbara; *Suspicion of* series
Connor, Lily 70, 71, 77–87; 88; *see also The Tentmaker*; Blake, Michelle
Contents Under Pressure 98–99; *see also* Buchanan, Edna; Montero, Britt
convents 69–70
The Cooking School Murders 31; *see also* Potter, Eugenia; Rich, Virginia
Cooper, Alexandra 66; *see also* Fairstein, Linda; *Fatal Jeopardy; Likely to Die*
Cooper, James: *An Illustrated Encyclopedia of Traditional Symbols* 40
corn, as symbol of regeneration 32
Cornwell, Patricia 14, 51–56; awards won 57; as commodity 65; *see also From Potter's Field, Kay Scarpetta's Winter Table; Point of Origin; Postmortem*; Scarpetta, Kay; *Southern Cross*
corpse, masked 14
cosmic egg 18, 51, 149–50
cosmology myths 149–151
costume 42–43
cozy mystery 25, 27; defined 4
creation myths, South Africa 155
Creative Mythology 19, 30, 32, 46, 48, 91, 92, 94, 98, 99, 113, 115, 133; *see also* Campbell, Joseph
creativity: images of 144; loss of 131, 133; renewal 89; thwarted 136; value of 128
creator goddess 150

Cretan labyrinth 123
Crone 153
Cross, Amanda 12, 94; *see also Death in a Tenured Position*; Fansler, Kate; Heilbrun, Carolyn G.; *The Puzzled Heart*
Crum, Laura 10; *see also Cutter*
Culinary Mystery 31–38
Cutter 10; *see also* Crum, Laura
cyberspace 117, 118, 121, 123

Daedalus 21; and Icarus 118
Daheim, Mary 31
Dalgliesh, Adam 67, 70–71; *see also Death in Holy Orders*, James, P.D.
Danae 38
Dante's *Inferno* 139
Dark Mother 37, 47, 153
Davidson, Diane Mott 29; 31–38; *see also* Bear, Goldy; *Dying for Chocolate*
Death DuJour 13, 55–56; *see also*, Reichs, Kathy; Brennan Temperance; *Déjà Dead*
Death in a Tenured Position 95; *see also* Cross, Amanda; Fansler, Kate; Heilbrun, Carolyn G.
Death in Holy Orders 68, 70, 83–89; *see also* Dalgliesh, Adam; James, P.D.
death penalty 112
Decker–Lazarus series 22; *see also* Kellerman, Faye
Deep South 116–17; *see also* Barr, Nevada; Pigeon, Anna
Déjà Dead 55; *see also* Brennan, Tempe; *Death DuJour*; Reichs, Kathy
Demeter 127; and Persephone 121, 125; *see also* myth of enclosure
Denvir, John 103
Detecting Women 3 10; *see also* Heising, Willetta
detective: as artist 157; as creator goddess 154–55; hero 16–17; killer 16; loner 28; ordinary life 27; poet 84–85; social outcast 36, 40, 45; social reformer 131; suffering of 24, 46; vision of 30, 33, 46, 154
Detective Agency: Women Rewriting the Hard-Boiled Tradition 130
Dial "M" for Murder 54
Dickinson, Emily 7, 9–98
Dietz, Denise 31
Dilley, Kimberly 27, 38, 39, 47
DiNunzio, Mary 106; *see also Moment of Truth*; Scottoline, Lisa
disguise 45, 53
DNA 14,112

Doc in the Box 99–102, 103; *see also* Vierling, Francesca; Viets, Elaine
domestic abuse 32–33, 36, 37
domestic mystery 31–44, 47–48
Döppelganger 51, 52, 53; *see also* alter-ego
dread 80
dream 66, 84, 122, 135–36; relation to fairy tales 30
drowning: daughter 48; infant 151; woman 111–12
duality of identity 148
Dundes, Alan 150
Dying for Chocolate 29, 31–38; *see also* Bear, Goldy; Davidson, Diane Mott

Earth Diver 18, 151–53
Ecclesiastical mystery 22
Echo 53; and Narcissus 56
Eden 84
Edwin of the Iron Shoes 9; *see also* McCone Sharon; Muller, Marcia
Eichler, Selma 31
82 Desire 121, 125
Electra 104
Eleusian ritual 125
Eliade, Mircea 5, 6, 74, 75; apocalypse 137; art and the divine 77; *axis mundi* 20; metaphysical expression 75; on rituals as time-markers 74; on stopping time 141; *see also The Myth of the Eternal Return*; *Myth and Reality*
Elias-Button, Karen 47; *see also Jungian Literary Criticism*
Eliot, Alexander 6; mythosphere 20
Eliot, T. S. 130, 142; *see also* "The Waste Land"
elixir 17
end of the world 137, 141
epilogue 156–57
epiphany 24, 80–81
Eros 89
erotetic narration 79–80; *see also* Carroll, Noel; *The Philosophy of Horror*
erotomania 53
eternal return, 137, 141
Ethos 103, 104, 106
Eumenides 105
Eurydice 133
Every Crooked Nanny 42; *see also* Garrity, Callahan; Trocheck, Kathy Hogan

Fairbanks, Nancy 31
Fairchild, Faith 28; *see also* Page, Katherine Hall; *The Body in the Belfry*

Index

Fairstein, Linda 14, 51, 53–54, 57; *see also* Cooper, Alexandra; *Fatal Jeopardy*; *Likely to Die*
fairy tale 26, 41, 44–45, 70, 79, 159; as not-understood dream 30
faith 70, 79
family life 18, 31, 33, 43–47, 76, 98–99, 104–05; 107–08, 109, 124, 131–32, 135, 145–148
Fansler, Kate 94–98; *see also* Cross, Amanda; Heilbrun, Carolyn G.; *The Puzzled Heart*
Fatal Jeopardy 51, 52–54; *see also* Cooper, Alexandra; Fairstein, Linda; *Likely to Die*
fear 79, 80, 81; degrees of 80; of sexuality 59, 108
feminine bonding 110
fertility rituals 41, 128
Finch, Atticus 103; *see also* Lee, Harper; *To Kill a Mockingbird*
Finnegans Wake 150; *see also* Joyce, James
Firestorm 115; *see also* Barr, Nevada; Pigeon, Anna
The Firm 103–04; *see also* Grisham, John
folklore, in American culture 31
food: as aphrodisiac 34; magic 32; mythic attitudes toward 33; as poison 34; power of 34, 36; psychology of 34; ritualistic power 32; tie with the natural world 34; as way out of domestic abuse 31, 37
forensic mystery 4, 49–66
forensic time 79, 83, 85
forensic timescape 72
Four Archetypes 28, 36, 47; *see also Aspects of the Feminine*; Jung, Carl G.; *Man and His Symbols*
From Potter's Field 57–59; *see also* Cornwell, Patricia; *Point of Origin*; *Postmortem*; Scarpetta, Kay
Frye, Northrop 2, 7; on demonic time 140; on epiphany 24; on eros 89; on movement of time 76; narrative rhythm and pattern 22; nonrepresentational fiction 20; on projecting problems onto God 77–78; role of the church as time-marker 74; on seasonal rhythms 23; transcendence 75; *see also Archetypes*; *Myth and Metaphor*
Fulford, Robert 159; *see also The Triumph of Narrative*
Furies 104, 111

"G" Is for Grafton 142, 143, 144, 153; *see also* Kaufman, Natalie Hevener

Garcia-Aguilera, Carolina 20; *see also* Solano, Lupe
Garrity, Callahan 29, 41–44, 47; *see also Strange Brew*; Trocheck, Kathy Hogan
The Gashleycrumb Tinies 143; *see also* Gorey, Edward
Gaudy Night 93; *see also* Sayers, Dorothy
gender-connected creation myths 151
God 77–78, 79, 82–83, 99–100, 141
god of good fortune 32; *see also* Agathodaemon
golden bowl 125
Goldilocks 30, 31, 33; and porridge 35
Gorey, Edward 143; *see also The Gashleycrumb Tinies*
Gorgons 39
Grafton, Sue 130, 142; character innocence 18; on choice of alphabet structure 143; contributions to genre 156–58; fictional landscape 20; on gender 153; and Jungian psychology 144; on Kinsey as alter-ego 153; use of myths word play 144
Grail legend 41, 91, 98
Grant, Michael 21
Graves, Robert 38, 143; *see also The White Goddess*
Gray Women 38–40
Greene, Graham 25
Grimm's Fairy Tales 31
Grisham, John 90, 103–04
guilt, in reader 15; in characters 18
Gur, Batya 94; *see also* Ohayon, Michael; *The Saturday Morning Murder*

Hades 125, 133
hair, as symbol of marriage 40
Hamilton, Edith 38, 39, 43–44, 51, 104, 118, 125
Hammett, Dashiell 56
Hard Time 131, 133–42; comparison to Dickens 139; depiction of media 124; emblem of the Waste Land 133, 140; futility of prison reform 141; journalism in 124
Hardware 118
Harmon, William (and C. Hugh Holman) 114
Harris, Lee 22, 67, 75–76, 88; *see also* Brooks, Christine Bennett; *The Thanksgiving Day Murder*
Hawthorne, Nathaniel 11
Heidegger, Martin 80; *see also History of the Concept of Time*
Heilbrun, Carolyn G. 12, 91, 94; *see also*

Cross, Amanda; Fansler, Kate; *Death in a Tenured Position*; *The Puzzled Heart*
Heising, Willetta 10, 14; see also *Detecting Women 3*
Henderson, Joseph 2
Hermes 39
The Hero with a Thousand Faces 6, 17, 95, 123; see also Campbell, Joseph
The Heroine's Journey 4; see also Murdoch, Maureen
Hindu cosmology 150
history 94, 137, 160
History of the Concept of Time 80; see also Heidegger, Martin
Hoffman, Daniel B. 6
Holmes, Sherlock 7
Homer 3
Hornet's Nest 65
horses 45
The Hound of the Baskervilles 11
House of Blues 121; see also Langdon, Skip; Smith, Julie
houses of worship, as settings for mystery 68–69, 78, 141
Huck Finn 131
Humpty Dumpty 149–50

identity 42–43; duality of 148; merging of 53, separation of 52
Ill Wind 115; see also Barr, Nevada; Pigeon, Anna
Illo tempore 75
illusion versus reality 145
initiation rites 102, 109, 110, 134
instant message 122
Iphigenia 104
Ishmael 131

James, P.D. 67, 83–89; see also Dalgliesh, Adam; *Death in Holy Orders*
Jane Doe 14
Janus 24, 157
Johnson, Samuel 114
journalism 92, 98–102
journalists 98–102, 160
journey 118
Joyce, James 150
Judging Amy 9
Jung Carl G. archetypes 8, 47, 51; with C. Kerenyi 158; the Dark Mother 47; on history 160; power of the mother 36; symbols of self and the body 51; on transformation 28; see also *Aspects of the Feminine*; *Essays on a Science of a Mythology*; *Four Archetypes*; *Man and His Symbols*
Jungian Literary Criticism 8, 47, 153–54
justice 103, 104, 112

"K" Is for Killer 144; see also Grafton, Sue; Millhone, Kinsey
Kaufman, Natalie Hevener (and Carol McGinnis Kay) 142, 143, 144, 153; see also *"G" Is for Grafton*
Kay Scarpetta's Winter Table 65; see also Cornwell, Patricia
Kellerman, Faye 22; see also Decker–Lazarus series
Kelly, Grace 54
Kemelman, Harry 22, 67; see also Rabbi David Small
killer unmasked 24
King Minos 21, 118
Klein, Kathleen Gregory 17
Kokopelli 154
Kongas, Elias 151

"L" Is for Lawless 144–45; see also Grafton, Sue; Millhone, Kinsey
labyrinth 82, 117, 118, 120, 124, 127, 128; Cretan 123
landscape 116, 149; blasted 128, 133, 141; death removed from 48
Langdon, Skip 117, 121–25; see also *82 Desire*; *New Orleans Beat*; Smith, Julie
Language and Myth 6; see also Cassirer, Ernst
Lar and Penates 43
law 92, 103–113
Law & Order 9
Lee, Harper 103; see also *To Kill a Mockingbird*
legal thriller 90, 103–113
Leitch, Vincent B. 6; see also *American Literary Criticism from the Thirties to the Eighties*
Leonardi, Susan 94
lesbianism 62–63
Levi-Strauss, Claude 33; see also *The Raw and the Cooked*
Liberty Falling 115–16; see also Barr, Nevada; Pigeon, Anna
librarians 160
Likely to Die 51, 53–54, 57; see also Cooper, Alexandra; Fairstein, Linda
linear time 22, 76, 85; relationship to mythic time 89
linear timescape 83
line-up 17–18, 78
Logos 19, 23

174 Index

Lord of the Abyss 32
Luminol 57

Macbeth 98; *see also* Shakespeare, William
The Machine in the Garden 136; *see also* Marx, Leo
magic 29–38, 41–47
Man and His Symbols 8; *see also* Jung, Carl G.
Manson, Cynthia 22; *see also* mystery, ecclesiastical; *Thou Shalt Not Kill*
Marlowe, Philip 15
Marple, Miss Jane 28
marriage 37, 44–46; hair as a symbol of 41
Martini, Steve 90
Marx, Leo 136; *see also The Machine in the Garden*
mask 14; and identity myths 14
Masks of God 14; *see also* Campbell, Joseph
McCarthy, Gail 10; *see also* Crum, Laura
McCone, Sharon 9, 20; *see also* Muller, Marcia
medieval imagery 134, 135
Medusa 38, 48
memory 84
Millhone, Kinsey: and androgyny 154; babies 151, 153; body of 155; childhood 148; compared with V.I. Warshawski 131, 144, 157; as Creator Goddess 150–55; food 152; gender 152; and Great Mother 152; on language 156; and men 147–48, 153; metaphoric daughter of 154; and money 152; Santa Teresa 20, self-creation 155; senior citizens 146–47; significance of name 150; on solitude 28; stuck in time 145, 147, 151, 152, as thief 155; vision of 154; wit 147; *see also "A" Is for Alibi; "G" Is for Grafton;* Grafton, Sue; *"K" Is for Killer; "L" Is for Lawless; "O" Is for Outlaw; "P" Is for Peril*
Minotaur 21, 119, 123
Moment of Truth 106; *see also Rough Justice;* Scottoline, Lisa
monster 123
Montero, Britt 98, 102–03; *see also* Buchanan, Edna; *Contents Under Pressure*
movies, transcendent value 82
Moyers, Bill 4
Muller, Marcia 9, 20; as innovator of women's PI novels 130; *see also Edwin of the Iron Shoes;* McCone, Sharon
Murder in Ordinary Time 69–70; 77–81; *see also* O'Marie, Sister Carol Anne; Sister Mary Helen

Murdock, Maureen 4; *see also The Heroine's Journey*
mutilation 38, 51, 54, 57
Myers, Tamar 31
mysteries: academic 19, 90, 92–98, 134; and aging 28; animals in 11, 16, 40–41, 139, 142, 145, 160; beginnings and endings 25; as business 160–61; and change 28, 41; computers in 117, 118; cozy 7; cozy as misnomer 48; culinary 31; domestic 160; ecclesiastical 67–89; of Eleusis 125; embedded truths 26; feminist 57, forensic 7, 49, 160; history in 94; journalism in 90, 99–102; as literature 2, 11, 12, 160–61; marketing of 22, 25, 143; materialism in 2, 160–61; in media 8, 9; paid for hire 7; police procedurals 7; religious 67–89; structure 13–26; of time 83; as wish fulfillment 27
myth: of apocalypse 137; cleansing effect of 16; of cosmology 149–51; of creation by theft 155; of Daedalus and Icarus 21, 118; critics 6; definitions 2, 4–6; of Demeter and Persephone 125, 127–28; of the Earth Diver 151, 152; of enclosure 125; of eternal return 74, 137; of identity 51; of Medusa 38–40; of Narcissus 56, 66; of Narcissus and Echo 50–51, 53; of Orestes 104–05, 111, 112; of Orpheus 132–33; power of 88, 132–33; relationship to linear time 89; of repetition 141; and time 21–24, 73, 76, 84, 87
Myth and Literature 6–7; *see also* Vickery, John B.
Myth and Metaphor 2, 74, 75, 89, 117, 140; *see also* Frye, Northrop
Myth and Reality 5, 20; *see also* Eliade, Mircea
Myth of the Eternal Return 74, 75, 77, 137, 141; *see also* Eliade, Mircea
mythic time 76, 84
mythology 4; classical 43
mythosphere 22

Narcissus 56; and Echo 53; vision of wholeness 66
narrative, as dream 30; as magic 30; and time 21– 24; as transformation 31
narrative time 21–24
"Narrative Time" 76, 77, 89; *see also* Ricoeur, Paul
narrator, first-person 14, 15, 154
natural world 35, 36, 114–117, 143; pets as a tie with 41
The Nature of Narrative 73–74, 78; *see also* Scholes, Robert (and Robert Kellogg)

Neumann, Erich 160
New Orleans Beat 121–25; *see also 82 Desire*; Langdon, Skip; Smith, Julie
New York Times 138
New Yorker 11–12
nightmare 30
"Nine Brothers Who Were Changed into Lambs, and Their Sister" 44–47
Noah and the Flood 137; as earth diver myth 151
Noir 139
Numina 43
nun 55, 69–70, 107
NYPD Blue 9, 62

"*O" Is for Outlaw* 145–46; *see also* Grafton, Sue; Millhone, Kinsey
Oates, Joyce Carol, on Raymond Chandler and Poe's "The Gold Bug" 14
Odysseus 3
The Odyssey 3
Ohayon, Michael 94; *see also* Gur, Batya; *The Saturday Morning Murder*
O'Marie, Sister Carol Anne 22, 67, 77–81, 88; *see also Murder in Ordinary Time*; Sister Mary Helen
ordinary time 81
Orestes 104–05, 111, 112
orphans 44, 131
Orpheus 132–33
Ovid 21, 50–51

"*P" Is for Peril* 131, 145–57; concepts of time in 150–51; cosmology myths in 149–50; creation myths in 151; Dark Mother 153, earth diver myth 151–52; lack of epilogue 156–57; landscape in 149, 157; money in 152; poetic qualities 157; significance of title 157; twins motif 152; vision in 157; White Goddess 153; writing metaphors in 156
Page, Katherine Hall 28; *see also The Body in the Belfry*; Fairchild, Faith
Pandora's box 29
Paretksy, Sara 129–43; contributions to genre 157–58; on the women's movement 10, 130, 131; on writing 138; *see also Hard Time; Tunnel Vision*; Warshawski, V.I.; *A Woman's Eye*
Parker, Barbara 91, 105, 109–112; *see also* Connor, Gail; *Suspicion of* series
Parzival 41, 91; *see also* Percival
Pence, Joanne 31
Percival 41, 91; *see also* Parzival
Permed to Death 38; *see also Bad Hair Day*

Mystery; Cohen, Nancy J.; Shore, Marla
Persephone 125, 127
Perseus 38–40
Pervushina, Lubya 12
Peters, Ellis 67; *see also* Brother Cadfael
Pickard, Nancy 31; *see also The 27–Ingredient Chile Con Carne Murders*
Pigeon, Anna 20, 115–17; *see also* Barr, Nevada; *Blind Descent; Blood Lure; Deep South; Liberty Falling*
Pilate 86
Pilpul 22
Pinocchio motif 31
plant lore 143
Plurabelle, Anna Livia 150
Poe, Edgar Allan 14, 15; "The Fall of the House of Usher" 69; "The Gold Bug" 14; innovator 159; "The Purloined Letter" 37
poetic imagination 158
poetry 22, 84, 85, 86, 89, 114, 132, 134, 157, 158; of Emily Dickinson 7; of William Blake 88; of Talba Wallis 127–28
Point of Origin 59–66; *see also* Cornwell, Patricia; *From Potter's Field; Kay Scarpetta's Winter Table; Postmortem*; Scarpetta, Kay; *Southern Cross*
Poirot, Hercule 22
poisoned cauldron 121, 125
police procedurals 160
Pollack, Rachel 51, 116
poppy, as symbol of altered consciousness 32
Postmortem 57; *see also* Cornwell, Patricia; *From Potter's Field; Kay Scarpetta's Winter Table*; Scarpetta, Kay; *Southern Cross*
Potter, Eugenia 31; *see also* Rich, Virginia
Power of Myth 6, 8, 17–19, 20, 24, 25, 56, 19, 102, 103, 126
Pratt, Annis 153–54; *see also Jungian Literary Criticism*
Prime Time Law 103, 112; *see also* Denvir, John; Rosenberg, Charles
Prince Charming 42
Private Eye Writers Convention 18
profane time 78
prostitution 144
The Puzzled Heart 94–98; *see also* Cross, Amanda; Fansler, Kate; Heilbrun, Carolyn G.

Quest 2, 16–17, 24, 90, 110

Rabbi series 22; *see also* Kemelman, Harry

Ragan, Kathleen 155
ratiocination 15
The Raw and the Cooked 33; *see also* Levi-Strauss, Claude
Razor's Edge 21, 115, 116
recipes 31, 100; as magic words 36
red herrings 18–19
Reichs, Kathy 13, 51, 55; *see also* Brennan, Temperance; *Death Du Jour*; *Déjà Dead*
resurrection 109
retribution 101, 111
Rich, Virginia 31; *see also The Cooking School Murders*
Richman, Phyllis 31
Richter, Marta 105; *see also* Scottoline, Lisa
Ricoeur, Paul: linear time defined 77; on time and memory 76, on time and storytelling 89; *see also* "Narrative Time"
Rig Veda 150
rites of passage 92, 145
ritual: 7; absolution 41; castration 54, 57; confession 15; death 54, 133; death and rebirth 27, 37, 78, 127–29, 131; death of the god 141; defined 7; of Eleusis 125; enactments 75; fertility 41, 125; guilt 23; the hunt 16, 51; initiation 91, 102, 109, 134; listening 101; masquerade 43; murder 106; mutilation 38, 51, 54, 57; of passage 92, 145; renewal 25–26, 126–27, 129; to repair disrupted time 89; re-purification 87; restoration 160; resurrection 109, 141; of scapegoat 16; transformation 30–31, 124
romance 11, 12, 33, 51, 117
Rosato and Associates 105, 106; *see also Moment of Truth*; *Rough Justice*; Scottoline, Lisa
Rosenberg, Charles 112; *see also Prime Time Law*
Rothenberg, Albert 158
Rough Justice 16, 105–06; *see also Moment of Truth*; Scottoline, Lisa
Rourke, Constance 6

Samuels, Andrew (and Bani Shorter and Fred Plant) 8; *see also Jungian Literary Criticism;* Pratt, Annis
The Saturday Morning Murder 94; *see also* Gur, Batya; Ohayon, Michael
Sayers, Dorothy 93; *see also Gaudy Night*; Harriet Vane
scapegoat 16
Scarpetta, Kay 56; *see also* Cornwell, Patricia; *From Potter's Field; Point of Origin; Postmortem*

Scholes, Robert (and Robert Kellogg) 73–74, 78; *see also The Nature of Narrative*
Scotland Yard 67
Scottoline, Lisa 16, 91, 105; *see also Moment of Truth; Rough Justice*
senior citizens 28, 43, 95, 95–99, 146–47
Shakespeare, William 98
Shore, Marla 38–41; *see also Bad Hair Day Mystery;* Cohen, Nancy J.; *Permed to Death*
silence 99, 102, 109, 138, 140–41, 142, 147
Simpson, O. J. 112
Sister Mary Helen 77–81, 88; *see also Death in Ordinary Time;* O'Marie, Carol Anne
Six Feet Under 9
sleuth, masked 14
sleuths: amateurs 10–11, 14, 27–48; journey of 30; occupations of 10–11, 14; users of magic 29–30
Small, Rabbi David 22, 67; *see also* Kemelman, Harry; Rabbi series
Smith, Henry Nash 6
Smith, Julie 115, 117, 121, 125; *see also 82 Desire;* Langdon, Skip; *New Orleans Beat*
Solano, Lupe 20; *see also* Garcia-Aguilera, Carolina
The Sopranos 9
Southern Cross 65; *see also* Cornwell, Patricia
Spender, Stephen 157
Spillane, Mickey 25
Stevens, Rosemary 31
Strange Brew 41; *see also* Garrity, Callahan; Trocheck, Kathy Hogan
suffering 25, 101, 102, 105
Sun-Sentinel newspaper 65
Superior Death 115; *see also* Barr, Nevada; Pigeon, Anna
Survivor 92
suspects 60, 78
suspense 64
Suspicion of series: *Betrayal* 110–112; *Innocence* 109–110; *Malice* 112; *Vengeance* 112; *see also* Connor, Gail; Parker, Barbara
symbolism: corn 32; hair 40; name 84, 150; poppy 32; ticking watch 152

tattoos 38
technology: cyberspace 117, 118, 121, 123; distrust of 6; as evil 136–38; and Pinocchio motif 31
television: courtroom dramas 9; crime dramas 8, 62; reality shows 9, 92
The Tentmaker 70, 81–83; *see also* Blake, Michelle; Connor, Lily

Index

terror 79–81
tests 95–98, 99, 102–03, 106
The Thanksgiving Day Murder 69, 75–76; see also Brooks, Christine Bennett; Harris, Lee
Theseus 21, 123
Thou Shalt Not Kill 22
thrillers: career 90; ecological 117; legal 90, 103; medical 160
time: "of the crime" 79; erasure of 139, 141; forensic 29, 83, 85; as killer 68; linear 76, 77, 78, 85; lost 24; man-made 22; mystery of 83; mythic 21–24; 73, 76, 84, 87; with no God 82; ordinary 81; profane 78; stopped 145, 147; and storytelling 89; suspended 23
timescape 24, 83
Tiresias 56, 154
To Kill a Mockingbird 103; see also Finch, Atticus; Lee, Harper
Tomc, Sandra 57
topographical poetry 114
Topoi 114–15, 116, 117
Track of the Cat 115; see also Barr, Nevada; Pigeon, Anna
transformation narratives 31, 42, 46, 47, 124; of landscape 128
Transformations of Myths Through Time 41, 91, 113; see also Campbell, Joseph
tree-alphabet 143
tree magic 143
Triumph of Narrative 159; see also Fulford, Robert
Trocheck, Kathy Hogan 29, 42, 47; see also Callahan Garrity; *Strange Brew*
Tunnel Vision 131, 139; myth of Orpheus 132–33; see also *Hard Time*; Paretsky, Sara; Warshawksi, V. I.
Turow, Scott 90
The 27-Ingredient Chile Con Carne Murders see Pickard, Nancy
twins motif 152
2001: Space Odyssey 118

uncanny 80
Uses of Enchantment 27, 33, 43; see also Bettelheim, Bruno

vampire 58
Vane, Harriet 93; see also *Gaudy Night*
Vaughan, Henry 114
vengeance 101, 104–05, 106, 111
Vickery, John B. 6–7; see also *Myth and Literature*

Vierling, Francesca 19, 99–102; see also *Doc in the Box;* Viets, Elaine
Viets, Elaine 19, 91, 99–102; see also *Doc in the Box*; Vierling, Francesca
violence 24, 26, 94, 104, 111–12
Virgin, Mad 134–35; and crone 153
vision, loss of 30, 52, 60–61, 131, 133, 154
Vogler, Christian 92; see also *The Writer's Journey: Mythic Structure for Writers*
voiceless people 138, 140–41
Von Franz, Maria 30, 41, 44–47, 48

Wallis, Talba 127; see also Baroness de Pontalba
Walton, Priscilla 153
Walton, Priscilla (and Manina Jones) 47, 130; see also *Detective Agency: Women Rewriting the Hard-Boiled Tradition*
Warshawski, V. I. 1, 131–43; as Joan of Arc 139; compared with Kinsey Millhone 131, 144, 157; lack of redemption 142; loss of creative vision 131–32; relationship with men 138, 142; ritual death 143; as solitary 28; see also *Hard Time*; Paretsky, Sara; *Tunnel Vision*
"The Waste Land" 130, 133, 142; see also Eliot, T. S.
"The Water-Fall" 114–115; see also Vaughan, Henry
The White Goddess 18, 153; see also Graves, Robert
Williams, Tennessee 126
Wilson, Edmund 11–12
wise guide 95, 108
witch 31, 36, 44–47
witches' brew 135; ritual 124
Wittig, Monique 154
wolf man 31
Woman in peril convention 16
A Woman's Eye 10; see also Paretsky, Sara; Warshawski, V.I.
women in law 90, 105–112; in law enforcement 2–3, 5, 49, 87, 88
women's movement 10, 130
Word Beyond Words 98–99, 102, 109
word magic 36, 74, 100
World of C. G. Jung 160; see also Berger, Merrill and Stephen Segaller
wound 25, 42, 99; significance of 46
The Writer's Journey: Mythic Structure for Writers 92; see also Vogler, Christian
writing, metaphors of 156

Zeus 38, 50, 125

www.ingramcontent.com/pod-product-compliance
Lightning Source LLC
Chambersburg PA
CBHW032103300426
44116CB00007B/873